In the
Unlikeliest
of Places

Nachman Libeskind, *Sonata*   Photo by Jeremy Berkovits

In the

Unlikeliest
of Places

How Nachman Libeskind
Survived the Nazis, Gulags,
and Soviet Communism

Annette Libeskind Berkovits
Foreword by Daniel Libeskind

WILFRID LAURIER
UNIVERSITY PRESS

Wilfrid Laurier University Press acknowledges the financial support of the Government of Canada through the Canada Book Fund for our publishing activities.

LAURIER
Inspiring Lives.

Library and Archives Canada Cataloguing in Publication

Berkovits, Annette Libeskind, [date], author
    In the unlikeliest of places: how Nachman Libeskind survived the Nazis, gulags, and Soviet communism / Annette Libeskind Berkovits; foreword by Daniel Libeskind.

(Life writing series)
Issued in print and electronic formats.
ISBN 978-1-77112-066-1 (bound).—ISBN 978-1-77112-248-1 (paperback)
ISBN 978-1-77112-068-5 (epub).—ISBN 978-1-77112-067-8 (pdf)

    1. Libeskind, Nachman. 2. Holocaust, Jewish (1939–1945)—
Biography. 3. Prisoners—Soviet Union—Biography. 4. Holocaust survivors—New York (State)—New York—Biography. 5. Jews—Poland—Biography. 6. Jews—New York (State)—New York—Biography. I. Title. II. Series: Life writing series

DS134.72.L52L52 2014   940.53'18092   C2014-902732-X
                                                 C2014-902733-8

Front-cover image: Nachman Libeskind in Poland, 1934. Cover design by Blakeley Words+Pictures. Text design by Angela Booth Malleau.

This book is printed on FSC recycled paper and is certified Ecologo. It is made from 100% post-consumer fibre, processed chlorine free, and manufactured using biogas energy.

Printed in Canada

Every reasonable effort has been made to acquire permission for copyright material used in this text, and to acknowledge all such indebtedness accurately. Any errors and omissions called to the publisher's attention will be corrected in future printings.

You can cage the singer but not the song.
—*Harry Belafonte*

Contents

Foreword by Daniel Libeskind
ix

Author's Note
xiii

Part 1: Before
1

Part 2: Purgatory
185

Part 3: After
265

Epilogue
371

Foreword

When my father died, I thought about a question someone once asked Goethe—what colour he liked best. "I like rainbows," he said. And that's when I thought of my father; for him, the world was full of rainbows. He painted in an explosion of colours, shapes and patterns with a disciplined and finely tuned eye. My father died in June 2001, and I was grateful three months later that his death preceded the World Trade Center bombings of September 11. I was glad he was never witness to that seminal destruction and that he never lived to see his beloved New York attacked. Perhaps of us all, he would have been the most horrified and devastated, not only because of the loss of life but because America represented to him all that was good, safe, and uplifting—and this was a vicious attack on all of that.

When my father died, a kind and decent soul left this world.

My first vision of New York was so iconic, that it is burned forever in my memory. In the summer of 1959, we sailed into New York Harbor on the SS *Constitution*. It was very early morning; my mother shook us awake and led us up to the deck to see the Statue of Liberty and the magnificent New York skyline. It was a most incredible sight; Lady Liberty pointing her torch to the sky. My father, who had arrived months earlier, had already fallen in love with the city. I remember his face, filled with love and beaming with excitement. Those images—the Statue of Liberty, the New York skyline, my father's gentle face filled with optimism—informed my view of how Ground Zero should be shaped. I won the competition for Ground Zero in February 2003. The last months of 2002 and the first months of 2003 were frenetic and intense, filled with unimaginable tension and emotion. So what held me steady? Well, you are, in many ways, who your parents are: their values, their ethics, their humanity. I often think that what set my winning proposal for Ground Zero apart was, in large measure, the symbolism and the pragmatism of my parents' lives.

Nachman worked on Stone Street, a few blocks from the original World Trade Center towers. While I was working on my proposal, I imagined my father walking past the site, almost on a daily basis and my mother in the fur-factory sweatshops. What would they expect from this tragic site? What would they experience as ordinary working people walking by those fateful blocks? Not for them the gleaming office towers, marble lobbies, sleek elevators. No, for Nachman and Dora, the site had to be public, had to be open, had to hold the memory of what happened there. It had to tell the story: the slurry wall, the bedrock, the memory of the Statue of Liberty. It had to have symbolism; the tallest tower soaring to 1,776 feet to commemorate the Declaration of Independence, the memorial plaza with the footprints of the fallen towers; waterfalls to bring nature and quietude. And a public plaza—the Wedge of Light—formed by the line of light striking every September 11, precisely at 8:46 a.m., when the first jet smashed into the first tower; and at 10:28 a.m., when the second tower collapsed into dust and debris. With the towers rising in a spiral echoing the torch in Lady Liberty's hand, all the elements would be like chapters of that dreadful day—the story that all New Yorkers would feel and see.

We moved to Berlin in 1989, to realize the Jewish Museum. Most members of our extended family were horrified. To willingly live in the city where the Holocaust was devised was a total anathema to them. But my father, ever the geographer, was not one to forget history. After the Berlin Wall fell, he walked with me through Potsdamer Platz; in its glory days, the commercial centre of Berlin. Now it was a site divided by the wall—a no man's land. We walked along until my father suddenly stopped. He stomped on the earth. "Look at me," he said. "Here I am. Hitler is nothing but ashes. But I am here and I am living, eating, sleeping in this city and below the Nazis' bones are rotting!" His eyes filled with tears but he sounded victorious.

Ten years later, in 1999, the Jewish Museum Berlin opened, empty. Chancellor Gerhard Schröeder attended. After the formal dinner, the chancellor went to the table where my ninety-year-old father sat so he would not have to get up, knelt before him, and took his hand. "Mr. Libeskind, you must be so proud. Thank you for being here." What a moment for my father and for me.

I applaud my sister's resolve to write this book. Striking a balance between oral history and recovered memory is complex and demanding. Nachman's story—in Lodz, Poland; in Russia; in Israel; and in New York is told not from an objective or independent point of view but rather from the insight, intelligence and love of a daughter.

—*Daniel Libeskind*

Author's Note

This memoir has been inspired by the remarkable survival and optimism of my father Nachman Libeskind whose tapes narrated in his native Yiddish and partially in English have served as a principal resource for this book. This story is also a product of a decades-long dialogue between father and daughter, reams of preserved correspondence, and my own research.

Nachman, an animated storyteller, was blessed with nearly total recall of people, places, and events over his ninety-two-year lifespan. His memory remained sharp until the end of his life. It is thanks to him I had a treasure trove of material recorded with exceptional freshness and colour. My father always believed that one should expose the evils wrought by war and repressive regimes, instead of consigning them to dark corners of memory. I hope that in writing this book I am fulfilling his wish to pass on the history he lived and to share, as best I can, his sense of positivity and belief that humans have a core of goodness, no matter their nationality, creed, colour, or gender, and that it is never too late to pursue one's dreams.

Nachman's earliest years are based on stories he related to me over the years. Nearly everything else is based on existing tapes and voluminous correspondence. These resources were my treasured assets in maintaining accuracy. I have been careful to reconstruct dialogue to the best of my recollection and strove to be faithful to the emotional content of every exchange. In some instances I abridged, without sacrificing accuracy, long passages from Nachman's narrative in the service of story pacing. I also changed some names to protect the privacy of certain individuals. Differences in the recollection of events from accounts of others are a function of the lenses through which each of us views the world. I have done everything in my power to respect the compact between reader and author to ensure the reliability of Nachman's remarkable experiences. Any errors of fact, omissions, or misstatements are entirely my own.

A note about transliteration: it is an imprecise science at best. Various native Yiddish speakers I consulted often differed on the "proper" phrasing, pronunciation, or transliteration of certain words. Indeed, some of the phrases my father used in his *Lodzer* Yiddish were not even known to them. I take all blame for any errors in transliteration, but am pleased to have been able to share a tiny fraction of my father's linguistic milieu.

My father's recorded narrative served as the primary resource for this memoir, but I also incorporated my recollections of many conversations that we had over the years. In addition, I wove in trips I took to Poland with my father and later my husband. The trips with my father took place in 1984 and 1992. They gave me critical insight into his persona. The 2007 trip with my husband to revisit my father's haunts gave me additional information that aided my understanding. As with any historical account, mine blends research that adds context for the reader.

All of these different sources and strands suggested a format that takes the reader back and forth in time as Nachman's life events unfold against a historical backdrop. But while his story is the predominant narrative thread, told in third person, it is sometimes interrupted by his first-person account. Similarly, the trips back to Poland are inserted into Nachman's story in places where a later event would shed light on events that took place years earlier. I hope that rather than disorienting the reader, the shifts into the different modes—Nachman mode in third and first person, Memory mode, Conversations with Dad mode—will enliven the overall narrative and make it feel more akin to the way memory works with its inevitable leaps into the past and future, almost simultaneously.

I dedicate this book to my mother, the aspiring author Dora Blaustein, a woman of uncommon substance, wisdom and indomitable spirit. We would have been an entirely different family without her feminist outlook. It is she more than any-one who influenced Nachman's life in ways great and small.

It may take a village to raise a child, but it took passionate people in many parts of the United States, Canada, and Europe to make this book a reality.

First and foremost, my husband David, has been my muse, my pillar of strength and my first critic. Without his exceptional love, staunch support, boundless patience, and deep friendship with my father, this book may never have come to fruition.

I also must acknowledge the unstinting encouragement and wise advice of my daughter Jessica Ursell, and thought-provoking discussions with my son Jeremy Berkovits. I draw great satisfaction knowing that both of them possess a deep and abiding respect for the written word.

My brother Daniel Libeskind and his wife and partner, the remarkable Nina Lewis Libeskind, have been behind this project from its inception. Daniel took time from his projects around the world to write the foreword. I will always be grateful to have these brilliant family members at my side.

Many other individuals also need to be credited with helping me complete this book. My Gotham workshop teachers: Kelly Caldwell, the late Cheryl Burke, Kyle Minor, and Kerry Cohen taught me most of what I know about memoir writing. My first superb editor, Bill Roorbach, boosted that knowledge to a different level. His generous guidance, insight, and respect for Nachman's story helped me more than he will ever know.

My fellow writers Tammy Dietz, Adrienne Totino, Ross Martin, Glenys Loewen Thomas, Gail Kretchmer, Tabitha Blankenbiller, and Jim Cooper have commented on early drafts of chapters and served as a font of support and encouragement throughout the six years it took me to complete this book.

Special thanks to the women who provided generous assistance with the foreign languages that made my manuscript a more realistic depiction of my father's world: Cilia Ebert-Libeskind (German) and Rebecca Friedman (Russian). There were even some who chose to keep their contributions anonymous.

I am also indebted to Ashley Allen at Duggal Visual Solutions for her tireless work on the artwork images.

This book might not have been published without the boundless energy of my dedicated literary agent, Nancy Rosenfeld, and the vision of acquisitions editor Lisa Quinn at Wilfrid Laurier University Press. I am also indebted to Carol Harrison for her diligent copy-edit and the amazing team at WLU Press: Rob Kohlmeier, Leslie Macredie, Clare Hitchens, Heather Blain-Yanke, and Darren Thompson.

Part 1
Before

Prologue

My father's visits gave me a chance to pick his brain and work at unearthing its tightly held secrets. I grabbed my briefcase and rushed out of my office heading to Gale Place in the Bronx to meet him. It was only a twelve-minute drive, but in the Friday-evening rush hour I wove in and out of traffic, glancing at the dashboard to check the time. I didn't want him to wait outside because already the air held the sting of winter.

It was getting dark and large droplets of rain rolled down the windshield as I pulled up in front of his apartment building, the Amalgamated Co-op adjacent to Van Cortlandt Park. He emerged smiling and holding a large stainless-steel pot wrapped in checkered kitchen towels, his overnight bag slung over the shoulder of his weatherproof parka, navy cap festooned with Chinese buttons from our trip to China. He looked youthful and fit, though he was nearly seventy-five.

Dad got in the car and we hugged over the centre console. "How are you, Tinku?" I asked.

"*Zeyer gut.*" Very well, he replied in Yiddish, then added, "*Der vinter kumt shoyn.*" Winter is almost here.

I pulled out of the cul-de-sac and noticed the wind twisting the branches of the trees in the park. *I better hurry before the weather worsens*, I thought. It worried me, but I knew that a storm meant nothing to my father. The gulag experience

3

prepared him to survive hardships, and weather was the least of it. The rain turned heavy as I merged onto the Major Deegan Expressway, the mad rush hour by now well underway and the road surface slick. Cars whizzed past us. I needed to speed up. The car was infused with the smell of my father's cooking. My stomach growled and I realized I was starving. I inhaled the pungent ginger aroma. It was pleasant and surprising.

"Dad, what did you make today?"

"Ginger meatballs."

"Did I give you that recipe?"

"No, your mama's friend gave it to me. It's very easy to make."

"You had ginger in the house?" I asked, surprised for this is not a common ingredient in Polish Jewish cooking.

A huge truck passed, making the road momentarily invisible. I pressed the gas.

Dad was oblivious. "No, I used ginger ale."

My husband, David, and I had been begging my father to move into our Larchmont home since Mama passed away nine years before. But Dad refused resolutely, saying only, "I need my Bronx headquarters." We settled for the weekend visits. It didn't matter how frustrating our workweeks may have been, what arguments we had with or about the children, the minute my father crossed our threshold something magical happened. Everyone was calmer. Problems that seemed impossible on Thursday would be solved by Monday.

After Friday dinners we often lingered in the dining area, the adults sipping tea, the kids moving their chairs closer to *Zayda*, all of us huddled around the proverbial fire, though the only glow came from the scarlet glass lamps that hung over the table.

Our daughter, about to graduate high school, usually got dibs on conversation first: "*Zayda*, tell me again about your marriage to *Bubby* under Stalin's portrait."

"Ach, vedding, shmedding," he'd say. "It's the love that counts."

Our son, two years younger than his sister, would pipe up next: "*Zayda*, can you tell us the story about when they threw you into that Polish prison?"

"But I have told it a hundred times," my father would say, waving his hands in frustration, while his smile invited more questions.

"Yes, but each time you tell us a different wrinkle. The part about the tattoo was new last time! I don't want to miss any part of it."

One weekend, when we were helping my father prepare for his annual migration to Florida, we gave him a new tape recorder to bring with him. I had had so many questions for my mother that I never thought to ask. I believed that she would always be there, that I could ask later, or the moment wasn't right and then ... she was gone. I wouldn't make that mistake again.

On Saturday morning, David struggled to open the impossible plastic packaging. He called to my father who was in his room busy practising a new tune on his electric keyboard. "Nachman, can you join us in the den? We want to show you something."

We heard the strains of the melody repeating. I knew he'd come in only once he had the tune exactly right. Finally, Dad appeared, triumphant. His eyes shone and his cheeks looked rosy as if he were suddenly younger. "I got it!" he said.

David presented the tape recorder,

Perplexed, my father asked, "What's this, when I want to play my music?"

"Dad, I hope you'll record stories from your life on this machine when you go to Florida."

"You know them already," he said.

"But I want them for the children, for the future ..." I didn't want to say *for when you are gone*. He seemed to understand. His face turned serious for a moment and all he said was, "Ach." I didn't know what to make of it.

And we showed him how the tape recorder worked.

"Why do they need all those buttons and why are they so small?" he asked. "Ania, have you seen my glasses?"

"Look, Nachman," David instructed. "This is the pause button, if you want to stop your narration for a moment and think."

I handed Dad his glasses. The lenses magnified his eyes into two blue pools.

"What should I think about? It's all in there." He tapped his head.

"Look Dad, this is the button to press if you want to rewind and hear what you have recorded," I chimed in.

"What are those double arrows?" he asked.

"Oh, I forgot to say, these are fast forward?" I told him.

"Who is in a hurry? I won't need these," he said.

Then David showed him the mini tape cassettes.

"This small thing will hold my whole story?"

"No, Dad, you will have to put in a new one when this one ends," I said.

He held his head with both hands. "Oy, is this necessary? I have told you enough stories already," he said.

My father pushed up the glasses slipping off his small nose and stared at the buttons. He pressed one tentatively, took a deep breath and began: "I was born in 1909 in Lodz, but my passport says Przedborz ..." He stopped suddenly and searched for a button.

I said, "What's wrong, Dad?"

"I ...: I what do you call it? I want to cancel, to go back."

"Why?"

"Ach, I forgot to explain this," he said utterly frustrated, then pushed the wrong button and erased what he had just recorded. "*Shayze!*" An uncharacteristic curse escaped his lips. He took off his glasses and said, "I think it's time to prepare lunch. Today I will make the broccoli with eggs. Good?"

Dad died in 2001. My grief abated slowly. Every time I stepped into his room, the funeral rushed at me as if it were only days before so I put off tackling his closet for three years. Now I stood in his room staring at the geometric rug he himself selected, the slippers still lined up like soldiers where he'd left them under the bed, everything still held his persona and seemed to scream, "Are you going to keep this bedroom like a museum?"

Not that my father's closet had much in it. He was very frugal and hadn't bought anything new for years. I was wracked by guilt because I knew what he would have said. "Take my coats and sweaters and give them to a charity, there are so many homeless people who could use them."

"But Dad, I need them here for a bit longer," I would have pleaded.

And surely he would have replied, "It has been three years! Ach, Ania it's such a *shande*. Take them to Goodwill now. Do me a favour."

But it was spring and the coats wouldn't help anyone now. I made a mental note to take them to the donation centre in the fall and started rummaging through the closet. I hugged his coats and sweaters and inhaled deeply hoping for his scent, but by then there was nothing of it left; just the slightest hint of mothballs. I took out his favourite blue shirt and noticed a tiny smear of paint on the sleeve. He wore it while he painted. It made me smile because he was so fastidious that he wouldn't have worn it had he noticed the yellow paint smudge. I went to hang it in my closet. This way every time I open it, I thought, just for a split second, I would have the illusion that he was still here.

I had sorted the clothes I would donate, some twill trousers, old flannel shirts, his blue terry bathrobe, a few sweaters he rarely wore. "Who is cold? I'm never cold," he'd say, and some ties that he'd only use to attend graduations and his show openings. It was unfortunate that David was too tall to use any of my father's things. My father's five-foot-four stature, perfectly normal in pre-war Europe, was decidedly below average in America. I was almost finished with the emotionally exhausting job when I noticed a shoebox, way at the back of the closet.

I opened the box and stared. It was full of cassette tapes neatly labelled with dates in my father's fine hand.

"Oh, my God!" I called out though no one was nearby to hear me. "So he did use the tape recorder!" How could I have doubted him? "David!"

David ran upstairs, office papers still in his hands, and stood at the door out of breath and wide-eyed. "Annette! What is it? Are you okay?"

"It's Dad," I said, showing him the tapes.

"All these years," David said. He chewed on his lip. "Drying out."

I handled the tapes gingerly, priceless, ancient treasure— my inheritance.

For weeks I agonized. The fragile tapes had to be transferred to CDs. It bothered me that some stranger in the lab would get to hear my father's voice before I did and I was wary of letting the shoebox out of my sight, but there were no appropriate conversion services in our immediate area. What if the tapes were to get lost in the mail? What if they were so brittle they crumbled when handled? After consultation with experts, I reluctantly decided to send them out for conversion to CDs, to a business whose reputation I verified as if I were a detective. In a few days I received a call from the recording company. "Who is calling? I asked, expecting to hear about some disaster that destroyed the tapes. Fire? Flood? Why would they be calling me otherwise?

"Mrs. B?"

"Yes, yes. What is it?"

"I am the technician converting your father's tapes. I am sorry to be disturbing you, but I just wanted to tell you something." He sounded nasal, young, inexperienced.

My heart pounded. He must have screwed up.

"What, what is it?"

"I just had to tell you how I enjoyed hearing your father sing."

"Sing?"

"Yes, he has such a beautiful voice and ... and his stories were better than many of the books I have read. I was deeply touched by them."

I unplugged the phone and turned off the dishwasher. I closed the windows. I wished I knew how to halt the sounds of traffic whizzing past our house. I didn't want to lose a single syllable. I wanted no sound mixing with his voice. I sat at his desk and pushed the start button. Goosebumps rose on my skin. Mesmerized by the sound of his voice, a melodious baritone, upbeat and conversational, I barely breathed. His rich Yiddish lexicon was peppered with expressions I knew so well: "*Nu, Anya, lomir shmuesen khaloymes.*" So, Ania, let us talk about dreams and reminisce. Or with urgency in his voice, "*Du darfst dos farshteyn.*" You have to understand this, he'd insist. He was with me, just in the next room, or on one of the long telephone calls from Florida. I listened with my whole body, every cell in my brain straining to absorb every word, every nuance, the said and the unsaid.

Chapter One

In the year of Nachman's birth, Piotrkowska Street, the boulevard that cut a long, wide swath through the city of Lodz, might have impressed a visitor from another part of Poland. Its elegant facades looked vaguely British. Compared to other towns, it was grand in its sweep and so modern, with a tram that ran along its length, and neo-Renaissance bourgeois villas, industrialist palaces, and public buildings adorned with dragons and dolphins. Smaller, less impressive streets branched off toward the east and west. Here tenements surrounded narrow shadowy courtyards that made dark play areas for the hordes of children who treasured them. In these yards, permanently infused with the pungent smells of poverty—refuse from the trash cans and urine wafting in from the staircases—they could, at last, run and stretch their muscles: freedom from cramped flats overfilled with the basics—a stove, a table, and several narrow beds wherein family members slept head to foot in pairs if they were lucky, or if they weren't, in foursomes arranged like sardines.

Nachman was luckier than most because his family's apartment was on the ground floor, in a corner near the courtyard entrance. Here on summer days, if the sun's rays were at just the right angle, light would seep into the apartment and make playful rainbows that bounced off the edges of a glass bowl above the stove. But in the winter when it was too cold to venture outside, he could perch on the windowsill looking at the comings and goings. Wiping the rivulets of steam from the high window with his sleeve, five-year-old Nachman could see wondrous things.

He sat for hours at the window hoping for the magical machine that had appeared for the first time weeks ago. Most days it was nowhere to be seen, but on this day he could tell from the racket at the gate's entrance that it was on its way. He held his breath. The sound came closer and now the machine and its owner stood before his widened eyes. A stooped man in a shabby black jacket and baggy pants cranked a shaft on the side of the barrel-shaped box and made sounds emerge out of its belly. Nachman did not know the box was an organ or that organ grinders were disdained because of the poor quality of the music. To Nachman and the poor children of his neighbourhood the tones emerging from the box were fairylike. The sounds bounced off the concrete walls and filled the courtyard, seeped into open windows and filled Nachman's lungs so that he could barely breathe. He had never heard anything so beautiful. He repeated the music in his mind long after the wondrous machine and its master were gone.

Other children were more fascinated by the monkey on the man's shoulder, but Nachman felt sad for the poor creature, a lively little thing wearing a tight-fitting suit. *If someone were to put me in the jungle,* he thought, *and make me wear a coat of fur I would feel equally uncomfortable!* But Nachman lived nowhere near a jungle. He lived off Piotrkowska Street in Lodz, Poland, smack in the centre of the country.

On some days, Nachman saw the ragman with his wagon tilting his head back and yelling, all the way to the top floors, "*Szmaty! Szmaty! Szmaty!*" Rags! Rags! Rags! or, "*Noże! Noże! Noże!*" Knives! Knives! Sharpen your knives! The words reverberated through the courtyard. Windows opened and sometimes people threw down bundles of rags, or knives wrapped in them for sharpening. Then children would run down to retrieve them and hand the ragman a few zloty, sparing their parents the many flights of stairs.

On Friday nights when his parents came home from the synagogue, the whole family would sit after dinner in the candle glow and sing. All of his siblings, two older brothers and two sisters, had lovely voices. They joined with their parents and their music made Nachman so pleased that he belonged to this particular family, not the others, whose loud arguments he could hear through the thin walls. His family was harmonious, like the sounds he had heard in the courtyard. One of these nights, still too young to join the others in the singing, Nachman crawled under the table, his favourite private spot and listened while he stared at the shadows dancing on the walls.

This is where he fell asleep, and if it weren't for his mother, Rachel Leah, scooping him off the floor and arranging him in the bed he shared with his brothers, he would have spent the night on the floor. It gave her immense pleasure to sing him her favourite lullaby: "*Shlof, mayn kind, mayn treyst mayn sheyner, Shlof-zhe, zunenyu. Shlof, mayn lebn, mayn Kaddish eyner, Shlof-zhe, lyu, lyu, lyu.*" Sleep, my child, my strength, my handsome sonny, Sleep, my life, my only Kaddish, Sleep, Lyu, Lyu, Lyu.

She must have experienced a brief moment of inner peace singing it, knowing that she was lucky to have a son who would recite the mourner's Kaddish three times a day, for eleven months after she was gone.

Nachman was her youngest child, arriving, as she often said, "with the last train." Nearing fifty, she hardly expected this baby and found more tenderness for Nachman than for her other children. With his big blue eyes, blond hair, and button nose, he struck her as an angel child. She wanted to keep him close to give herself the illusion that she wasn't growing older. As was the custom then, she clothed him in dresses but for longer than her other two boys, and nursed him till he was almost four. She had never seen such a contented, happy child. It was as if *HaShem* smiled at her and sent her this one last gift. All his life Nachman would remember her telling him this. He was a constitutionally good-natured child and nothing much could upset him. Some things, like the organ grinder and their Sabbath singalongs, could make him feel positively jubilant. For him the world was perpetually filled with sunshine and music.

Rachel Leah knew that if he had just those two things— light and music—he might not even need food. This notion made her heart swell because she could be sure that those were things he could get without worrying about money. Money was something she and Chaim Chaskel, her husband, worried about each and every day of their lives.

They migrated to Lodz from the village of Przedborz shortly before the birth of their fourth child, Rosa. Folks back in Przedborz always talked about the opportunities in the big city. Lodz was known as the Polish Manchester because of its industrial base and the multitude of textile manufacturers. No one told Nachman's parents about the smokestacks that rose high into the sky, higher than the tallest trees back home; that they spewed foul clouds into the sky that settled onto the buildings and into lungs.

Chaim Chaskel's old friends still called him the *Tishler.* He brought his Przedborz carpentry tool chest filled with planes, saws, and hammers, but couldn't make a go of it. It seemed no one needed him to build tables, or benches, or to repair anything. The fancy city folk preferred to buy modern, factory-made furniture. After a while Chaim pushed the tool chest under the bed where it gathered dust.

After a time in the big city, he and Rachel Leah opened a tiny grocery that adjoined their one-room apartment and faced the street. In provincial Przedborz , a shop this minuscule might have seemed like a real business, but in a city like Lodz, it was too small and understocked to be anything but an insignificant hole in the wall. They struggled to scrape a few zlotys together to buy the merchandise—mostly vegetables and fruit—at the market. They went to the stalls before closing time and managed to negotiate a better price on the unsold fruit and vegetables—a few apples with too many spots, a wilted cabbage, onions pungent with incipient rot, or potatoes that started to grow roots. For most of their meagre clientele these would be all right because they could buy them for less than at the bigger markets.

The *gevelbl* (little shop), as they called it with a dose of irony, also carried tea that had sat in the boxes so long that its aroma was a distant memory. There were also some rusted tins of herring, and *cykoria*, a cheap coffee substitute made of ground chicory roots, because who in their neighbourhood could afford real coffee?

"Rachel Leah, look, I need a few potatoes. Can you put them on my tab? I will pay you next week, I promise," old Sarah, their next-door neighbour, said, pulling off the roots that were starting to sprout from them.

"*Farvos nisht?*" Why not? Rachel Leah answered with a smile. "What's another week?"

"*A gezunt oyf dayn kop, Rokhele.*" Health onto your head, Rachel, said Sarah, and shut the squeaky door as she shuffled out.

When Nachman turned seven, his parents wanted to send him to study at a *cheder*, a small religious school for Jewish children. As soon as he overheard the start of a discussion on the subject between his two older brothers and his father, Nachman knew to make himself scarce. They always took Nachman's side and he knew instinctively to keep quiet. He picked up his pencil, the one with the chewed up end, and crawled under the table to draw while keeping his ears pricked up to catch every word. The two older brothers, old enough to argue with their parents, would have none of this *cheder* business for their youngest sibling.

"Poppa," said Yankel, the oldest, "let Nachman go to the new Vladimir Medem School. It's just a few blocks from our home."

"What's the matter with the *cheder*? You went there, your brother went there," Chaim Chaskel replied, raising his eyebrows and putting aside his pipe. He was surprised that his oldest son, the one who still followed the traditions, would make such a radical suggestion. Chaim Chaskel had heard about the new school. It was the talk of their neighbourhood. The Jewish Labor Bund party was opening up free schools in the poor sections of the city and it had become a powerful socialist voice in Lodz.

Like Chaim Chaskel's family, most Lodz Jews barely scraped by. They were tailors, shoemakers, hat makers, small grocers, but most of all, weavers and dyers, because Lodz was the capital of textile manufacturing in Europe. Jewish factory labourers constituted more than a third of all workers. Dramatic and bitter class differences had turned Lodz into a hotbed of political activity, with the Jewish Labor Bund as a major player. It was a city whose industrial growth was unprecedented in Europe, but this rapid burgeoning spawned abject poverty for the workers while for the factory owners it generated untold wealth. Polish, German, and Jewish industrialists vied to build bigger and better factories, filling blocks and blocks with brick edifices whose chimneys reached ever higher to spew black clouds. Like germ-encrusted living tissue, the city's lopsided social layers were a ripe breeding ground for political turmoil. Abysmal factory conditions and indecent wages spawned constant labour unrest, strikes, demonstrations, protests, and brutal confrontations with the police. The Bund fought with factory owners to reduce the workdays from eleven hours to eight and to increase starvation wages by a few kopecks.

As Yankel was making his argument about the Medem School, Chaim Chaskel reflected on how even he, an old man, engaged in a bit of subversive activity on behalf of the Jewish Labor Bund. His mind spun to the recent elections and on how when he went to pray at the Great Synagogue on Zachodnia Street he furtively distributed slips of paper with the number four written on them. Number four promoted the Bund party's slate of candidates. Chaim Chaskel knew that political activities in the synagogue were not welcome, but he believed in the Bund party's ideals because they stood for the rights of the working poor. He believed in the Bund's values as much as he believed in God.

Chaim Chaskel decided to give his oldest son a hearing. He adjusted his glasses and said, "*Nu*, so tell me why a *cheder* isn't good enough for Nachman."

"I learned the prayers, but not much else," Yankel said quietly, looking down. It was not his way to be pushy with his ideas. By now the early religious training he'd received had become so ingrained that he followed its precepts, but without much enthusiasm. He wished he had learned something about the world around him. If his parents would relent, at least his little brother could have his eyes opened. Yankel, twelve years Nachman's senior, was a Bundist, though looking at him one couldn't tell. He wore the usual black garb of Orthodox Jews, but on the inside he was different. As soon as he learned of the Medem School's creation he promised himself he'd convince his father to send his little brother there. He wanted Nachman to come under its positive influence while he was still impressionable and open. Though he himself continued to attend the synagogue and pray for a better life, he could see that prayer did little to fill empty stomachs. Deep down, Yankel suspected that people needed to take matters into their own hands if they wanted to see changes on earth, not wait for rewards in the other world. He couldn't quite bring himself to break out of the religious habits that had been ingrained in him, but he wanted his youngest brother to look at the world through a different lens. The Bund's socialist teachings and emphasis on equality among people, including women, were enticing. The Medem School would grow a new kind of Jew— proud, unassimilated, socially engaged, and deeply steeped in Yiddish culture.

Nachman shifted around in his spot. His legs were getting numb from trying to keep still and not attract attention. He was glad that Yankel was trying to talk Poppa out of the *cheder*. Playing with older boys in the courtyard he had heard how the rabbi rapped on their knuckles with the Torah pointer when they misread the Hebrew prayers.

Natan, six years older than Nachman, had been listening to the conversation quietly, but now he itched to add his voice to this discussion. He, too, had known about the Medem School and wished he had gone there. It sounded so exciting. The classes would all be taught in Yiddish, the language they spoke at home. There would be music and art and sports, subjects never included in his religious school. Nachman would love it. It was as if the Medem School's founders had anticipated a student like his little brother—thirsty for all things artistic.

"Poppa, listen to Yankel. He is right. Don't you support the Bund? Aren't you always encouraging your friends at the synagogue to vote for Bund candidates for the city council?"

"What does that have to do with anything?" For the moment Chaim Chaskel couldn't grasp the link.

"They will teach Nachman to believe in himself, not to depend on anyone, to be a strong Jew who won't be afraid of the goyim. They will teach him about fairness and about being decent to others, no matter who they are," Natan launched into his speech repeating exactly what he had read in the paper.

Chaim Chaskel didn't mind having Nachman introduced to these ideas. He believed in them himself. The way the Bund stood up for the workingman's dignity, well, he couldn't argue with that. He was beginning to soften, but wasn't ready to give in so easily.

"Imagine," Yankel said, emboldened by Natan's comments, "Nachman can learn world history and science, not like the *cheder* kids who only learn how to pray in Hebrew. Nothing else. They don't even learn the meaning of the words they mouth."

The brothers argued late into the night on behalf of Nachman. Rachel Leah had been listening to her boys. They made sense. She had high hopes for her youngest son. She wanted him to become a man of the world. Maybe he, more than any of her other children, could break out of their poor neighbourhood and taste the world. She knew that the Medem School was to be a secular place for learning unlike any other, and she knew her husband like no one else. He wouldn't exactly like it, but his expression told her that he could be persuaded.

"It's late," she said, pointing to the grandfather clock. "Let's sleep on it. We'll figure it out later," she added with a wink. "Come to bed Chaim." Then she glanced under the table and saw that Nachman had fallen asleep. He breathed so quietly that engrossed in their big debate they had almost forgotten he was there. She lifted him up as she used to do when he was a baby and put him in bed. He was small for his age and light as a feather.

Despite his deep religious values, in the end, Chaim Chaskel relented. Yankel and Natan had won. Nachman was enrolled in the Medem School along with twenty other neighbourhood boys and girls from poor working Jewish families for whom religious instruction was secondary to their financial woes.

As I listen for hours on end to my father narrating his story, sometimes the mind plays tricks. It deceives me into thinking we are sitting on the balcony of his Florida condo, drinking tea, and he is telling me these stories. I catch myself and then hit the back button to hear some of his phrases again. "*Yo, Anya. Emes. S'iz azoy geven.*" Yes, Ania, it was really like that. I can see him nodding with a faraway look as if he were seeing himself as that slight blond schoolboy in knee-length trousers and a cloth cap.

By the time Nachman began school, Lodz was a bustling, industrial city with its population roughly divided into thirds: Jews, Poles, and ethnic Germans. The rapid technological growth had made it a modern city in many respects. Many religious Jews had abandoned their Hassidic attire. A substantial number had become modernized and politically active in the Jewish Labor Bund and the various Zionist parties. This meant that even those who were still somewhat religious no longer wore the wide-brimmed black fedoras or fur *shtramls* of the Orthodox. Instead, they wore black wool caps that made them look much more like Greek fishermen than Hassidim.

Trams criss-crossed the wide streets and wagons hitched to horses were seen mostly on market days. Poles shopped in stores owned by Jewish merchants. Jews bought produce from Polish farmers and hired Poles to turn on their lights on the Sabbath when this action by the pious was forbidden.

The school was like a rebirth to Nachman. All day long he sat spellbound by the amazing things teachers taught him. He learned about faraway lands where people spoke different languages; ate raw fish and rice with sticks, or snails, or noodles as long and thin as his sisters' hair. He swallowed stories about composers who wrote music when they were still boys; the mysteries of the constellations in the night sky, and how fancy artists from fancy countries made pictures in which people's faces looked as if the features had been scrambled.

No longer confined to observing the world through his window, he felt as if he were finally a participant. Everything interested him but music and art most of all. He loved drawing with the coloured pencils the teacher distributed during art classes and felt embarrassed when the teacher held up his pictures as examples for the class. In music class, he waited anxiously for the operas and concertos the teacher played for them on the scratchy gramophone. It was stunning to learn that real people, not unearthly creatures, could sequence sounds that transported him beyond the classroom and beyond the city. The dance class with Miss Zina was his favourite because here he not only listened to the music but watched her execute elegant dance steps as she twirled to the rhythm. He could watch and watch, but then she called the children to join her and he jumped up with joy to skip and dance with his friends.

Nachman began to dream of owning an instrument of his own. He wanted to see if he, too, could make music. But this was an unattainable dream. The school's tiny budget could not support instruments. They were lucky that someone donated an old piano that allowed teachers to offer musical accompaniment to dance lessons. At first Nachman fancied a piano because of the way Miss Chana, the music teacher, coaxed out sounds with her long, delicate fingers gliding gracefully along the black and white keys. Soon enough it became clear to him that his parents could never afford one even if they saved every *groshen*. He realized that his piano idea was quite laughable. Even if by some miracle they found one on the street just begging to be taken in, it would no more fit in their one-room apartment than a goat, though the goat would be far more useful.

One day Nachman took a different route home from school and on the way passed a store that sold all manner of musical instruments. He pressed his nose to the display window and stared at the guitars with their graceful necks, the drums he could almost hear tapping out a march, the cymbals like golden suns. But it was the bugle in one corner of the window that captured his imagination more than the rest. Its gleam bounced off the shiny surface, reflecting on the window. Its shimmer exuded a magical pull. Nachman pursed his lips and imagined blowing in it. He wondered how he could get it to emit different notes. "Maybe I would have to vary the intake of my breath," he speculated, but he had no idea though he desperately wanted to know.

While his friends liked to play games in the street, or run directly to the lady who sold bagels on the corner, Nachman ran to spend time before the instrument display. It made his imagination soar and just the sight of it satisfied him for a while, but then his longing became so intense that he got a pain in the pit of his stomach. On some days he stood there until it became dark. On those days he thought that his ache for an instrument was the fault of the organ grinder with his monkey and music machine that he spied in the courtyard all those years ago. Then he ran home faster because he knew he would get a scolding from his worried mother.

Nachman's two sisters were busy around the kitchen rushing to set up the Shabbat table before Friday sundown. The older one, Pola, with her round, thick glasses, looked as if she were meant to perform this ritual. She polished the utensils with the corner of the kitchen towel knowing they would never shine quite like silver, yet she enjoyed the illusion that some-day they may have a silver set and then she would be ready.

Rosa, at sixteen, five years Pola's junior, stepped into the alcove of the large room that served as the bedroom, living room, dining room, and kitchen. Over the cot covered in a worn green coverlet she shared with her sister, hung a small round mirror. Yankel had found it in the courtyard, discarded by a family who had moved out. He brought it in like a cat dragging in an unusual offering. He banged a nail into the wall, hung the mirror on it, and said to Rosa, "Here, you can now style your auburn tresses."

She looked at the mirror satisfied. *Yes*, she thought, *my hair is definitely my best feature.*

"Stop primping and help me," Pola called out. "Mama and Poppa will be back from the synagogue any minute."

Not a moment later, Rachel Leah opened the door; her usually pink cheeks reddened a shade more from the cool air. "The winter will be here before you know it," she said, and asked of no one in particular, "how many pairs of socks have we knitted?"

Poppa came in right behind her and greeted his daughters, "*A gutn shabes!*" He pulled out his pocket watch and glanced at it. "Where are the boys? They should have been home by now."

"Don't worry, Poppa, Yankel will make sure that Natan and Nachman will be here by the time Mama blesses the candles."

"Yes, yes," he said, not sounding convinced.

His oldest child, Yankel, was the one Chaim Chaskel could understand best. He still dressed like a decent Jew: the black coat, a hat and, of course, the vest with *tzitzes,* whose white strands reminded him of the daily *mitzvot* (good deeds) every good Jew had to perform. But even Yankl had changed lately. Change seemed to be in the city's air, in its water, in its people. *Not that all change was bad,* thought Chaim. He could actually agree that working from dawn to dusk and barely eking out a life was not fair, especially when the factory owners owned mansions, right in this city, as if they were royalty. It was Yankel's involvement with the Jewish Labor Bund that put these fancy new ideas in his head, but those ideas were easy enough to accept, even for Chaim.

Lately, Yankel had joined the painters union where he and his fellow house painters could negotiate better conditions from the landlords of the buildings in which they worked. Yankel was an artist in his trade. He seemed to treat every room as if it were a canvas. He would stroke the flat blade of his trowel carefully over any unevenness, applying the plaster generously, two coats or three, whatever it took to make sure the wall was more perfect than new. But this painstaking attention to detail cost him dearly. It took him twice as long as the next guy to complete a paint job. Still, he didn't care: better a perfect job than a fast one. That could have been his motto.

The door burst open bringing in a gust of wind, and Nachman ran in heading straight to the sink to wash his hands. Rosa tousled his hair.

"What are you doing? I am not a baby anymore," he said, but only half-heartedly. She knew he really didn't mind. He was her baby brother, her favourite sibling, and so much like her that had she been a boy and born later, they could have been identical twins.

Rosa looked at the shriveled snap peas Mama had brought in from their little grocery this morning. "They are wilted already, they'll be rotten by Monday. We might as well use them," Mama had said.

Natan, the middle son, whose place in the family hierarchy fell between Pola and Rosa, felt he was the most sophisticated and modern in his family. He came through the door waving the evening edition of the newspaper. "Another strike is planned for Monday. I hope you will all be joining me," he said.

"Stop saying nonsense, Natan," Rachel Leah said. "You are giving Nachman bad ideas."

"I was only speaking to the adults here," Natan defended himself and winked at Nachman.

With his round wire-rimmed glasses Natan looked like a professor. He always spoke of politics and was more serious than Rosa and more outspoken than Yankel. Nachman worshipped him because Natan always brought a whiff of excitement when he came home and did not treat Nachman as if he were too young to hear about awful things like street fights with the police, or about arrests of the strikers. Natan always spoke of these events with passion and fire in his green eyes and Nachman knew that if it were up to his brother the world would be a fairer place.

Pola looked out the window and confirmed that the first star had appeared in the sky. They all sat around the long table Chaim had made before any of them were born. A hush fell over the room as Rachel Leah covered her eyes with her hands and recited the Sabbath blessing, swaying slightly in rhythm to the holy words: "*Barukh atah Adonoi, Eloheinu, melekh ha'olam asher kidshanu b'mitzvotav v'tzivanu l'ehadlik ner shel shabat. Amen.*" She lit the candles sitting in the silver candlesticks she inherited from her mother, a piece of finery that made the rest of the table look shabby by comparison.

On Friday nights the meal started with gefilte fish when inexpensive carp was available. It was accompanied by a beautiful braided challah baked by the sisters. Rosa, especially, was an expert at braiding the dough. When the smell of the baking challah filled the room, one could have been forgiven for thinking this was a home where food was plentiful. The divine smell alone stood for all the delicacies in the world, at least that was what Nachman thought whenever he came into the apartment on Fridays and saw the plump challah cooling under a cloth embroidered by Mama. After the blessing of the food and the bread, they were at last free to savour the fish and the chicken soup.

Rachel Leah distributed small pieces of chicken according to family hierarchy. Father and Yankel got the legs, Natan and Nachman got pieces of the breast, and the girls got the wings, while Mama ate the neck and gizzard. The bony back along with some of the breast meat and the fatty part near the chicken's tail were saved for another day.

Nachman couldn't wait for the meal to end. His favourite part of Friday-night dinners was not the food, but the singing. After Rosa and Pola cleared the table they all sat around the table singing old Yiddish songs. Some were full of longing for a better day, some spoke to the drudgery of the daily work and the joy of the Sabbath, others were lullabies, but the ones Nachman loved the most were the ones about love gained and lost, like "Volt ikh zayn a feygele":

> Were I a bird, were I to have wings
> I would fly straight to you
> But I am no bird and I have no wings
> I long for you

Nachman didn't know much about love or girls yet. It was probably the faraway look in Rosa's eyes as she stretched the high notes. She seemed to be looking somewhere beyond the ceiling, beyond the street outside the window, to a world unknown to him. He could always pick out Rosa's honeyed tones from the rest of the voices. He knew for sure that if his family had had the means for her musical education, Rosa would have been an opera singer. Her voice could transport him to places far away from Lodz. He wasn't sure where, but it was like sitting on a magic carpet and sailing the skies. Most Fridays he joined in the singing and when they all harmonized, nothing was sweeter.

As night fell, they all scrambled to their beds arranged around the perimeter of the room. They had slept two to a bed while Nachman was very small and still fit in a cradle. But when he turned five, he had to join his brothers and they tried their best to lay straight and still on their sides as to not to push the others out of the narrow metal cot. In minutes Nachman could tell who was sound asleep because he recognized the distinct character of their snores, but it was never Pola. From his position he couldn't really see her, but he knew that the eerie glow near his sisters' bed was Pola's candle. She had a habit of placing it strategically on the floor so as not to wake their parents while she was reading. She read so much and often in the dim light of the candle that Nachman was convinced those were the reasons for her poor eyesight and thick lenses. Pola was sweet and quiet, but she was so much older than he that he thought of her as his second mother. Rosa on the other hand was beautiful, and lively. She always had something interesting to say. She laughed at the slightest provocation and Nachman always felt happier when he came home from school and she was there. He knew that soon Rosa would get a job and then who could tell how their close-knit family would change?

Yankel already had a girlfriend and soon he would marry Balcia, or at least that was Nachman's assumption. It was obvious that the young couple couldn't move in with them into the one-room apartment, so Yankel, too, might soon be gone. Nachman worried about all of them flying out of the nest. He knew his mama would be sad and he couldn't stand that thought. He squeezed his eyes shut and listened to the wind rattling the covers on the tin trash cans outside.

Though Nachman didn't lack for love and attention from his own family, the Medem School fostered such close and warm relationships among its students and teachers that they all became part of an extended family. The school's philosophy espoused brotherhood among all peoples, and those were not empty sentiments. The curriculum included studies of cultures from around the world, and the annual international dance festival featured students in national costumes. Nachman was selected to be the Dutch boy and perform the *klompen* dance wearing wooden clogs. He never forgot this experience. It fuelled a thirst for knowledge about music and the world beyond his school.

Nachman had an easygoing nature. He considered all of his classmates a friend. Most of the time they all hung out together. Students would go home after school for a little while, then return to school to do homework, to work on group projects like making sets for a school performance or just to play with friends and to engage in spirited discussions with teachers who seemed to be there at all hours.

One day Nachman's fourth-grade class received a letter from the art teacher who was visiting Paris. The principal, Shlomo Itche Ravin, came into the classroom. The children stood up at attention and said in unison, "*Gut morgn, Khaver Ravin.*" Good morning, Friend Ravin. They called their teachers "friend," as a sign of respect and to minimize the distance between students and teachers. A hush fell over the room. The principal didn't visit often. *Khaver* Ravin held up a long blue envelope covered with stamps.

"*Ikh hob do a briv fun Pariz, fun undzere Liza Holtzman.*" I have a letter here from Paris from our own Liza Holtzman.

The children's eyes widened in surprise. This was surely a first. None of them had ever gotten a letter from such an exotic place. Nachman remembered that Miss Liza, the art teacher, had a sister who lived in Paris and that she was planning a trip there to see the renowned museums and art galleries. He was bursting with curiosity about what was in the letter. Then *Khaver* Ravin started reading it to the class in his deep bass:

> *Mayne tayere kinder*—my dear children—I wish I could have brought you all with me to see this city that is just exploding with artistic energy. I have spent hours at the Louvre and can't get enough of it. There are artists sketching along the Seine and the sounds of accordion played by the street musicians makes it feel like one grand party. I would need a year to see all the art galleries here. And the Eiffel tower, you would not believe it. I didn't exactly measure it, but I think it's a hundred stories high.

Every now and then one student or another uttered *oohs* and *ahhs* and was shushed by the others. They were all mesmerized by their teacher's wondrous accounts. It was as if someone on a different planet had communicated with them. Miss Liza ended her letter saying, "I truly hope that each and every one of you will get a taste of Paris one day, but Niemele, most of all, because of his artistic talent." Like all his classmates the teachers called Nachman by this nickname, derived from a poem the students had read in school, about a blond, blue-eyed child called Niemele. The child's description matched Nachman and the nickname stuck for life.

Nachman's face reddened up to his ears.

After *Khaver* Ravin read the postscript, Nachman vowed he would do his best not to disappoint Miss Liza. Her words, "I am sure that one day Niemele's artwork will hang in a museum," stayed in his mind for the rest of his life. And it wasn't just the words that tugged at his imagination. The letter made Nachman realize that the world was bigger than his neighbourhood, bigger than Lodz; that it held mysteries, which once uncovered, could make one look at the world with new eyes.

The Vladimir Medem School went up only to the eighth grade and in 1924 Nachman was in its first graduating class. But for him graduation was a big letdown. His friends scattered. Like Nachman, most of them looked for jobs to supplement the meagre family incomes. Nachman pined for the camaraderie and he still longed for an instrument. But with the end of school, music lessons ceased. Nachman moped for a while, but then an idea struck him and he thought, *A bisl mazl is vert mer vi a ton gold.* A bit of luck is worth more than a ton of gold.

He went to see the school principal. The principal was not in the building so Nachman moved on to his plan B. He headed to see the head secretary of the administration, Mr. Freidenreich. The man greeted him warmly.

"What brings you back to school, Nachman, now that you have graduated?"

"I am looking for a job," Nachman replied directly, as was his style.

"A job? We don't hire fifteen-year-old teachers."

"It's not the job I had in mind."

"What then? What could you be thinking about?"

"Mr. Freidenreich, don't you have too much to do? Aren't you just swamped by the paperwork?"

"What's it to you?" the secretary said, clearly taken aback.

"I can help you," Nachman said confidently.

"You? Help me?"

"Yes. Me! Oh, Mr. Freidenreich, you won't regret hiring me. Never. You'll see, I will work harder than anyone. You have so much work that the teachers here have to take turns helping you out, keeping them from the students. I know I can do some of this work. I would be a good assistant secretary."

"Chutzpah," Mr. Freidenreich breathed. But he knew of Nachman's extraordinary penmanship. He wrinkled his brow and puffed out his cheeks. "All right, Libeskind, I'll give you a try, but I can't pay much."

Nachman beamed. "You won't be sorry," he said.

In 1924, the fifteen-year-old Nachman took on his responsibilities at the Medem School with relish. In a short time he became indispensable to the functioning of the office. He handled calls from parents, typed lesson plans, processed forms, filed papers and student records, all while staying in close contact with his beloved teachers. And the few zloty he earned were a great help to his family. He tried, but could not save enough to buy an instrument. There was not even enough for a small harmonica.

To round out his education, he studied on his own in the school's library, attended free public lectures, and became active in the Sotsyalistisher Kinder Farband (SKIF), the Union of Socialist Children, a division of the Jewish Labor Bund. Like its parent organization, SKIF emphasized *khavershaft*, friendship, equality, and empathy among people. Of all its principles, this was the one that most appealed to Nachman's sensibilities.

Nachman tried to satisfy his yearning for learning about the world beyond his city by helping his father. In his family, storytelling was a personal enterprise. It wasn't just a matter of passing off fables told by others. Nachman's father could spin stories endlessly. He often started the telling with a twinkle in his eye and the Yiddish phrase *"S'iz an emese mayse."* This is a true story.

For Chaim Chaskel, storytelling was a way to supplement the family's meagre earnings. On weekends, he was a *badkhn*—an itinerant storyteller and entertainer at weddings, bar mitzvahs, and other *shtetl* celebrations. He would get into a horse-drawn wagon and travel many miles to neighbouring villages in central Poland, making sure he arrived before the Sabbath. He would then sit on a rickety chair in a humble home or a room in a local synagogue where celebrations would be held and wait for his fellow entertainers, the fiddlers, and harmonica players. Occasionally, Nachman joined him.

Most of the yarns Nachman's father told in Yiddish were what he himself had heard as a child. Some were folk tales or allegories with bits of moral instruction woven in; others were parables and humorous epigrams whose clever wordplay revealed the meaning. The guests at the celebrations where Chaim Chaskel performed could see themselves in the stories and would easily laugh, or cry, as the story demanded.Young Nachman not only loved the tales, he wanted to help preserve them. They weren't written down anywhere. As it happened, in 1926, the Institute for Jewish Research (YIVO) in Vilna (now Vilnius) Lithuania, issued a call to Jews throughout Eastern Europe to collect Yiddish folklore and other ethnographic material. At the age of seventeen Nachman responded enthusiastically to the call. He volunteered as a *zamler*, a collector of Yiddish oral traditions. He sought out his father on every free moment and wrote down what he heard using the tiniest Hebrew characters to save as much paper as possible and to reduce postage cost. Each time he collected a substantial sheaf, he would run to the post office, carefully affix the stamps using the few kopeks he managed to save, and mailed them off to YIVO's headquarters. He was happy that he could play a part in saving his father's wonderful tales.

Soon, however, the tranquil Libeskind household was shaken to its core. Nachman had just turned eighteen when his father died. This was the first death in his family, and Nachman took it hard. The only thing that cheered him was that he still had his job and could contribute his earnings, now needed more than ever, to the running of the household. Chaim Chaskel's refusal to submit to surgery sealed his fate when an untreated abdominal hernia led to gangrene. Shocked and saddened as they were about his passing, his absence changed the family dynamics. Rachel Leah retreated into her private grief and let her children make decisions. And it seemed as if the death of the patriarch unleashed a cascade of misfortunes.

By 1927, Joseph Stalin became the undisputed dictator of the Soviet empire, Bavaria lifted the ban on Adolph Hitler's speeches, and the Chinese civil war was in full swing. The following year, in Italy, Benito Mussolini flexed his muscles, abolishing the electoral system and taking away women's rights. The Japanese committed unspeakable atrocities in China. The world bubbled with unrest. By 1929 German president Paul von Hindenburg refused to pay Germany's war debt and when the stock market crashed in America, it sent ripples across the Atlantic unleashing a worldwide depression.

The Medem School could no longer afford even its low-waged assistant secretary and had to let Nachman and even some teachers go. *Worse than being evicted from your home*, he thought. He was now almost twenty and decided to seek his fortune in the world of people who worked with their hands. *For now I must put aside my dreams of music and art*, he thought. Isn't that what men do, put their minds to practical concerns?

He took a job at a chocolate factory. Initially, he was excited at the notion that he might get samples—chocolate was a delicacy his family could not even dream of—but when he got there on his first day, he was overwhelmed by the intense sickening sweet odour that filled the entire building. It permanently changed his attitude toward chocolate. He quit after three days. Next, he took a job in a textile dye works. Vats of ever-boiling coloured water made the walls drip with moisture. It was beastly hot because the boilers operated day and night. The men were perpetually shovelling coal into the open mouths of the ovens. The only redeeming aspect of the job was watching the different colours swirling about in the vats. They formed designs that fuelled Nachman's imagination.

Then Yankel offered him work as a house painter, in his own business. Nachman tried it, but instead of painting the wild images that churned in his head he had to paint most walls a bland beige. He knew that this could not be his life's work either. He wondered if music or art could be a viable way to survive, but without education in a conservatory or an art school, he knew it was useless. Careers in those fields were for aristocrats, not boys from the slums of Lodz.

Time and again he pondered how to find his way to a musical instrument then struggled to shove this idea to the back of his mind, but it asserted itself at the most unexpected times. He knew he would not rest until that glorious day it finally happened, but he had to try and live life as it was, not as he wished it to be. In the meantime, he joined a Yiddish-language amateur theatre group. Here his musical soul found an outlet and kindred spirits. He sang and performed in musicals. Nachman felt honoured that most of the audience was made up of working-class folk, like his own family, not comfortable middle-class people, like those who filled Polish theatres. His was a theatre of the people. It was the facet of his life that filled his heart with joy and muffled the ominous political winds swirling in Poland and neighbouring nations.

As Nachman grew older he watched as all his friends had per-fected clever schemes to avoid being drafted into the Polish military. Because men had to meet a minimum weight of 110 pounds in order to be accepted for service, some starved them-selves so as to be underweight. For the poor boys, perennially hungry, this was an easy task. Others finagled new birth certifi-cates showing them to be younger, or older, or just the wrong birth month for the current year's draft. They walked in feign-ing limps, or spoke incoherently, hoping to be mistaken for idiots. Despite peer pressure, Nachman would have none of it.

His friends and relatives didn't get it. He was the only one in his circle who actually wanted to join the army. He knew they all wondered. Why does a peaceful, artistic young Jew like him want to subject himself to the rigour, the brutal exercise regimen and the anti-Semitism of the Polish military? But such things were not discussed even among friends. It was a given that most Jewish young men would stop at nothing to avoid service. What was the point of serving a country that rejected them?

Nachman had his reasons for wanting to join the military, but he would not reveal them lest his friends think him shallow or stupid. In his heart he knew, he hoped, he imagined that he could persuade his way to becoming his company's bugler, just as he had convinced his school to hire him just a few years before. The very thought made him giddy. He would set his hands on the golden instrument and caress it as if it were the skin of a woman. For years he had dreamed of having this magical instrument in his possession and learning its secrets, in getting it to produce beautiful melodies.

When his family expressed reservations about the army Nachman told them it was his opinion that Jews, as Polish citizens, had an obligation to serve just like any other Polish men. No, in fact they had more of an obligation! Jews had to prove the Poles wrong, to show that they had courage and could handle weapons; that they were not only good at books and business!

"Why can't you be more like Yankel?" his mother said. "Why can't you put your mind in the Torah instead?"

"*Oy, mamenyu, du kenst mir nisht?*" Mama, don't you know me? he asked. Nachman could tell by her soft tone that she didn't really mean it. He knew that she always liked him to be himself. And what he wanted was to go into the army.

And that was the end of it.

He knew just what he would do when the draft notice arrived. He would eat salty herring for all of his meals, day in and day out, for a whole week. The herring would make him so thirsty that on the day of his weigh in he would tip the scale at just the right weight. He was small in stature, just

about five-foot-four, but he was healthy. They'd take him. Of
course they would!

When the medical screening date finally arrived, Nachman
was ready. He entered the building with an extra spring in
his step, confident that he would emerge with his orders. But
when the doctor told him to step on the scale, Nachman could
tell by the dissatisfaction on the man's face that he wasn't
going to make it. "You are several pounds short, young man,"
he said gruffly, and called for the next applicant.

Nachman was upset, but he would not give up. He would
stick to his salty diet, eat even more potatoes, and drink even
more water before the next screening. Months later he stood
before the second medical commission. But he was still a
couple of pounds short of the minimum weight. He vowed to
try again in the near future.

I paused the CD and smiled remembering how diligently my
father observed his diabetic diet. As soon as his doctor told him
he could no longer eat soups so thick the soup spoon could
stand up in them, my father went cold turkey. No more heavy
meals, or butter, or cake with his evening tea. He was as relentless in his quest to lose weight as he once was in trying to gain
it. I glanced at the clock and thought of my early-morning staff
meeting. It was past midnight, but I couldn't stop. I turned the
CD back on.

Always passionately interested in politics, at the end of
1929 young Nachman attended a major meeting at the Philharmonic Hall to protest the formation of a new constitution
by the ultra-conservative Polish government. Everyone was
talking about how it would make life worse for the working

class and limit personal freedoms that were already quite restricted. The meeting, organized jointly by the Jewish Labor Bund, the Polish Socialist Party (PPS), and the German social-ists, was packed and boisterous. People were tired of wide-spread unemployment and abysmal working conditions for those lucky to get jobs. Emotions ran high. Police stormed the auditorium arresting speakers and participants. A brawl erupted as police swung batons and cracked people over their heads.

Nachman managed to push his way out unscathed. Outside, he inhaled the cold air and felt good that the people stood up for their beliefs. He headed home. As he neared the corner of Zielona Street, two men grabbed him by his arms and dragged him into a nearby courtyard. One of them pulled a crumpled flyer out of his pocket, shoved it toward Nachman's face, and accused him of having distributed such flyers at the meeting. Nachman recognized the flyer as a piece of communist propaganda agitating against the government and realized that the men who stopped him were agents of the *defensywa*, the Polish secret police.

"I saw you distribute these at the meeting," one agent said calmly, holding Nachman's arm in a vice grip.

"You couldn't have," Nachman said. "The only use I'd have for it is to wipe my ass. I'm not a communist."

"I was at that meeting and I saw you distribute these with my own eyes. Don't lie to me!" the agent spat the words out with venom. Nachman hadn't seen these agents at the meeting, but he thought that if he explained it all rationally, the agents would let him go.

"Look, I am a Bundist. How can you think I'd have anything to do with this communist garbage?" Nachman asked in a somewhat calmer tone.

"Shut up and tell me the truth," the agent barked, tightening his grip. "I was there and I saw you, admit it, you lying scum, or else." Again he waved the leaflet in front of Nachman.

He motioned the second agent and in an instant handcuffs dug into Nachman's wrists and his arms were pulled so tightly behind him, he thought his shoulders would come out of their sockets. The agents threw him into a van and drove him to the police station. Nachman spent the night in detention. His head ached from the fall he took when they dumped him into the cell. He told himself that in the light of day someone would hear him out, they would realize their mistake and let him go.

In the morning, he was transferred to the prison at 13 Gdanska Street.

I remember the first time we talked about my father's imprisonment when I was a young teenager and felt that somehow he wasn't telling me the whole story. I wanted to know the details of the treatment he received and how he ended up there in the first place. I would urge him. "So tell me more," again and again, I repeated, like a broken record. I didn't want to tell him that in the absence of the gory details I was imagining flogging, water torture, electrical prods, even rapes and all manner of torture I couldn't even name. Once I even glanced at his nails to see any traces that they may have been pulled with rusty pliers, but his fingernails were cut neat and square and spotlessly clean as always with nary a sign of violence. He always managed to parry my questions like a skilled fencer.

One phrase my father used frequently when watching certain news stories played in my head, over and over. If the story had anything to do with crime, or incarceration, or most especially, recidivism, he would just shake his head and say, "If American prisons were anything like the prison in which I landed, believe me, none of these characters would want to end up there again." He was not a dedicated TV watcher, except for news, but whenever he'd channel surf and come across reality shows, like *COPS*, he would be especially incensed by the ineffective prison practices, one of the very few flaws he'd ever observe about America. "Look at this, Ania, the prisoners have a TV and entertainment. *A gelekhter!* It makes me want to laugh. What else do they need, a cruise?"

But I had read about political prisons and I knew that there were things he was not telling me, so I urged in the nicest, sweetest daughter voice I could muster when I reached adulthood. He would sit in his Stressless leather chair in his apartment with the *New York Times* in his lap because he just had to read it from cover to cover each day. He would push his gold wire-rimmed glasses down on his nose and get a faraway look in his blue eyes, the rhythmic rubbing of his fingertips on his knee the only betrayal of his apparent calm. His voice was tranquil as if he were telling me about a book he'd just read and his gaze fixed over the sofa at my brother's painting of a still life. Light from the wide window overlooking Van Cortlandt Park illuminated his face. "Okay. First, I will tell you how it happened, how your father became—what do you call it in English? A jailbird? And with that he told me the story of his arrest by the *defensywa*.

My husband David and I boarded a crowded tram in October 2007 and made our way through Lodz streets that looked as grim as the last time I had seen them in 1992. Buildings covered dark grey by decades of soot and grime, uncared for and unloved. As we got off the tram and walked toward our destination, the wind had picked up, swirling the leaves in little eddies rustling at our feet. There were a few people gathered near the tram stop lifting their collars to keep out the premature whiff of winter. On the corner, workmen in helmets were digging up the street in a fit of urban reconstruction fuelled by new money from the European Union. For the residents it was the ordinary tempo of city life, but for me, each step closer to what I knew was the address of the prison on Gdanska Street made this an occasion fraught with anxiety. With each step, my heart beat faster, my palms turned sweaty.

I was pretty sure that the prison would be long gone, but I wanted to walk on that very street and imagine what my father might have felt then and understand how the experience had changed him.

A short walk past the neo-baroque Poznanski palace then past the Academy of Music along EU-funded road construction brought us close to the address we were looking for when I noticed an L-shaped edifice with a two-story wing perpendicular to a three-storey section. It was painted fresh white with sunny yellow trim. It could have been a school or an office building. "I wonder what this building is?" I said, thinking it looked too new and cared for to be our destination. "This can't be the prison."

"Annette, I think we are here," David said.

"I don't think so."

We stepped closer to the entrance to read a sign: Museum of Independence Traditions. *What sort of a museum is it*, I wondered. I was in no mood to visit any art or history museums just then.

"Annette, this has to be it. See? It is 13. It's the right address." He pointed to the number that I hadn't noticed.

I entered the museum cautiously and David followed. A young Polish woman was seated at a blond wooden desk in the entry vestibule. *Everything here is blond, just like all the people*, I growled in my mind, knowingly stereotyping the Poles, just as they had done to my mother all those years ago. I addressed her in perfect, unaccented Polish. She smiled and informed me that, indeed, this was the infamous Gdanska Street prison, now converted to a museum highlighting the atrocities that took place there. I froze. My leg muscles became rigid. Tension choked my neck. *Oh, my God, it was here! The place still exists, the very place where all those stories happened*. After a moment I asked if we could visit. The woman glanced at her watch and said that they would close in a half an hour. "Maybe you can come back another day?" she suggested.

"No, I can't. We are leaving the day after tomorrow, and you are closed tomorrow," I said, my voice rising.

"Do you live far from here?" she asked.

"I live in America."

"America?" she almost gasped. "So what brings you here?" She looked at me as if I were an apparition from another world.

"My father was a prisoner here in 1929," I stated with emphasis on here. Her eyes widened, registering surprise as if she couldn't quite get her mind around such an ancient date.

"Wait a moment, I will call the director," she said, and I could tell by her animated voice that she was really trying to help.

A few minutes later a short middle-aged woman in a white blouse and calf-length pleated skirt came down the stairs.

"Did you say your father was here before the war?"

"Yes, I did."

Her face was small and round, her eyes widened with curiosity. "Are you sure it was before, not during the war?" she asked as if this were an essential piece of information.

"Yes, I am absolutely sure, but why does it make a difference?"

"Because all of our pre-war records were destroyed by the Nazis and we are desperately searching for any information we can find from that period. We know this was a prison for political dissidents."

After I told her my father's name she raised her eyebrows and said, "Just like the architect of the Jewish Museum in Berlin! Our mayor hosted him in the city just two days ago," she said with obvious pride. I smiled enjoying how my brother's fame had spread around the world and knew how much my father would have loved knowing that people in his beloved city now knew his surname.

"He is my brother," I said. "Your prisoner was his father," I added for clarification. She looked as if she would faint.

"No, I can't believe that!" she exclaimed.

"Yes, it's true," I reassured her.

With that she rummaged in the desk drawer for keys and took us on a tour of the museum that lasted well past its official closing time. The cruelty unfolded in an orderly progression. First we saw an exhibit on prisoner restraints: manacles, shackles, chains, cuffs; then weapons used for executions; and guard's uniforms. On the second floor we saw an exhibition on the atrocities that took place in this prison during the Nazi occupation—executions and photos of skeletal prisoners. It housed women in numbers that exceeded the capacity tenfold. We saw the very gallows where they had been executed. I could hear their screams in my head.

I felt nauseous.

Upon his transfer to the prison, Nachman wanted to explain again, but there was no one who would listen. It became clear that if he uttered another word, his punishment would be worse. He scrambled in his mind for options, wondering how to get word to his family or friends about his situation, but nothing that made sense came to his brain. Prisoners were not allowed to contact anyone. They had no rights.

Inmate processing proceeded apace. Nachman's head was shaved. He was issued a striped prison uniform: baggy pants and a large shirt that hung on his small frame as if he were a beggar. The burlap itched his fair skin. He was led to a cell that housed about two dozen men. They were bearded and dirty, and sat on the cement floor, leaning against the wall and one another. They looked Nachman over and shifted their positions just enough to give him a place to sit. Soon Nachman learned that all of his cellmates were communists. For the most part, they were Gentiles. But there were two or three Jewish young men like him. Nachman was the only Bundist. They all wondered why Nachman, whose political beliefs were so different from theirs, was to share their cell and their fate, but they were friendly. Nachman concluded that these were not hardened criminals but men, like himself, who were unhappy with the reactionary political system.

After a few days Nachman told his fellow prisoners how he found himself in their midst. He explained how the *defensywa* agents had falsely accused him of being a communist. For some reason the men found this amusing.

"You are one of us now," a burly, dark-haired man said.

Never, never, Nachman thought, but didn't say anything. He knew that in such minuscule quarters they had to maintain a semblance of civility.

Like Cain and Abel, business partners, or even close neighbours, rivalries between groups or individuals who share something important are often the most acrimonious. This is the way it was between socialists and communists. They competed for the supremacy of their ideas, each believing their ideology would best heal the injustice heaped upon workers by factory owners. Socialists believed first and foremost in economic reforms in which the workers would own the means of production, the factories. The communists' ideas however were more political in nature. They wanted to overthrow the government and have it own the factories.

Despite the vehement hatred between socialists and communists on the outside, on the inside Nachman and his cellmates had cordial relations. They shared anything their family members managed to get through the prison guards. Needless to say, generous bribes were required to slip in even the most minor items. The prison cell was like a commune, everything belonged to everyone. Despite the utter misery of losing his freedom, Nachman liked the spirit of the men who shared his cell.

The prison food was slop and the coffee a bitter imitation, but food had never been Nachman's great interest. The hunger, the mould, and maggots in the food weren't the worst of the prison experience. For Nachman, not knowing what was happening on the outside, and not having any idea if his family knew what had happened to him was far worse. Except for brief daily walks around the prison yard, he saw no one from the other side of the thick walls.

"Now I'll take you down to the first floor to see the prisoner's cells," the museum director said. Our three sets of footsteps reverberated on the polished hallways. The odour of fresh paint hung vaguely in the air. "We are installing a new exhibition and have refreshed the paint in this gallery," the director explained. The cleanliness and care of the building were such that I couldn't square them with the images my father described: the filth, the sour stench emanating from the buckets of human waste, the lice and bugs that ate the prisoners' bodies. I felt my guts doing somersaults. What would my father say knowing what had become of the place where he first learned, on his own skin, about injustice? Knowing it has become a place for education and enlightenment? Knowing him, it wouldn't surprise me if he said, "See, young Poles will learn something important here, so history wouldn't repeat itself."

The director jangled a bunch of keys and put a large iron key into the lock of a cell. "Here it is, your father most likely would have been in a cell just like this." I stood there open-mouthed holding David's hand. He squeezed my hand tighter and by the look in his eyes I could tell he wanted to kill the people who put my father in this hellhole. The cell was no more than seven by twelve feet, with a tiny window at the narrow wall opposite the door. How was it possible for these inmates to survive on three square feet per person? Just enough to sit cross-legged or to stand, no way to lie down.

The director stepped closer and touched my arm. "This prison opened in 1885 by the tsar to accommodate the huge numbers of leftist political prisoners," she said. "The tsar tried to muzzle the opposition forces, but he failed and eventually they ignited the Russian revolution."

I forced myself to be attentive. It dawned on me that by the time my father was an inmate, this prison would have been operated by the repressive Polish regime whose colonels, just like the tsar, wanted to eliminate all political opponents.

"This prison doesn't look so large," I said. "How did they fit them all in?"

Raising her eyebrows, she said, "When the prison became overcrowded and there was no space in the annex, they just shot them." I must have gasped. Then she added, "On one day in 1909, they executed 104 prisoners in one day. Right there," she pointed to the yard outside. I shivered. 1909 was the year of my father's birth. He would arrive in this prison some two decades later, a young man. I hoped that the jailer's approaches to detention had become more humane by then, but I had no idea and didn't want to talk about it anymore. I just wanted to absorb the cell.

Nachman lived with the hope that news of the police round-ups at the Philharmonic Hall meeting would get around and that his Bund friends would come to his aid. The first sign from the outside was a pot of meatballs his mother brought wrapped in towels to the prison gate. Nachman was astonished that she managed to get a care package past the guards and it wasn't until much later that he found out about the huge bribe she paid. He never found out how she scraped up such a princely sum. That pot of food was like a ray of sunshine, it was the very first sign that his family knew what had happened to Nachman. He shared the meat with the men in his cell. Greedily, they grabbed every last morsel, dripping the gravy and noisily sucking every last drop off their fingers.

Like other prisoners, Nachman was constantly called in for interrogations. Hearing the false charges made Nachman's blood boil. In addition to prison officials, *defensywa* agents showed up to question him. Each time Nachman repeated the truth: "Can't you see that a Bundist couldn't possibly distribute communist literature?" He wanted to scream, "Don't you know that socialists and communists have vastly different philosophies?" but he didn't want to get beaten any more. The usual portion of lashes meted out to encourage confessions was enough. What was there to confess? Nothing!

After several months of imprisonment, Nachman discovered that one of the most prominent Jewish attorneys of the day, Henryk Ehrlich, an influential member of the Bund, had accepted his case. It seemed incomprehensible that someone of his fame would have any interest in a young man without money or clout. But Nachman's Bund colleagues brought his case to Ehrlich's attention and the attorney was incensed by the absurdity of the allegations. He took the case on a pro bono basis.

Ehrlich visited Nachman in prison twice to discuss the case. The visits gave Nachman a glimmer of hope that he might be freed. Now he dared think again of trying out for the military when he regained his freedom. He even gave himself permission to dream about getting an instrument. These thoughts helped him survive the misery of the nights spent in the cold cell, cramped on fetid straw, struggling to hang on to his bit of space and dignity. Some nights he dreamed of Jadwiga, one of his many female friends. In the long dark nights he had to admit to himself something he'd never told her: she was his favourite, more a girlfriend than just a friend.

I sat with my father in his Bronx living room. By then he must have been in his late seventies. "Keep talking, I'm listening," I said as once again I pressed him about the prison story. The sky outside the window darkened and I hoped for rain so that the construction noise would stop. I got up and turned on the light. The room now bathed in the glow of his modern Italian lamp formed such a contrast to that long-ago cell.

Despite the grimness of his story, a light shone in his eyes. When he came to the part of the story when his mother brought food to prison, my father smiled at me as if he could still taste those meatballs. I wanted to go over and hug him, but didn't want to risk him getting on to another subject or getting up to start dinner.

"Tinek, tell me how it was really? Did they beat you during the interrogations? Don't spare the details, please." I wanted to understand all the nuances of his story, to ease his pain retroactively. I wanted to learn even the tiniest details and didn't want anything to interrupt our discussion, not the phone or the next-door neighbour. Most of all, I hoped he wasn't getting too tired.

But he looked ready for this storytelling marathon. He clapped his hands once, then opened them and held them up in the air for a moment, as if to say, "You see?" then he said, "Okay, Ania. I can sum up the essence of my time in prison in one Yiddish phrase: *mir hobn nisht gelekt keyn honik*—we didn't get to lick honey."

I laughed.

He laughed, too, in short staccato bursts and said, "I wasn't the only one. The other guys got the same treatment."

I cast my eyes down and focused on the intricate geometric designs on the white wool rug and once again his presence in this cozy modern apartment and his life in the pigsty that was his cell seemed ridiculously incongruous. I tried again, "Aside from being deprived of your freedom, were you tortured?"

"Ach," he said, "You are so naive, Ania, it was a prison, not a resort. You had to expect some beatings."

The museum director continued to drone on about the prison history. It had held some famous Polish political prisoners. Josef Pilsudski, the chief of state of the Second Polish Republic had

been an inmate there in 1890; and Wladyslaw Gomulka, the
first secretary of the Polish United Worker's Party, had been held
there in the 1930s. President Pilsudski wrote in his journal about
the inhumane conditions: the midnight executions, the naked
cement floors on which prisoners slept, the slop they were fed.
The first Bundist, Zurek Frenkiel, a man who had shared my father's political passions, was executed in the yard on the other side
of the wall from where we stood. And the courtyard that was
playground to the executioner still reverberated with the laughter of the drunken orgies hosted by the director as preamble to
each midnight slaughter.

I did my best to focus on the cell. It was painted a bright
white. A shaft of light from the slit of a tiny window near the
ceiling flickered on the wall. Surely, this was the Disney version
of the prison, a sanitized room, suitable for two or three men.
How could two dozen men sleep here, defecate, fight, or
communicate in code with prisoners in adjoining cells? How
could they preserve vestiges of their humanity? A huge rusty
lock on the door and old shackles bolted to the wall were the
only hints of the grim past. David held my hand throughout the
visit. It made it easier for me to face the stark reality of the cell.
The gentle warmth and pressure of his hand were reassuring.
I knew then that his feelings mirrored mine and that when
the whole episode was over he and I could look back on this
moment with a level of understanding between us.

I turned around abruptly and thanked the director. I felt a
desperate need to get out of there, as if, were I to linger another
moment, I would be locked in that cell. The director looked as
if she understood.

When we parted I mentioned to her that I had recordings of
my father speaking about his experience in the prison and the
famous trial that followed. She was stunned and begged me to
send her a copy. "We will use it," she said. "You have a priceless
piece of history in your hands."

I felt odd about her request. On the one hand, I was glad that
the story of my father's imprisonment could serve as a lesson

to a new generation, but I felt possessive about my father's narrative. It was my gift and I was reluctant to share it with the country that cared so little about its Jewish citizens. The whole mess was too painful for me to contemplate though I knew in my heart of hearts that my father would be glad to have his story reside in the city he never ceased to love.

Early one morning in June 1930, a metallic sound of keys jangling at the cell door and loud voices of guards woke Nachman from deep sleep. The guards barged into the cell, turned on a bright light and threw Nachman a bundle of his street clothes.

"Get dressed. Now!" they shouted. There was no explanation. The men, all awake now stared bleary eyed, not comprehending. Nachman had barely buttoned his shirt when the armed guards handcuffed him and led him to the prison van in silence. In the thin morning light the prison yard looked grey. A chill went through Nachman's thin jacket. *What now?* he wondered.

After a short ride, Nachman saw that they were approaching the brand-new courthouse that had recently been inaugurated. Soon, he learned that his political trial would be the very first to be held in the new building. *Why,* he asked himself, *did they choose him for this "honour"?* He was not a big fish, after all.

Escorted by the guards, Nachman was led to the defendant's seat. His heart leaped when he spotted his mother, then Jadwiga, in the courthouse. They sat in the visitor's gallery, with bunches of flowers in their laps. Apparently, they expected Nachman's imminent release. After all, he had such an extraordinary jurist to defend him.

First, the prosecutor presented the case. He repeated the ridiculous charges against Nachman and called the *defensywa* agents as witnesses to assure the jury that they saw him in the act distributing communist literature. Then it was Ehrlich's turn. He was brilliant in his passionate delivery of the defence. There was fire in his words, brimming with outrage about the underhanded lies perpetrated by the prosecutor all in the name of squelching any opposition to the government. Ehrlich called many witnesses who testified that Nachman was an active Bundist and thus it was out of the question that he would have distributed communist flyers. One of the witnesses for the defence was a prominent Lodz city councilman, Shmuel Millman. It moved Nachman deeply that such important people came to speak on his behalf, but he was most touched that so many family members and Medem School classmates were there to support him. He hadn't seen them for almost half a year.

Yankel, Natan, Pola, and Rosa were all there. Jadwiga sat in the front row! Sergei, Shymon, Motl, Blima, and Sara were there too. They all came through for him. But when Nachman glanced toward his mother he felt a pang of regret that he had put her through this ordeal. She looked older than her years. Grey strands of hair escaped her headscarf and hung limply against her cheeks. He saw her lips moving and imagined she was praying for his release. *Mama*, he thought, *there is no power that will get me out of here but Ehrlich.*

The judge called for recess. With the overwhelming volume of exculpatory testimony on his behalf, Nachman was sure that in just a few minutes he would be a free man. Still, waiting for the verdict made him anxious. Finally, the judge walked into the courtroom with a solemn expression on his face. He must have been aware that the press would scrutinize the very first trial held in the newest courthouse in the city.

A hush fell over the room. Nachman could hear himself breathing. He looked over at his family, friends, and Jadwiga. Looking at their faces he had a strong gut feeling that things would turn out in his favour. The judge cleared his throat and said it was plain that Nachman was not a communist. Then he paused.

My father and I resumed our prison discussion. I looked at the silver hair curling above his ear and made a mental note to remind him to get a haircut. He straightened up in the chair and I noticed a slight grimace on his face. I could tell that his back was giving him trouble and that this conversation would soon come to an end. Still I wanted him to get to the verdict and leaned forward looking at him with rapt attention. Strange, I knew that he had gotten out, but I felt as if I were there with him in the courtroom awaiting the verdict. It was like seeing a movie you've seen a hundred times, yet you still get chilled to the bone at all the critical junctures. "Go, on Tinek," I begged. "What else did the judge say?

"Guilty!" the judge pronounced and pounded the gavel. People in the gallery gasped. The verdict made no sense whatsoever. Everyone knew that Bundists and communists were bitter adversaries. How could a non-communist be guilty of distributing communist literature? Nachman's mind raced, he felt sick to his stomach. The judge's statement defied logic. What would happen now? Years more of imprisonment?

Before he had a chance to turn and see the reaction of his family and friends, the police pushed him into the rear of the courtroom, clamped on the shackles and returned him to prison. After all that, Nachman was still not a free man. *If Ehrlich couldn't get me out*, he thought, *no one would.*

I was at the edge of my seat. It was time to start dinner but I had to know. "Dad, did you consider plotting an escape?"

He pressed his lips together, looked at me and shook his head.

"Ania, this was not an American movie. There was no tunneling out. If you so much as looked at the guards cross-eyed you'd be thrown into the solitary and kept there in total darkness for months, but only if you were lucky. Otherwise there were gallows just waiting to be put to use."

"Okay. Okay. I get it. Tell me ... tell me."

"Well, you know I was eventually freed."

An ear-to-ear grin erupted on his face as he recalled that moment he stepped out of the prison gate and breathed fresh air.

Attorney Ehrlich filed an appeal and several weeks later Nachman was released on bail after his friends donated the huge sum of three hundred zloty. It would have been impossible for Nachman, or his family to come up with such a pile of money. For the moment, Nachman celebrated his freedom, but the thought that he hadn't been cleared of all charges ate at him. He could not stand the idea that his family's good name would, forever, be tarnished by lies.

It wasn't until years later that I discovered what a towering jurist Ehrlich was. Eleanor Roosevelt and Albert Einstein made direct appeals for Ehrlich's release when he was captured and imprisoned by the Soviets. He was executed nevertheless. I remembered how my father said with reverence, "Henryk Ehrlich was a man of exceptional intelligence *and* conscience."

"And then ... Dad? What happened afterwards?"

"Oh, it's boring after that."

"No, it's not," I protested.

"Four months after I was released on bail—victory! The court of appeals in Warsaw cleared me of all charges."

In my mind's eye I saw him: jubilant, tougher, and wiser. He could resume his life and his quest to enter the military. Now, more than ever, he wanted to prove that no setback would derail him from serving his country. I raised both my hands, my fingers making V's for victory. "But, still! You had served all that time. How did you feel about that, Tinek?"

And he explained that the humiliation of losing his freedom and the utter sense of powerlessness were lessons he'd never forget. "The prison was my college education," he said. As a result, he became even more impassioned about justice and involved in the Jewish socialist youth movement. He became the secretary general of SKIF.

"After you were freed did you want to be alone for a while?" I asked my father.

He laughed his characteristic resonant laughter that seemed to come straight from his gut without a trace of bitterness. "No, not at all."

"Oy, Ania, you should have seen the surprise party my friends threw to welcome me. One of Bund's main leaders, a man equivalent in stature to the head of the American Democratic party—Froim Luzer Zelmanowitz—hosted a reception in my honour. Suddenly I was a celebrity. Me, a celebrity? Can you believe that, Ania? They bombarded me with questions. Most of all they wanted to know how I managed to get along with the communists."

"So what did you tell them, Dad?"

And he replied, "They are people, like us, and that though I could never agree with them, I respect their right to differ."

"So what else did you do at the party? Did you dance with Jadwiga?"

He looked at me as if I had lost my mind. "I did think about her a lot in prison, but dance? You know I think dancing is for *puste kep.*"

"*Puste kep?*"

"It means 'empty heads.'"

I laughed. He raised his eyebrows surprised that I hadn't remembered this phrase. "So what did you do?"

"We argued, we discussed, we laughed, we sang and, of course, we ate. Ach ... such food, not exactly what I had been eating in prison."

❧

It helped that after the meagre, tasteless prison diet Nachman developed a voracious appetite. He hoped that it would help him gain enough weight to meet the military's minimum standards. Despite his imprisonment by the repressive regime, he had not lost his desire to serve. In fact, he was more determined than ever to prove that Jews were as able as their Polish peers to handle military discipline and weapons. Each time his mother served him a portion of food he would say, "Mama I am hungry as a bear. I need some more," then immediately felt guilty because food was not plentiful.

Nachman arrived at his third medical commission with trepidation because he knew it was his last chance. When the military physician asked him to step on the scale Nachman, undaunted, trained his eyes on the upper weight as the doctor slid it along the increments of the metal beam. He exhaled when it came to rest two notches higher than ever before.

"You made it, finally!" the doctor said, and signed the requisite form. "Report to the officer down the hall with this document." Nachman felt as if he had won the lottery. He sashayed into an office full of young men who had passed their medicals and approached the desk, proffering his prize document. The officer on duty looked up and said, "Libeskind? Are you of German extraction?"

Now, I'll be sunk, Nachman thought, but he answered looking directly into the officer's face.

"No, sir, I am a Jew."

The officer smiled. "Are you sure you want to serve?"

"I believe I have some talents the army might find useful," Nachman said. "If you won't accept me you will never know."

The officer raised his eyebrows in surprise, visibly chose to overlook the impertinence. "All right, then," he said. "Here is a list of things you need to bring when you are called up for service." And then he called out, "Next!"

Nachman counted the days until he had to report for basic training. His friends thought he had gone mad. At last,

in March 1933 the military called him. A three-hour journey
by train took him to join the Fifty-sixth Infantry Regiment
in Krotoszyn, a town southwest of Lodz, dominated by an
old Prussian castle. When Nachman arrived at his base he
was processed and issued a uniform. He was dazzled by it. He
couldn't believe his image when he saw himself in it in the
mirror for the first time. He admired his reflection and felt as
if he had gained a foot in height. How different he looked from
his days as a prison inmate. He smiled to himself: *If Jadwiga or
the other girls would see me now, they'd go crazy.*

Soon he was called in to see the commanding officer.
"Libeskind, I am putting you in charge of my horse," he said.

A horse? He'd expected to be given a weapon, or to be given
some special instructions, but a horse? What did animals have
to do with anything?

Nachman had never been to the country and the only time
he had seen a horse it had nearly run him over at the May
Day parade demonstration. The animal towered over him and
flared its nostrils. He still remembered its hot breath and huge
eyes with surprisingly long eyelashes. He had no idea how one
would even approach such an animal, but to think of feeding
it and harnessing it was terrifying. He wasn't sure he was up to
such an overwhelming task, but immediately started to think
about how he would deal with it.

"Okay, sir," he said. "Is there anything else?"

"Now that you mention it, there is one more thing. I
need a bugler for my company, someone who will play the
morning reveille and evening taps. Do you know how to play
an instrument?"

Nachman's heart stopped. "No, sir," he said, "but I can
learn quickly. I have a good ear."

"If you do a good job of handling my horse, private,
you will be enrolled in our training program for buglers.
Dismissed."

Nachman saluted smartly and marched out, hoping he
would not wake up from what surely must be a dream. Being

a bugler would mean that he would have a bugle. He didn't have to do anything to acquire it, except for dealing with the horse. Getting an instrument in exchange for taking care of a horse now seemed like a great bargain. He would learn how to do it if it killed him.

First, I'll have to make friends with the horse. It's a living creature, surely it would respond well to gentle handling, he thought. After all, it would be his ticket to the bugle. A horse couldn't be that different from, Filozof, his childhood canine companion. Nachman remembered how no one else in the courtyard wanted the mutt who hung around for days looking dolefully for scraps. Their neighbours had no pets, they were just mouths to feed, but Nachman's mother eventually relented and allowed him to bring the dog home. Nachman vowed to befriend the horse. Like Filozof, it might not need more than food and love, he thought.

The old stable hand on base gave him some tips on horse care and Nachman listened as if his life depended on it. Then he walked to the stall where his officer's stallion was kept. The pungent smell of hay hit his nostrils as he entered the dim space. It was unfamiliar, but not unpleasant. When he saw the animal up close he was astonished by its grace and elegance. It was a chestnut Arabian with a white blaze on its forehead and socks to match. Something about the animal's calm demeanour made Nachman approach slowly but with more confidence than he thought he had in him. He kept his eyes lowered as the stable hand instructed. The horse towered over him but turned its head toward Nachman, which he read it as an invitation to make contact. He reached up and stroked the animal's neck and flank, intoning gently in Yiddish, *"Du bist a guter ferd, aza min shayner ferd."* You are a good horse and a handsome one, too. The animal's skin twitched, but it stood there serene and royal in its demeanour. Nachman was surprised by the warmth and softness of the coat.

He wanted to offer the horse some treats as a sign of his good intentions, but he had no idea how to do it without losing his fingers to those large teeth. The sugar cubes in his pocket now felt sticky in his hand. Nachman stepped backwards toward the horse's rear attempting to come around toward its face, but the horse kicked its back leg nearly knocking him down. Nachman stumbled and returned to the right flank, gently inching forward and repeating his Yiddish praises. When he neared the animal's head he raised his arm and opened his palm. The horse lowered its head and picked up the sugar cubes with its wet, raspy tongue. Nachman was elated. He felt he had made a real connection with this huge creature.

After that, learning how to harness, feed, and lead it by the reins would prove to be easier than Nachman expected. When he next saw the stable hand, the old man said, "You are cut out for this, Libeskind, not everyone takes to a horse as well as you, not without being kicked in the ass or the head, God forbid." After a short while Nachman could manage the horse without too much trouble. He always whispered Yiddish endearments to him and never treated him roughly. The animal responded as if Yiddish were his language. When Nachman accompanied his officer on assignments and had to take charge of the horse while the officer went inside barracks to conduct business, Nachman stood proudly holding the reins, wishing his friends could see him.

I sat there in front of the player marvelling at my father's incredible luck—a musical instrument! I paused the CD and thought about his passion for music, not just listening to it but to making it. If he had no instrument, he'd sing, whistle, or tap out a march with the palms of his hands. I chuckled remembering how he insisted on Daniel, my brother, practising *Cavalleria rusticana* on his accordion when he was just a little boy, then returned to the story.

The bugle, even more than his success with the horse, was the crowning glory of this chapter of Nachman's life. The three-month buglers' training course was sheer joy and the instructor, a portly sergeant, told Nachman he had a natural musical talent. Nachman took to the instrument as if all those years of thinking about it had been lessons in disguise. From the very first moment when the instructor handed him his shiny instrument it was as if he was always meant to play it. He felt its weight in his hands and the way it made him feel inside, rich and warm, it might as well have been real gold. His lips pressed the mouthpiece and conformed to it with ease. He did not experience the uncomfortable tingling the other students complained about. He could pucker his lips perfectly and blow the air in evenly. His tongue worked like a stopper, making staccato sounds.

Nachman spent every spare moment playing songs he had heard at home, in school and later, on the radio. Sometimes he played when he had a moment alone when he felt lonely for his family. The music always closed the distance between them. At times, fellow soldiers in his barrack asked him to play. He felt like a movie star, a real celebrity. With a little practice he discovered that once he heard a new tune he could play it himself after just a few minutes of experimenting. After the months of training and daily practice Nachman's commanding officer told him he played the best taps and reveille in all of Poland.

The military was not only about music and animals, however. Nachman had to be a soldier, as well. As with almost everything he undertook, he wanted to excel, wanted to show his officers and Polish colleagues that a Jew could be as good as they were. He wanted to upend their expectations. Soon he could take apart his weapon and clean it faster than anyone in his company. In a short time he became an outstanding marksman.

One day he was summoned to see his commanding officer. What could it be this time? An opportunity to learn a new instrument? Another animal chore? He stepped into the small cluttered office with more confidence than on his first day on base.

"Libeskind, you have earned a special distinction for your excellent marksmanship," the officer said. "We don't issue these often, but you have exceeded all records."

"Thank you, sir." Nachman saluted and turned to go, not expecting that there was more to this meeting.

"Where are you off to? Have I dismissed you yet?"

"I am sorry, sir."

"I am issuing a one-week pass for leave in recognition of your fine performance. Few soldiers ever see one!"

"Sir!"

"But I must caution you," the officer said, "there is too much political upheaval in the large cities, including your city, Lodz. You cannot go there. Do you have any relatives in a small village somewhere? I would approve that."

Nachman had read that in Lodz there were skirmishes among the communists, socialists, and the reactionary right-wing parties. He didn't protest, but thought fast: "Yes, sir, I have an uncle in Przedborz, I could go to visit him."

"I think Przedborz will be fine. I will approve it, but I warn you, be sure not to set foot in Lodz. Do you understand, soldier?"

"Of course, sir. Thank you very much, sir."

Nachman had never been to Przedborz, but knew that there were Libeskind aunts, uncles, and cousins there. He didn't know any of them and felt awkward about visiting so unannounced. *Still, a pass is a pass*, he thought. He would have loved to go to Lodz to see his mother, brothers, and his special girlfriend. He missed his city. It was vibrant, noisy, and dirty, but so alive. He thought of the street vendors vying for attention, *beigalakh, heyse beigalakh, tsygareten, shmakedyke tsygareten*, the cacophony of voices selling hot bagels and cigarettes, mingled with the shouts and laughter of street urchins.

When he returned to his barracks and told his friend Jan Majchrowski that he'd won a pass, Jan was speechless. But finally he said, "Did you say Przedborz?"

"Why do you look so surprised, because I don't live there?"

"No, no, because that's *my* village," Jan said. "My girlfriend lives there. Oh, I miss her."

"I wish Jadwiga lived there," Nachman sighed.

"Who is she?" Jan asked.

"She is a girlfriend. I have many, but Jadwiga is special," Nachman said with a smile.

"Listen, Nachman, I have a favour to ask of you," Jan said slowly.

"Sure, anything," Nachman said. He liked Jan. He was a big blond Pole, with blazing green eyes and large hands that bore gnarled veins and calluses, signs of farm labour.

Jan pulled a small package out of his trunk and handed it over.

"Would you take it to my girlfriend? It's a gift for her birthday. I planned to give it to her when my tour of duty ends, but I would be glad to know she received it sooner."

"Why not? Sure I'll take it to her, give me her address."

Nachman started out for Przedborz, increasingly uncomfortable about meeting family members whose names he hardly knew. They were religious and never wrote letters. Contact was non-existent. He would be visiting strangers.

I'll drop off the present to Jan's girl, stop by to say hello to my relatives and then maybe, maybe, if I am very careful I can sneak into Lodz, Nachman thought. He was eager for his family to see him in uniform and he had missed them so much in the eighteen months he had been away he could not afford to waste this leave. Most of all he wanted to tell them about his bugle. He didn't know if he would get another pass before the end of his three-year service commitment. He had to take the chance.

Jan's girlfriend's house turned out to be a very modest house, a hut almost. A bearded Jew opened the door and was surprised to see a soldier at his door. Nachman addressed him in Yiddish to put the man at ease.

"*Rokhele!*" the man called.

A young woman, practically a girl, appeared at the door. Nachman considered her thick, blond braids and the way they were wrapped around her head. Like a halo! Her cheeks glowed pink in embarrassment. Nachman explained his mission, handed over the gift, and left.

Then, after a perfunctory stop in Przedborz (where he duly introduced himself to his uncle, the hat maker and was invited to a family wedding, which he attended) he climbed on a train, timed to arrive in Lodz under cover of darkness. The streets of his city were strangely silent. There must be a curfew in place, he thought. He quickened his pace and made it to his apartment late, nearly scaring his mother to death.

"Nachman, you are here," she exclaimed. "Just look at you, you have become a man." Tears streamed down her tired face. "You could have been arrested. What a strange hour for a visit."

"I wasn't arrested, don't worry Mama, everything will be fine," he said and thought how lucky he was.

Next morning Nachman slept late and by evening, he was delighted to be at home eating his mother's soup. He relished each spoonful for it not only filled his stomach; it filled his heart with daring. "Let's go out. I want to walk the streets to inhale my city's air. And I want to see Jadwiga."

"Are you crazy?" asked his brother, Natan. "Do you know what can happen if you are discovered? The canaries will arrest you. They are everywhere. And if you've violated an order from your commanding officer you could be court-martialled." Natan pushed up the wire-rimmed glasses on his nose and looked up from *Haynt*, the Yiddish daily. He was an inveterate consumer of news. They called the police canaries because of the yellow band on their caps.

"Nah, I'll be careful. Mama, come with me. You will be my lookout and warn me of the canaries."

"I suppose I have to go with you to save your skin," his mother said, wrapping her grey shawl around her shoulders as they both headed toward the door.

In the fading light they traversed the city's streets ducking into doorways and behind building gates whenever his mother warned, "Canary." The tense political situation was palpable. The Soviet Union concerned about the threat from Nazi Germany had just joined the League of Nations, but the Polish government had signed the German–Polish non-aggression pact just months before, leaving the government nervous and suspicious about anyone who might upset the tenuous situation. Most of all, the government did not want the soldiers to be infected by communist ideas. The police were under strict orders to arrest any soldiers violating the terms of their leave.

Nachman knew every corner of his beloved city. He knew almost each building's facade and every park. He could draw an accurate map from memory. Where most people took Lodz as a foul industrial mess, Nachman saw beauty in it. He loved the cobblestone streets and the laughter of children playing in the courtyards and alleyways. In particular, on this day, Nachman wanted to pass the Medem School. They arrived in front of the eight-storey building as dusk fell. He stood there for a few moments looking up to the sixth floor occupied by the school and basked in the glow of the lights coming from the windows. As usual, the teachers are there late, Nachman thought with satisfaction and knew that even if he were arrested this trip home would have been well worth it.

He dropped his mother off at her gate and headed for a quick stop at Jadwiga's. A kiss from her would make this day perfect.

⚜ ⚜ ⚜

When my father and I first arrived in Lodz in 1984 he was keen to look up all of his old friends and he encouraged me to find my old classmates. "But, Dad," I said, "all my Jewish girlfriends emigrated. Remember?"

"What about Danuta? She is Polish."

"Well ..." I hesitated.

"What's wrong?" He seemed alarmed by my lack of enthusiasm but I wasn't in the mood to discuss my forgotten childhood friendships.

"Danuta is probably married and goes by her husband's surname. There is no way to find her now," I said.

"Yes, there is," he said with a smile. "I remember exactly where she used to live. Maybe her mother still lives there."

He was right, as usual. When we arrived at her building she was just coming in to visit her elderly mother, though she did marry and change her name. Danuta met my father at the foot of the staircase while I climbed up to her old apartment to look for her. I heard her screams of joy. She couldn't stop hugging us. "Nachman, you haven't changed at all. I'd know that smile anywhere," she kept saying. "And your eyes are bluer than ever."

When we woke up the next morning my father said, "Ania, I would like to visit Przedborz before we leave."

"Why? What's there?" I asked because I knew that even though his documents said he was born there, they were incorrect. When he was born, in Lodz, his parents, like many Jews of that generation schemed how to register a child's birth to minimize chances he'd be conscripted into the army. They had come from Przedborz so they gave that to the authorities as Nachman's birthplace.

I called Danuta to inquire how we might get there: fifty miles into the countryside. Immediately, she said, "It would be our pleasure to drive you. My husband is a great driver."

I was grateful, as it would have been nearly impossible for us to get to Przedborz without a car and her warmth after so many years apart touched me.

After we got off the main highway onto the local rural route we passed many bedraggled farms with barns on the verge of collapse, skinny cows meandering among chickens and mangy dogs lolling about without any incentive to guard. The images reminded me of my childhood summers spent in the country and reawakened an anxiety that always sat just beneath the surface. Luckily, Danuta's steady patter about the weak Polish economy and my father's conversation with her husband distracted me.

Przedborz is an ancient town whose existence dates back to the twelfth century. A Jewish community there dates back to mid-sixteenth century, though several pogroms and fires had decimated it in the seventeenth century. Each time it rebounded so that on the eve of World War II 60 per cent, or 4,500 of the residents, my relatives among them, were Jewish. The town's wooden synagogue was considered one of the most beautiful in Poland.

Low buildings in the distance announced our arrival in town.

"Let's drive as close as possible to the town centre," Danuta suggested. "That way we can inquire what's what, because we have never been here."

"I seem to remember a marketplace right in the centre," my father said.

"Okay, I think I see it just up ahead," Danuta's husband said and sped up.

We pulled into a nearly empty square and parked the car. It looked very much out of place against the forlorn, dusty cobblestones. A few men sat around on a low stone wall as if their job was to stare at intruders from beyond town limits.

"It's so quiet here," my father said looking around. "I remember this place bustling with activity."

"You probably came here on a market day," Danuta said.

"Yes, you must be right," he replied and pointed at an elderly woman emerging from under the archway in the circle of buildings surrounding the plaza. "Maybe she would know something about the Libeskind family."

"I'll ask," Danuta volunteered and ran ahead to chat with the woman. I could tell the old woman wasn't going to help us because I saw her shaking her head from side to side as her shawl slipped down her shoulders. She was gesticulating, pointing to various spots on the square.

"Let's go over to them," I tugged on my father's sleeve. "We'll be back in a few minutes," I told Danuta's husband.

We approached the women and Danuta introduced us. In a few short minutes the two acted as if they had known one another forever.

"These are my friends from America," she said sweeping her hand gallantly toward us.

"Ooh, America!" The old woman raised her eyebrows and was now suitably impressed. There were not many visiting Poland yet and certainly even fewer ventured out to out-of-the-way towns like Przedborz. She launched into an animated explanation.

"Like I told your friend, the Nazis decimated the Jews during the war," she said. I wondered how she knew we were Jewish. Did we have Stars of David engraved on our foreheads?

My father spoke first, "I had a Polish friend living here before the war, Pan Majchrowski, maybe you know something about him or his family? He and I served in the army together."

"Majchrowski ... Majchrowski ..." She looked toward the sky as if the answer was written in the clouds. "Was his first name Jan?" she said suddenly with a glimmer of recognition on her face.

"Yes, yes, definitely, my friend was Jan Majchrowski," my father replied enthusiastically. "Did you know him?"

"Yeees, I did." She drew out the answer and shook her head. "You don't want to know. I'm sure you don't."

"*Oczywiscie ze chcę.*" Of course I do, my father said with a dose of irritation in his voice. "It's why I came."

"*Pan będzie bardzo smutny jak Panu powiem.*" You will be very sad when I tell you, she said. "*Niemcy zabili go razem z żoną. Zastrzelili ich tutaj, w tym rynku.*" The Germans killed him together with his wife and children. They shot them here, right here in this market place. She pointed at the ground with her gnarled finger.

My father's face fell. He might have been prepared to learn that his Jewish relatives were killed. That was no surprise, but a Pole?

The woman told us that Majchrowski eventually married the beautiful young Jewish woman to whom my father had delivered the gift all those years ago. Marriages between Poles and Jews were extremely rare, especially in small towns where everyone knew everyone's business. It is almost certain that both sets of parents opposed such a union and that the community frowned upon this marriage.

She told us that when the Nazis rounded up the town's Jews to be executed on the town square someone had ratted out Rachel Majchrowski. She could have passed for a Pole with her blond braids and two blond little girls, but evil tongues would have none of it. Jan walked out onto the square with his wife and little girls, but a German officer upon hearing his name barked, "*Sind Sie ein Jude?*" Are you a Jew? When he told them he was a Pole, in a rare act of mercy the officer yelled, "*Gehen Sie nach Hause.*" Go home.

Jan refused to leave his family. They were shot in the square that very day. Afterwards the whole town talked about the stupid Pole who gave up his life for a Jewess.

The old woman ended the story and asked us if we'd like to have a cup of tea in her home. We agreed, though I worried about Danuta's husband waiting for us. "Don't worry he'll be napping in the car," she assured me. We walked over to the building abutting the square. Its age showed by the peeling paint. The old woman dug out an ancient-looking key from her pocket and opened a door on the ground floor. The whitewashed room was tiny but tidy. A table covered with a plastic tablecloth stood near the window facing the square. "This is where I sat and watched when they conducted the selection," she said and lit the stove to put on the kettle. After a while she set before us four chipped china cups whose saucers didn't match.

"I only have some tea biscuits," she said. "I wasn't expecting company."

"That's just fine," my father said. "Please, sit down and tell us about life in this town before the war."

A half hour passed swiftly, if uncomfortably. I wasn't used to being hosted in the homes of Polish strangers, but my father gobbled up every last morsel of information. It drizzled while we sat inside. Small pools of water formed among the cobblestones. My mind was still on the square thinking about the executions and how neither Jan nor his wife nor children had a burial place. Unlike my grandparents, their bones rested nowhere. No one would need to tend their graves. We thanked the woman and stood up to leave.

We walked outside in silence. Slowly, I began stepping around the puddles because they seemed to be filled with blood.

"Ania, hurry up," my father said. "Danuta's husband is waiting."

As we drove back to Lodz, I stared at the fields and a single thought filled my mind. All of Polish soil is drenched in blood. I couldn't leave soon enough. And I didn't see how I could ever return.

Chapter Two

2005

I sat at the dining room table and watched David leisurely sipping his Sunday-morning coffee. We argued over our upcoming travel plans. I wanted to go to Argentina and learn how to tango. David had other ideas. "I want to see all the places that made you who you are today," he said, pinning me down with a twinkle in his hazel eyes.

"Well, you have already been to Israel, David. That was probably the most important country," I said.

"That has nothing to do with the price of beans. Poland and Israel—it's like apples and oranges. I want you to come with me to Poland."

"Beans, apples, oranges, that's a lot of produce," I said, pouting, but deep down David's Poland fixation made me feel warm right down to my toes: after forty-two years of marriage, he still wanted to know more about me, thought there were still discoveries to be made.

"Ania, look at me," he said. The greying hair at his temples was silver and still thick at the sides. It made me think of the masses of black ringlets on his head when I first met him. I liked him to shave, but for the moment he looked handsome with the shadow of morning stubble and sleep on his lids. He smiled and stretched his arm across the table, putting his hand over mine. "We won't only visit your old home and school. You can show me landmarks from your parents' lives too."

Now, that's better, I thought. I hadn't considered the notion of retracing my parents' haunts. "I'll try to get over my resistance," I sighed.

In 2006, I retired from my position as senior vice-president for education at the Wildlife Conservation Society. David had retired nearly a decade before to pursue consulting and worked hard to get me to retire as well, but I was reluctant to leave a job I had loved for thirty-four years. He prevailed, promising we'd spend winters in the Florida condo and travel the world. "You'd have time to write and research too," he had said, and that was the most tantalizing possibility.

One of the mysteries I wanted to dig into was my father. I had long been preoccupied with looking for clues to his inner world because he so carefully guarded his emotions that I rarely glimpsed them all. For years I wondered if his sunny exterior was some sort of a special device that kept his inner dogs muzzled. But he had a boundless ability to find something positive in just about everyone, no matter how unpleasant, angry, or obnoxious they might be. On our first trip back to Poland, a Warsaw hotel desk clerk threw the keys on the counter as my father and I checked in, tired from the long journey. She barely lifted her head to acknowledge us. I inquired about room service because it was late and we were hungry, but she barely dignified my question with an answer. We then walked toward the elevator with our bags and I berated her: "Stupid anti-Semite."

My father turned toward me and said, "Couldn't you see the dark circles under her eyes? Maybe she had to work an extra shift and was more tired than we are. You should give people a break, Ania."

"She sure didn't get a medal in customer service," I said.

He pressed the elevator button and said, "Just let it go, let it go, Ania. It's not important."

Maybe another trip to Poland, the third in the fifty years since we left it would help me see things in a new light because my father would not be there to guide me, to obscure reality with his rosy glow of love for the city of his birth.

By the time David and I made that 2007 visit to Lodz I was more organized than in 1992. I had made a list of places to visit and put the notorious Gdanska Street prison at the top.

The night of the unexpected prison tour I lay in bed rehashing conversations I'd had with my father over the years. I also found I could recall entire segments of his tapes, nearly verbatim. I wanted to overlay my impressions of the prison on my father's words so as to extract the wisdom that he squeezed from the harrowing experience.

Someone who didn't know much about the way the repressive pre-war Polish government administered "justice" might have found my father's story very tame and possibly even somewhat amusing to hear him tell it. I don't know if this was my father's way of sugar-coating the worst experiences of his life so as not to upset me, or if he really, truly managed to bury the pain and humiliation so deeply that he himself could no longer summon it to the surface. After all, fifty-eight years had elapsed between the time he was captured and imprisoned and the time he recorded the story. Was it possible, I wondered, that the scars from such an experience could have healed so well that only a slightly acidic taste remained, not too bitter, more like the slight bite of lemon rind?

Among the two dozen or so men from across Poland who shared Nachman's cell Antoni Russak stood out. With his bountiful mop of jet-black hair, he towered over Nachman. His broad torso and bulging muscles projected strength that must have been handy in his line of work as a marine and a sailor. Nachman liked his face: it radiated openness and honesty, especially when Antoni erupted in a rousing belly laugh. Nachman had never seen a man quite like him. Almost a neighbour, Antoni hailed from Pabianice, a town not far from Lodz. There was only one problem: like all prisoners in this cell, Antoni was a communist. Nachman and Antoni had no meeting ground politically, but they were two human beings in a similar predicament.

When Nachman first heard Antoni sing Russian songs in his deep, resonant voice, he knew they could be friends. During periods of numbing prison boredom Antoni made flags out of torn newspapers and taught Nachman semaphore communication. After Nachman became familiar with the entire alphabet, the two communicated using this code whenever they were forbidden to speak. Antoni used it to tell about his crazy adventures at sea. Years later Nachman would often say, "If not for Antoni, I don't know what I'd would have done."

Between interrogations and exercise walks in the yard, the prisoners smoked whenever someone smuggled in cigarettes. Adding to the stench of waste and sweat, the cigarette smoke made it hard to breathe. For some reason, everyone in Nachman's cell thought that smoking was good even though they had to line up at the door to inhale, through the keyhole, fresher air from the hallway. On some days the stench and lack of air in the cell was suffocating.

"It will relax you," his cellmates told Nachman encouraging him to take a puff.

"I am already relaxed," Nachman would reply. "Smoking is not for me." Still, they pressured him relentlessly until one day he took a drag of a foul cigarette remnant. It choked him and it stank. After a prolonged fit of coughing, Nachman vowed never to pursue this habit.

Another prison pastime involved getting tattooed. Dirty needles and ink were smuggled in, though not frequently. One of Nachman's cellmates said, "How about a picture of a rowboat on your forearm?'

"What for?" Nachman asked.

"Aren't you a citizen of Lodz? It's our city's symbol." Nachman was well aware of the logo, a rowboat with oars at its sides.

"Yes, of course, I was born here and have lived here all my life," he replied.

"How about it then?" Nachman's cellmate asked in an encouraging tone. Nachman thought for a moment: I do love this city. Maybe it would be a nice idea to always show where I belong.

"Well, why not?" Nachman responded.

The tattoo artist assembled his tools on a rag and started to push the inked needle into Nachman's forearm. A tiny design began to emerge. Nachman didn't so much mind the pain, but a growing sense of irritation grew in his gut. He felt angry with himself for giving in to the pressure. In a moment, he yanked his arm away. "Stop!" he said to the tattoo man.

"Why?" The man looked at Nachman as if he were crazy. "What's come over you, Libeskind?"

"Nothing, I just don't want to decorate my arm," he said, but inside he was very annoyed with himself for having given in, for not trusting his instincts. The other guys laughed. "You should have known you can't persuade Nachman to do anything he doesn't want to," they said to the disappointed tattoo artist.

Years later, whenever Nachman noticed that tiny remnant of the oar on his arm, he showed it to me and his grandchildren

as proof that it is possible to stand up to pressure from others
and to be guided by one's own beliefs.

Though I was bone-tired, my thoughts kept me awake. The tour
of the prison in the fall of 2007 turned out to be more emotionally draining than I expected. I tiptoed out of the bed to avoid
waking David, but the floorboards creaked loudly so I slid back
under the covers and gave up the idea of sleeping. In my mind,
I walked again the long, whitewashed corridors of the Museum
of Independence Traditions, a ghost of my father's past.

The happy ending of my father's story reinforced what my
mother had been saying to my father for years: "Nachman, you
must have been born in a caul. This is why luck is always on your
side." In Poland I had heard the lucky caul adage many times,
but as sleep eluded me I began to understand the depth of
my mother's pronouncement. My father did survive the prison,
and managed to have his name cleared. He escaped the Lodz
"canaries" while on his leave from the army. Later there were
more perilous tests of his fortitude. There just may be something
to the old wives' tale.

The moon shone brightly and illuminated the desk where
my camera sat. I wondered if the photos I took would be any
good. I decided to give sleep another try and fluffed the pillow
inhaling its odd scent—a mixture of mildew and lavender.
Now I'd have to look at his life in a whole new way. Was he
exceptionally lucky, or was it something essential in his character
that made him emerge unscathed from the most harrowing of
circumstances?

The sky outside the hotel window pinkened. I hadn't slept
even for a minute. I glanced at my travel clock and knew the
sun would be up soon. David's even breathing and the warmth
of his shoulder next to mine was calming. I was glad one of us
was getting rest.

Dad had called his time at Gdanska Prison his college education. And not ironically, for sarcasm was a concept alien to my father. His fellow inmates—holders of different political beliefs—were his classmates, the way he saw it. From their passionate debates about politics he must have learned to craft persuasive arguments. Maybe political science became his major and communications, with Antoni's semaphore lessons, his minor.

The next day David and I took the train to Warsaw and then the plane home. I never stopped hearing my father's voice in my head, but I was glad to be on American soil. Besides giving me deeper insight into my father, the trip had satisfied David's burning curiosity about my childhood.

Safe in our living room, David said, "You know, Annette, seeing the courtyard where all of your worst childhood fears resided made me understand you better. Seeing that grand staircase in your elementary school where you led a rebellion against the school authorities who wanted to make you and your little Jewish girlfriends recite Catholic prayers, gave me a whole new picture of you."

"Oh, so now you won't think I'm such an ogre," I teased him, "because you see there is reason for my madness."

"No, I always admired your guts, but now I know just where you grew them. What would Tinek say?" David asked.

"I don't know. Maybe, '*An epl falt nisht vayt fun dem boym.*'" An apple doesn't fall far from the tree," I said. "But that would be giving me far too much credit, David. Compared to my father, I'm a chicken."

Upon his honourable discharge from the military, Nachman returned to Lodz where he managed to find a job with a Jewish textile distributor. Though the work did not satisfy Nachman's artistic urges, it put food on the table. Rosa and Nachman's widowed mother came to depend on his income. In his spare time, he threw himself passionately into performing with the Ararat amateur theatre group. The Yiddish musicals were an ideal distraction from the gloomy world events unfolding in Europe. Rumours reached them that signs stating "Jews Not Welcome Here" began appearing in many German cities. Nachman thought it was more important than ever to keep Jewish culture thriving. And after the rigours of military life, Nachman found himself seeking out his family. He enjoyed visiting his married brothers and sister, roughhousing with his nieces and nephews, and teaching Isser, his oldest nephew, how to draw. Isser showed great promise as an artist and in him Nachman saw himself.

Jadwiga and Nachman became regulars at meetings organized by the Bund. Their circle of like-minded Bundists grew large and vibrant. Coffee houses and each other's homes buzzed with their endless political debates and discussion of news events. After the death of the Polish president Joseph Pilsudski in 1935, anti-Semitism skyrocketed. Parliamentary democracy was abolished in the new constitution. The government, the political parties, the Polish Catholic Church, and the press called for boycotts of Jewish businesses. Violence against Jews increased and anti-Jewish riots erupted in universities.

In 1936, personal disaster struck again. Rachel Leah succumbed to an undiagnosed illness because money for doctors was in short supply and like Chaim Chaskel, she did not have much faith in modern medicine. Guided by her religious beliefs, she was resigned to accept the fate inscribed by God in the Book of Life and sealed on the Day of Atonement. Everyone in the family missed the easygoing woman who never uttered a bad word about anyone, but Nachman, her youngest child, was most affected by her passing. How he missed the sweet smile that bloomed on her

pink cheeks whenever he sang or told her stories about how
he cared for the horse. He remembered how she stood by him
during his imprisonment, and served as his lookout when he
snuck into Lodz on his military leave. He realized too late that
if he were caught, she might have faced arrest for aiding and
abetting his violation of military orders. The thought sickened
him in retrospect.

Nachman immersed himself in his work for the SKIF,
the youth division of the Jewish Labor Bund. As its secretary
general, he knew that many of the children benefiting from
SKIF-supported camps were orphans. Now he knew their pain
better than ever, he was an orphan himself. He spent hours
fundraising for the summer camps and planning free after-
school activities for children living in Baluty, the poorest
neighbourhood in Lodz. He painted posters, made board
games, wrote skits and lyrics for Yiddish songs the children
would perform. But even his community work and Ararat's
busy performance schedule could not muffle the worry about
the future. Each evening Nachman was glued to the radio,
catching then parsing every bit of news. The air itself seemed
to crackle with instability.

In 1937, an exhibition of expressionist works by important
artists like Marc Chagall, Paul Klee, Wassily Kandinsky, Pablo
Picasso, and many others was held in Munich. The Nazis called
it "degenerate art" and exhibited it with the sole purpose of
showing the German public that art inconsistent with Hitler's ideology was unacceptable. Of the dynamic changes in
the art world of the time, the Nazis viewed modernism in
particular as a product of a deranged mind. Cubist, surrealist,
and Dadaist works were subjected to the greatest scorn. Deri-
sive text accompanied the paintings calling them Jewish or
Bolshevik. Art robbery was legalized so that the Nazis could
take possession and sell any artworks they wanted. Nachman
was horrified by these events in the art world. He expected

such works to be destroyed. He remembered the marvellous modernist canvases exploding with innovation at the Lodz Museum of Art in 1931. They made him long for those Paris museums his teacher had written about. Now he'd never have the opportunity to see them.

By 1938, Hitler seized control of the army and put Nazis in key posts. German troops entered Austria and annexed it. Jewish lawyers were forbidden to practise and all Jews were required to have a *J* stamped in their passports. The Nazi ideology rejected any ideas that did not comport with their beliefs of purity and Aryan ideals. Life became increasingly difficult for Jews in many European countries. By September 1938, Italy barred Jewish teachers from work in public schools and Mussolini cancelled the rights of Jews.

All these ominous signs of repression culminated on 9 November 1938, with the first organized assault on the Jewish population in Germany and its Austrian territories. Kristallnacht, the night of broken glass, resulted in 30,000 Jewish men being deported to concentration camps, 7,500 Jewish businesses destroyed, 200 synagogues burned and more than 1,000 desecrated. In its wake all German Jews were required to wear the Star of David. The *J* in their passports was no longer a sufficient marker of them as undesirable. Almost immediately after Kristallnacht, Jews were forced to transfer their businesses to Aryan hands and all Jewish students were expelled from German schools. German and Polish Jews who had the financial means emigrated in large numbers.

After their mother died, Rosa and Nachman continued to live in the apartment they had shared with her. Rosa put her mind to brightening the place and succeeded so well that Nachman couldn't quite believe it was still the same home. She used her earnings to buy new lace curtains and discarded the old-fashioned overstuffed mattresses. She bought a new radio and kept it tuned to the liveliest songs. By now her girlfriends thought of her as an old maid, but no, Rosa was in tune with the times. "No need to saddle myself with a husband and a bunch of snot-nosed kids," she would say, laughing her bubbly laugh. "I would much rather experience the world, work a little, save some money, be free to come and go as I wish." Heady talk about women's rights circulated in Bundist meetings and newspapers. The world seemed to be changing, though not always for the better. Unlike religious Jewish girls in Przedborz, who married in their early teens, the sophisticated Jewish women of Lodz put marriage off. Rosa knew that if her father had still been alive, he would have blamed it on the ideas of the Bundists, or even the communists, heaven forbid. Somewhere deep in her heart Rosa dreamed of finding "the one," but she was sufficiently satisfied with her job and the life she shared with her favourite sibling, Nachman, that she was a contented woman.

Privately, both Nachman and his sister had wondered what would happen if and when one of them had found a mate. How would they break the good news to the other? But lately their minds were more attuned to listen for bad news. With Hitler's rise to power, things had steadily grown worse. Nachman read the papers daily with apprehension and wondered what would happen to Jews in Poland as the Nazis and their ideas asserted more influence beyond their borders. Judging from what was reported in the Jewish press, the black clouds on the horizon were coalescing. They were impossible to ignore.

Already in 1936 Jewish doctors were barred from practising medicine in Germany. In Poland severe quotas on the number of Jewish students admitted to universities shrank those numbers to a mere handful. Since 1937, students in Warsaw, Cracow, and Poznan were required to sit, under threat of expulsion, in segregated areas of the lecture halls, called "ghetto benches." Jews were not allowed to hold any civil service jobs. Boycotts and looting of Jewish businesses became a daily occurrence. Kosher slaughtering of meat was outlawed.

In the meantime, anti-Jewish riots in small Polish towns like Przytyk, Dabrowa, and Przemysl resulted in dozens killed and hundreds injured. Soon the pogroms spread to larger cities like Czestochowa, Lublin, and even to the capital. The Jewish Labor Bund in Warsaw and Lodz worked to organize self-defence units, but the police routinely sided with the Poles who perpetrated the attacks.

One day on his evening walk home, a bunch of hoodlums accosted Nachman, grabbed him by the arms and yanked so quickly he hardly knew what had happened. They dragged him into the nearest courtyard. "Stinking Jew, what makes you walk and whistle as if you own this city?" they screamed. While the larger ones pinned Nachman's arms behind his back, others came so close to Nachman's face he could smell their foul breath. Nachman was such a habitual whistler he hadn't even been aware of it. He had to come up with something fast.

"What makes you think I'm a Jew? *Psia krew! Cholera jasna!*" He cursed at them in Polish and struggled to get out of their grasp.

"Filthy swine, show us your dick, then we'll know for sure."

Nachman yanked his arms free and shouted back at them.

"Yeah, you want to see it? Okay, here it comes!" With that he reached for his belt buckle, started to open it and made it look as if he were about to drop his pants. They stepped away. Surely a Jew wouldn't dare to expose his circumcised *shwantz!* Hell, they'd made a mistake this time. They ran out of the courtyard.

"*Idź do diabla!*" The devil take you! the leader yelled. "Next time stay out of our neighbourhood, *idiota.*"

Nachman's hands shook as he buckled his belt. He continued on his way home and made a conscious effort not to whistle.

⚘

Several days later, Nachman sat scanning the newspaper after work and debated with himself whether he should tell Rosa what had happened to him, but figured that it would upset her too much and decided to keep it to himself. Still, he couldn't get the incident out of his mind and thought, *If this can happen to a fair, blue-eyed guy like me, what about the men with beards and peyes?* The incident was only a small taste, almost innocent by comparison, of what was in store for Jews when Germany invaded Poland on 1 September 1939. The nation was paralyzed momentarily, but soon made a valiant effort to repel the invaders. Polish president Ignacy Moscicki issued an order that all able-bodied men must head toward Warsaw to help defend the capital from the German onslaught. It didn't matter if they had any experience or weapons. They just had to show up and then, who knew? Maybe the Polish army would use them as volunteers. It didn't sound very promising, but their country was being attacked. They had to do something.

On September 6, Natan and his good friend, Bloyfarb, came early in the morning and knocked on Nachman's door.

He knew why they came and he was ready, but Natan was in a hurry. "Let's go. Let's go," he kept saying as they descended the stairs. Even before they emerged onto the street they could hear the tumult. Men of all ages and sizes were gathered in groups, all moving north, toward the capital. After a few blocks the procession gathered strength, with each successive building spitting out more men. Entire squadrons of police and soldiers, all heading toward Warsaw, joined them along the way. Now the civilians mixed with uniformed men in an unruly, huge mass, like a single organism. The disorder was unbelievable, but they kept advancing forward. They flowed like a river in one direction. No man could swim against this current. There was no turning back: eighty-six miles to Warsaw.

As soon as the men neared the Lodz outskirts, German aircraft darkened the heavens. At first the Germans flew low, their deafening noise making communication on the ground impossible. Men looked up at the sky wondering if they would be attacked. The war was only six days old. Would the Germans be more aggressive this time around than in the First World War?

Soon the strafing by the Luftwaffe began. Machine-gun fire from low-flying aircraft mowed men down. They fell onto fields like rag dolls: legs splayed, blood trickling or gushing from open wounds. Others were only grazed. Nachman and his brother were among the lucky. As the crowds scattered, Nachman struggled to keep in visual contact with Natan, but it was nearly impossible in the havoc of men screaming and running for cover. Already Bloyfarb was nowhere to be seen. Nachman and Natan sought shelter behind anything—trees, rocks, barns. When a new barrage of fire erupted, they dropped to the ground and crawled toward the tree line. Bloyfarb was still missing. When the raid abated, those who survived kept advancing toward Warsaw. They had seen the enemy's intent to terrify the population and were now more determined than ever to do their small part. Exhausted and frightened, they kept walking and walking under cover of night until they could no longer feel their feet. They hid in the woods during the day and caught anxious minutes of sleep under the trees.

Nachman and Natan and scores of others—hundreds, thousands—marched in a weary daze from village to village for a couple of days. At last they reached Skierniewice, halfway between Lodz and Warsaw. A large part of the town was on fire. Nachman was unfamiliar with this place, but Natan told him that about a third of its population was Jewish. The Jewish section of town was engulfed in flames.

They moved on.

Other villages, many predominantly Jewish, were also on fire. Twenty-five miles south of Warsaw, bedraggled groups of men straggled into the town of Grojec. Nachman tried to ask what was happening, but confusion reigned and no one had any answers. Soon, rumours that Warsaw was already cut off proved to be true. German troops were everywhere distributing flyers asking people to return to their cities and villages, to open shops, return to work, and resume normal life. Normal life? In his exhausted state Nachman felt as if he had hallucinated. But it was a bitter, new reality. The new normal.

Dispirited and bone-tired, Nachman and Natan had no choice but to embark on the return journey back to Lodz along with hundreds of other men who had responded to the call for defence of their capital. The thought that Bloyfarb had fallen victim so early ate at Nachman's gut. He knew by looking at his brother's haggard face that Natan must have felt as guilty as he for having lost sight of their friend. Now it was clear that the strafing and the killings of defenders streaming toward Warsaw were intended to terrify the Polish people into a quick surrender. The invaders sent a deadly signal that life for the citizens of Poland would be easier if they capitulated and complied. Despite their patriotic hearts, the men could not deter an invasion by more than two thousand German tanks and one thousand planes. The incursion was swift. While Nachman and his companions struggled to get to Warsaw, by September 8 the Germans had already occupied Lodz. Ten days later, President Moscicki's government was exiled to Romania, leaving Warsaw and the country in the hands of the enemy.

On the way back to Lodz, Nachman and Natan found Bloyfarb. He was so bedgraggled they almost didn't recognize him among a group of other young men who all walked with their last vestiges of energy, like a band of old beggars. Bloyfarb had been lost in the tumult, but they were together once more and reunited in a hug that for a single instant was a taste of victory to savour in a week of tragedy.

As they returned to the outskirts of Lodz, in the field where so many were killed on that first day, they ran into another line of German troops. The officers stopped them and ordered them to remove the bodies of horses and men who had fallen. Until this moment Nachman was numb with exhaustion, but now, the full extent of the horror bore into his consciousness though his eyes and nostrils. The stench of decaying bodies, the flies buzzing, the despair in the open eyes of the dead: Nachman felt as if by some cosmic mistake he had stepped directly into hell. Guttural shouts of the Germans mixed with the barking of their dogs. *I have got to get out of here, the sooner the better,* was the singular thought filling his brain.

Once the men completed the gruesome cleanup, the Germans allowed them to move on to the city centre. They hadn't spoken during the march, but now Nachman had to speak with his brother. "Natan, can't you see what will become of us?" Nachman pleaded. "Let's get out of here together, as a family, as many of us as possible."

"What are you talking about, Nachman? Where would we go anyway?"

"Across the River Bug, at the Soviet border," Nachman didn't have the details worked out, but he thought he'd see what his brother said to such a radical proposal.

"*Bist meshuge!*" You are mad! Natan said. "Besides, you know I can't go without my Dorka. She's in Warsaw and you saw for yourself there is no getting there now."

"But you must find a way to send her a message." Nachman knew his newly married brother would not leave without his wife.

"I'll try, Nachman, but she and her family are tired of running." Dorka's family had recently escaped from Berlin and Nachman knew it, but the very notion of running from impending disaster lodged in Nachman's head like a painful splinter. It was all he could think of. He was nearly certain he would do it, but he couldn't shake the need to persuade his family to join him.

By the time Nachman returned to Lodz, eight days after the failed march, the Germans were fully in command. Only two weeks into this war they had ordered Jews to keep their shops open on Rosh Hashanah and closed the synagogues. They confiscated all Jewish bank accounts, issued orders forbidding Jews from owning radios, using public transportation, or leaving the city without permission. No, he wasn't going to hang around to see them defile his city and his people even more. *A broken spirit is difficult to heal*, Nachman thought. He would not allow anyone or anything to break it. Ever. A terrible disaster would unfold for the Polish people. And for the Jews ...

The Polish people, emboldened by the Nazi invasion, gave themselves permission to harass Jews whenever the opportunity presented itself. Not that they didn't do this before the war, but now their hatred had been given an open invitation to spew out. Had those hoodlums caught him now, not a few weeks before, and called his bluff, Nachman was certain they would have denounced him to the Germans. Soon after his return to Lodz, Nachman learned of yet another German edict. Jews were no longer permitted to own businesses, especially those that dealt in textiles. Nachman did not own much of anything, much less a business, but he knew that for each repressive German decree there would be ten others. They would multiply like rats.

We should all get away from Poland as quickly as possible, he thought. *Tomorrow might be too late.* But his siblings and friends discouraged him. More than discouraged, they said he was crazy and rash and illogical. Last time they had dinner together, Yankel cautioned, "Nachman, don't gamble with your life. It may all blow over in a few more months. The Germans and the Soviets made a non-aggression pact just this past August. God willing, they may do it again."

Pola, who was always serious and thoughtful, launched into a non-stop tirade when Nachman came over for Shabbat dinner. She said, "What about all of your belongings? Your books? Your photo albums? How could you leave everything behind and run, like prey? I would never abandon our home. Who in their right mind leaves all the furniture behind? The china? The silverware? You are crazy, Nachman. I beseech you, don't go."

Natan still could not reach his wife in Warsaw so he would not even discuss escape. Yankel and Pola were totally against it. "Take the children to schlep somewhere, who knows where?" Yankel had said. *But Rosa, she might yet relent*, Nachman thought. *I have got to convince her.*

Rosa was unattached and Nachman felt that after a few more conversations she would change her mind, but that was until the day she met their mutual friend Szymon. No sooner had Nachman begun his harangue, when Rosa cut him off sharply.

"Nachman, haven't you heard about Max's escape?"

"No, what happened?"

"He was killed."

Nachman gulped though he wasn't very surprised. Not eager for Rosa's reply nevertheless he asked how.

"Szymon heard that the Germans were stationed on one side of the river and the Soviet soldiers on the opposite bank. Both sides are poised to kill any idiot who thinks he can outwit them. Still want to run, Nachman?"

He did not reply, but he knew his answer—and that she wouldn't want to hear it.

Since 1935, Nachman had been working in Ziame Davidson's textile shop on Zielona Street, taking care of orders and keeping meticulous records of sales. It wasn't ideal employment, but given the terrible state of the economy, it was the best Nachman could do and it brought just enough income to live on. The best thing about the job at the shop was that his boss was a Bundist so they could pass the day discussing politics in between customers. On hearing that the confiscation of his boss's business was imminent, Nachman headed straight for the shop. He knew that Davidson was out of town and worried that his frail wife would go to pieces knowing their business was about to be destroyed. He decided to get to the shop before the German soldiers and see if he could salvage some goods for her; as a trusted employee he had a set of keys.

He unlocked the store and quickly scanned the shelves for bolts of the most valuable fabrics: silks, woollens, and brocades. If Davidson didn't show up by the next day, Nachman planned to hire a droshky and fill it up with as many bolts as the horse and carriage could carry. If the war didn't end soon, the Davidsons could barter these for necessities, he thought.

It was still morning when he heard someone enter the store. He stepped off the ladder from which he was inspecting the fabrics on the higher shelves and smiled. Herr Boltz had entered the shop. Nachman had known him well. He was a business associate of Davidson's. Though he was an ethnic German, a *volksdeutsch*, Boltz, was always a friendly man whose portly stature imbued him with an air of provincial comfort.

"Where is Davidson?" Boltz asked abruptly without his usual jovial greeting.

"Herr Boltz, I don't know," Nachman replied, taken aback by Boltz's changed demeanour and stiff stance.

"Well, I don't give a damn where he is. He owes me money. If he doesn't pay it by tomorrow, I will be back to confiscate all of this merchandise." Boltz raised his hand and swept his pointed, bejeweled finger across the shelves. Nachman was stunned at Boltz's transformation. It was as if empowered by the new Nazi edict, Boltz had suddenly taken off a mask he wore all along.

"I will do my best to convey your message, Herr Boltz," Nachman said calmly, seething inside. He knew he had to hurry with his plan to deliver the fabric to Mrs. Davidson. When evening fell Nachman loaded the droshky as full as he could. He tipped the driver generously to keep him quiet, locked the shop and they sped off. Except for the clip-clopping of the hooves and the squeaking of the carriage wheels, the street was eerily quiet. He rang the bell at the Davidson's address and wondered if Mrs. Davidson would let him in. Since the outbreak of the war everyone was so cautious, and she had no reason to expect him. When he heard nothing, he knocked loudly several times with his one free hand. In the other, he was balancing several bolts of woollens. He hoped no one else would show up in the hallway. *"Froy Davidson, dos iz Nachman fun dem gesheft,"* he called out. "Open the door, please."

"Vos iz geshen?" she asked, opening the door a crack. She looked frightened and smaller than he remembered her. When she noticed his armload of fabrics she gasped with disbelief. "What are these doing here, Nachman? What?"

"Here, take these, take them and stash them away. Don't ask any questions. Your husband will know what to do when he returns."

Mrs. Davidson opened the door wider and gestured toward the living room. Nachman realized instantly she couldn't possibly handle the heavy bolts on her own. He walked in and dropped them on the sofa, then ran back to the droshky for the remainder. Before he departed, Nachman handed her the keys to the shop, wished her well and headed to the door. She stood in the living room with her hands at her temples so overwhelmed that she could hardly utter one word.

The Boltz episode only hardened Nachman's determination to flee though he had no success in changing the minds of his siblings to join him. Even Jadwiga wanted to stay with her ailing mother. But since that harrowing march to Warsaw, Nachman had been planning his escape and it had become clearer in recent days. He studied the atlas. He felt he could do it. He would cross into the Soviet Union at Poland's eastern border on the River Bug. Sure, he could get killed at the crossing, either on the Polish side, or by Russian bullets flying from across the river. Increasingly, grim news made its way back to Lodz: many of those who attempted the crossing were shot.

Nachman still thought it was worth the risk. A person needed to think fast, and swiftly peel off the layers of spurious arguments obstructing the one thing that mattered—survival. Nachman had read enough about Hitler and his startling rise to power. He knew in his marrow that millions of ordinary Germans disillusioned with their lives would follow their leader's dreams.

The date of 10 November 1939 would remain etched in Nachman's memory. Returning from Mrs. Davidson's after dropping off the bolts of cloth, he stepped across the threshold of the apartment he shared with his sister. A gust of wind from the darkened landing blew in. Nachman flipped on the hall light switch and hung his coat on the hook.

"*A gutn ovnt, Rayzl.*" Good evening, Rosie, he said, stepping into the living room. Rosa sat stiffly at the edge of the corner easy chair, a hand-knit wool shawl wrapped around her thinning shoulders.

"Look, Nachman, I have given your idea a lot of thought. There is every reason why *you* should go." Nachman looked at her and was taken aback by the serious tone in her voice. He saw the shadows beneath her eyes. She hadn't been sleeping much. Neither of them had since the Germans invaded Poland ten weeks before. He was surprised at Rosa's unexpected turn around.

"Go where? What are you talking about?"

"Oy, Nachman, let's not speak in riddles. You know what I'm talking about."

"What changed your mind?" Nachman asked, his eyebrows arched.

"I saw something appalling today," Rosa said, and turned to walk into the kitchen to light a fire in the stove. It was dinnertime. With most stores now shuttered, it was already difficult to buy anything decent to cook, but she found some soup ingredients and dry goods for Nachman's journey.

"Wait, Rosa. Where are you going? Aren't you going to tell me what it was you saw?" Reluctantly, Rosa stepped back into the living room and sat down heavily on the divan. Her eyes were glued to the floor.

"What? Why are you so strange? What was it you saw?"

They were both silent for a moment and then she began, her voice trembling. "Two German officers stormed into our offices today and dragged outside a man who was waiting to speak with me."

"What did they want?"

"They asked nothing and said nothing, just dragged him by the beard down the stairs like a sack of potatoes. I looked out the window and saw them punching him. Then they shoved him into the sewer and put the metal cover on."

"Were there any people there? Did anyone try to stop them?" Nachman asked.

"Stop men with guns? No, Nachman. Passersby stepped back. No one dared speak."

"And then what?" Nachman was impatient for the outcome.

"Then the Nazis began to laugh, a terrible bellowing that resembled animals at a feeding frenzy. It gave them such joy to torture this man. You should have seen their faces, Nachman. Goose-stepping in unison they left, and all we could hear was the sound of their knee-high black boots clicking on the pavement."

"You saw a Jew killed?" Nachman interrupted her torrent of words.

"No, but almost." Rosa regained her composure and continued. "When it seemed they were far enough away, a young man approached the sewer and pried open the cover. He lay on the ground and stuck his arm down the sewer hole. Then he dragged out the poor old man gasping for air and coughing. The sewer gasses would have suffocated him if he had been there a few more minutes. He almost choked to death."

Nachman was quiet. What could he say? That he knew the *Szwaby* (Krauts) would be cruel?

Rosa stood up from the divan and smoothed her apron. She walked into the kitchen and Nachman could hear the clattering of pots. He inhaled the aroma of the beef barley soup as if it were perfume and sat in the dimly lit room contemplating how life could change so abruptly. He unfolded the evening newspaper and set it on the coffee table. The headlines screamed danger. He didn't want to read on. His mind was swirling with the one crazy, dangerous idea that had been burning in his brain for days.

Only yesterday Hitler had annexed Lodz to Germany, just like that! It was clear to Nachman, if not to his relatives, that this time around the Germans would behave differently than in the First World War: no more being nice to little Jewish boys. How well he remembered them from his childhood. Nachman at six, playing with an improvised rag ball, kicking it down the block with his friends. Out of nowhere a German officer appeared and lifted him up into the air. Nachman kicked and screamed with all his might. He was small for his age, but his voice was loud. The officer laughed, then put him down gently and said, *"Seien Sie nicht erschroken junger Mann. Ich versuchte gerade, mit Ihnen zu spielen."* German and Yiddish were not so different. Nachman knew what it meant. The officer had told him not to be frightened. The officer just wanted to play with him. His ankle boots and brown knickers with shiny metal buckles still evoked the soldier with incredible clarity.

"Hier ist etwas Süßes für Sie!" Here's a sweet for you! Nachman understood it perfectly. And the man pulled a chocolate bar from his pocket.

Nachman threw the chocolate down and ran so fast that rivulets of sweat trickled down his forehead. The next day a woman who sold newspapers in the area told everyone who came by her stand how she picked up the chocolate and laughed that the silly boy hadn't taken it. Yankel heard the story and told it to the family when he came home.

No one guessed that the boy was Nachman.

He didn't trust the Germans then and he certainly wouldn't trust them now. His mind bubbled with questions. How had they transformed from mere soldiers in the last war to beasts like the ones Rosa just described? Was it the humiliation they suffered after the Treaty of Versailles?

The memory of the benign encounters with German soldiers haunted him. The contrast between then and now was so dramatic, it defied reason. He recalled another childhood incident with the Germans. He had lived at 24 Nowocegielniana Street, next to Kolczycki's Pharmacy, where he'd bought cough drops for his mother. Nearby was Zelenovka Square, where the Germans carried out manoeuvres and parked their planes. Then they had flown in with small Fokkers, nothing like the more powerful, sleeker Dornier and Junker airplanes that rained bombs on Poland this time around.

Nachman and the neighbourhood kids were playing soccer at the square when a German pilot appeared and asked them to clear the area because he was going to practise with his plane. Nachman was too engrossed in the game. He didn't hear the pilot's instructions. The next thing he knew, a large pair of strong hands lifted him up into the air and put him into the cockpit. He screamed at the top of his lungs, kicked at the dashboard instruments, and flailed his arms wildly because he thought the pilot was going to fly away with him.

It occurred to Nachman that the Prussian soldier might have been a father himself, simply trying to entertain a child who reminded him of his young son back home. Maybe this is why people refused to leave Poland: they remembered German soldiers as proper gentlemen, behaving with civility toward non-combatants.

⚘

It should have been obvious to anyone who read the news and kept their eyes opened that the invaders would be very different this time around. *Why didn't they all see it his way*, Nachman wondered.

Rosa had always been his defender. Now she would be his only ally and might explain to the rest of the family that his action was not insane. Dear Rosa.

She appeared from the kitchen carrying a tray of bowls. "Come Nachman, eat some soup before you get on the road," she said wearily sitting at the table.

"Will you consider coming with me?" Nachman asked once again, knowing her answer before she replied.

And of course it came: "You know I can't go. I don't want to leave my boss in the lurch. Besides, someone has to keep an eye on our apartment."

Nachman wasn't surprised at her answer. Rosa was a very dutiful employee at Tomkhei Orkhim, a social service agency that served the poor.

"God knows they will need me now more than ever," she added.

"But what meaning do material possessions have when your very life is in danger? Rosa, please!" Futile: she would not relent. None of them would. They will all stay here and be sorry, he thought bitterly.

She pushed her chair back and stood, leaving the soup spoon in her steaming bowl, marched into the bedroom, shuffled around in there. After a long time, she emerged distraught handing him an unexpected package—a khaki-green satchel.

"Take this and go. Forget the soup. Go now."

He took the bag from her, flustered, said, "Where did you get it? Aren't the shops all closed?"

"Never mind where. I put in a little food and a few items of clothing to keep you going until ..." Her voice trailed off. The tears in her eyes looked like large raindrops. She willed them not to roll down her cheeks. She turned away and kept talking as if nothing was the matter.

"Remember Resnick?" she asked.

"The Yiddish teacher?"

"Yes."

"What about him?"

"I heard that he is living in Kobryń. If you can make it to his place, he might help you. He is a good man. You won't be so alone." Abruptly, she turned around. "On second thought, eat the soup. Who knows when you'll eat next?" She sat down tentatively at the edge of the chair and lifted up the soup spoon. He smiled at her concern. But a deep regret that she wouldn't be joining him stabbed him somewhere below his breastbone. Kobryń was a city in southwestern Lithuania. Just three weeks prior the German and the Polish armies had fought a bitter battle over it, but for now it was squarely in Soviet hands. Nachman didn't speak much Russian, but hoped that he would find enough Yiddish-speaking Jews there so that he could communicate and find work.

The next morning, 11 November 1939, dawned cloudless and blue, as clear as his decision to run. He tiptoed out of his room so not to wake Rosa, but she followed him to the door in her long flannel nightgown, sleep still on her face, and whispered, "Be safe, little brother. Don't forget to write."

Six days later, the Jews of Lodz were ordered to wear yellow Stars of David on their front and back with the word *Jude* written across. The borders were tightened as well, making escape nearly impossible.

If it weren't for the brilliance of the day, Nachman would have felt far worse, but the brisk air and bright blue sky swept the gloom to the back of his mind. Not far back, but enough so that he could marshal his inner resources to execute his plan. He had to snap out of the despair that none of his family would be joining him in his decision to sneak across the border to

Russia. If he weren't his own advocate, he wouldn't make it. He marched briskly toward the train station. At five in the morning, except for an old woman wrapped in a shawl sweeping the entrance to a courtyard, there was hardly a soul on the street. The citizens of his city hadn't yet awakened. *Maybe they will not until the* Szwaby *leave and the city will be Lodz once again*, he thought.

Nachman made a sudden turn away from the station because something pushed him to stop at Yankel's home. True, it was early, an ungodly hour for visitors, but it was worth waking them up. Nachman thought he would try to persuade Yankel to let Isser come with him. If the rest of the family wouldn't come, maybe the boy could. Isser was fifteen and Nachman's favourite nephew. Not that Nachman didn't delight in little Esther and Chaskele, Yankel's other children, but they were young kids. Isser was already a man. Nachman could discuss anything with him: politics, music, even theatre. His black eyes had an unusual spark in them, and he wanted to learn from his uncle. Nachman could tell from Isser's drawings that he might become an artist one day if only there would be enough money for him to study. But now, with the war underway, all plans had to be put on the highest shelf.

Nachman rang the bell. In the silence of the morning it sounded loud, like an alarm. Nachman heard Yankel shuffling toward the door in his slippers and turning the many locks. He stood at the door confused, his hair tousled. "*Vos iz geshen?*" he asked.

Oh, brother, don't you know what happened, Nachman wanted to scream, but all he said was "*A gut morgn, bruderl*," and stepped inside. He saw Balcia, Yankel's wife coming down the corridor barefoot, tying her robe, her eyes like black saucers. *Just like Isser's*, Nachman thought.

"Look, Yankel," he said slowly, "I know you refused to take your family and come with me, but I have a proposal for you." Nachman spoke calmly, trying to keep his nervousness enclosed in a tight bundle inside his chest.

"A proposal? This early in the morning?"

"You know how much Isser enjoys spending time with me, don't you?" Nachman replied.

"It's too early in the morning, Nachman. This is *mishuga*. Can't we talk later?"

Nachman had arranged to meet his friends Adek and Regina at the train station. He glanced at his watch and knew it was getting late, very late. "All right, I'll come right out with it. I want to take Isser along with me. He is young, agile, resourceful. I will take care of him. I promise."

Yankel looked puzzled and stood silent for a moment, stroking his beard. Balcia started speaking, "Yankel, I think ..."

"Shh, I'm thinking. Don't distract me."

Balcia pouted.

Isser came out of the bedroom looking fully awake and ready to go. He was dressed but his hair stood at odd angles and begged to be combed. His dark eyes glowed with anticipation of adventure. He was not used to seeing his uncle this early.

"Hi, Uncle Nachman. What brings you here?"

Yankel stepped toward Nachman and leaned forward, as if he wanted to be certain that his reply would be heard. "Isser stays with us. You will have to go on your own, Nachman."

"Go? Go where?" Isser sounded agitated. The smile on his face disappeared. He suddenly looked younger with his chubby, pink cheeks and incipient fuzz on his upper lip.

His father gave him an unyielding look and pointed toward the bedroom.

Isser's voice turned to a whine. "I don't care where. I want to go with Uncle Nachman."

"Quiet, Isser," Yankel said sternly. "This is between Nachman and me, no one else."

Nachman tried once more, though he could tell by the steel in his brother's voice that he could not prevail. "Isser can bring along his sketchbook. I have room in my satchel."

"Dad, please let me go," Isser was now pleading like a child.

"No. Whatever happens with us, we will stick together. I'm not splitting up the family. We will live together, or die together." Then his voice softened, and he said, "Brother, I'll pray for your safety. Go. Go now … and be well."

Isser and Balcia's sobs were too much for Nachman. At this moment Yankel's anger was preferable. It was no use. He turned toward the door and left without a further word.

1976

I hesitated before sitting down to complete the applications for my children's summer camp. My children were eight and ten, respectively. They were bright, but I wasn't sure they were emotionally prepared to be apart from us for two whole months. Would they feel abandoned in some rickety cabin in the woods? What about all the mosquitoes and ticks?

Our daughter and son had lived a sheltered existence until that point, supervised by carefully screened babysitters when not with their family. I realized that I hadn't questioned the camp director sufficiently about the counsellors' qualifications, but the familiar voice in the back of my brain reminded me that I was behaving like a typical overanxious, guilt-ridden, working mother. A phone call from my father interrupted the task at hand.

"Have you sent in the application for Camp Hemshekh?" my father asked with obvious pressure in his voice. "They have a limit on the number of children they'll accept," he said pointedly. "You don't want to wait until the last moment."

He knew me too well and sensed I had hesitated. For him, that summer had been a long time coming. Camp Hemshekh (*hemshekh* means "continuation") had been formed by a group of American and Canadian Jews, mostly Holocaust survivors, in an effort to rekindle interest in secular Jewish culture in the new generation. The American grandchildren of these survivors had no idea of the rich pre-war cultural lives of Jews in Eastern Europe. The vibrant youth of the grandparents lay shrouded in silence and covered by thorny weeds much like the graves of their ancestors.

My father was on a mission to undo all of that. He wanted to peel back the years, expose the long-vanished lives, and reanimate them for his grandchildren through their attendance in Camp Hemshekh. They were finally old enough to go and he was as excited as a kid himself about the prospect of visiting them there in the verdant countryside in upstate New York. In them he would see his young self and the children he had supervised while he was a camp director more than forty years before.

The stories of my father's camping experience had become a part of family lore. He had repeated them many times, not because he was forgetful—he wanted to be sure I did not forget. But his tales were not limited to the enjoyable parts of life. He spoke about the brutality of war and about the fate of his family. In our family's circle of friends and survivors he was in the minority that applied a missionary zeal to the "telling." He was upset by their reticence to speak about the Holocaust. "Soon our generation will be gone," he would to say. "Who will believe then that the inhumanity we experienced actually happened if we first-hand witnesses are silent?"

Unlike many Jews for whom the experiences of the war had completely soured all the fond pre-war memories, my father maintained a warm memory of his exciting days organizing summer camps for poor city children in pre-war Poland. His summer camp stories were among my favourite. Despite the elapsed years, his enthusiasm for camp fun was infectious. I had caught this bug myself and loved camp as a child. This is why I persuaded David to consider the idea for our kids as soon as they reached the age of eligibility. I had promoted the idea ardently, so why was I hesitating now? Perhaps aside from the practical issues of health and safety, I wondered what exactly was it my children would do with the knowledge gleaned from camp. Would they be able to integrate their grandfather's culture into their modern American lives?

꘎ ꘎ ꘎

On our last night in Lodz during that 1984 trip Mrs. Olczak invited us for dinner to her home. I would have preferred a quiet meal in a restaurant and a chance to sort out my feelings, but my father was delighted to accept her invitation. We sat in the Olczak's cozy parlour after dinner when I noticed a cabinet filled with crystal pieces and other knick-knacks. As I looked at the treasures in the display case my eye caught a brass menorah, silver Sabbath candlesticks, and then a kiddush cup. What were these things doing here? This was a Catholic home. A moment later I looked at the lower shelf and saw several other Jewish ritual objects: a Torah pointer and two silver filigree mezuzot, doorpost Torah scrolls. I stared at them intently and Mrs. Olczak noticed.

"You must be wondering about these," she'd said.

"Well ... yes, I am," I replied, my eyes glued to the objects.

"Shortly after the war, I was at the market and spotted a stall filled with Jewish artifacts. A grubby man stood in front of the table hawking them," Mrs. Olczak launched into her explanation.

"Oh, so they were for sale," I said, offering the obvious. "Who would have wanted them? There were so few Jews left."

"Exactly," she said. "I felt that I needed to rescue these objects from people who would defile the memory of our Jewish neighbours who perished. It pained me to see these ritual artifacts manhandled by people who had no idea what they were."

"What a nice thing to do," my father said. Mrs. Olczak smiled at him. I remained silent.

When we returned to the hotel I discussed this with my father. "I know she meant well," I had said, "but it bothers me somehow. These objects belong in a Jewish home or a museum."

"Oy, Ania, can't you see? She took them out of the hands of those whose only idea was to make money on them. I'm sure he had no clue what else to do with them."

"Yes, he may have been the very one who looted them after the families to whom these things belonged were rounded up and shoved into ovens."

"Look, can't you see that Mrs. Olczak and her husband were treating these things with respect?"

"Yeah, I guess. Still ... it bothers me. Why didn't she offer for us to take them if she's such a goody-goody?"

"And what would we do with them? We are not religious."

The Jewish Labor Bund's lofty ideals—the cultural primacy of the Yiddish language for Jews, socialist principles of fairness and equality for all, brotherhood of people, and secular national identity—were the very ones on which Camp Hemshekh's program was built. They rang as unrealistic in the last quarter of twentieth century America, but my father believed them with every fibre of his being. He had studied Esperanto, the almost extinct universal language that was supposed to make all people brethren. He still counted for me in Esperanto: *unu, du, tri, kvar, kvin* ...

"Why did you study it, Dad?" I would ask.

And he would say, "You could use it to communicate with people across the globe who spoke it too. They could teach you so much about their way of life."

These idealistic notions never left him. He believed that not only would his grandchildren have fun in camp, but that much more importantly, they would learn how to function in society, to get along, to empathize, and to value their culture. I set the applications aside and stood folding a pile of laundry on the dining table. I listened to my father on the speakerphone, anxious for the conversation to end because I was dead tired, but I could tell from his animated tone that my father was eager to talk.

"Have I told you about the Children's Republic?" He knew that would capture my attention.

One of my favourites of his stories. "Okay, Dad, tell me." I threw the laundry into a basket and settled into the easy chair because I knew this would be a long telephone call.

"I don't remember if it was the ninth or tenth Children's Republic, but it was held near Zakopane in place called Bundowki." He said this with such a burst of youthful energy that I could almost hear the sound of his voice vibrating the telephone wire.

"The village name was especially fitting because it was so similar to the word *bund*. Do you see what a lucky coincidence this was?"

"Yes, I do, but why did you call it a republic instead of camp, Dad?"

"Because we tried to create a country for these tenement kids. They were all dirt poor like I had been. In our republics, for at least two months, no one was hungry, and everyone was accepted despite the holes in their shoes."

"Who ran this country?" I asked thinking about the role of chaos in *Lord of the Flies.*

"The children elected a mayor and created their own court where disputes were settled. It worked so well. We never had any problems."

Though it was getting quite late I had more questions. I wasn't sure how his answers would help me finalize my decision, but I wanted, once and for all, to know all I could about the magical country my father tried to cobble together each spring.

"Wait a minute, Tinek," I asked. "Where did the money for all this come from?"

"Ah, money. Ania, you are thinking like an American," he said. "You call it ... what? 'Fundraising,' right?"

"Well, it takes money to feed several hundred kids, doesn't it?"

"Ania, if you have the will, you can do it even without the money."

Now I was even more curious. "So how did you do it?"

He was ready with the reply. "We organized huge spring collection campaigns with the help of hundreds of teenagers who volunteered to work with us."

Teenagers. I had an image of motley mobs of undisciplined ninth graders in my mind.

"How did *that* work out?" I asked.

"Very well. They were great. I organized them into teams and trained them," he said proudly. Then he paused and recalled, "The campaign for the last republic took place in March 1939, just five months before World War II broke out."

"So, Dad, who were the contributors?"

"Ah, this is also a very good question."

I could practically see the grin on his remarkably unlined face. This seemed to be the question he wanted to answer.

"You see, most Jews in Lodz were poor themselves, none of them had much to give, but for kids, who could turn us down?"

"Did you write letters asking for support?"

"What letters? We didn't want to waste money on postage. We went from door to door speaking with excitement about what their children and their neighbours' children would experience."

"What was the most persuasive argument you used?"

"*Nu*, it's obvious. We told the parents how the kids would breathe sweet country air and leave behind the smog of the city, how they would swim and throw balls without worrying about breaking windows."

I heard the excitement in his voice as if he were ready to make the pitch right then and there.

"So, in the end, what did your teens collect?"

"Food contributions were the most common. Some people gave half a pound of sugar, others a can of oil, others some canned goods. Very few gave us a couple of zlotys. Somehow, we always managed to collect enough."

"And the money? What did you use it for?"

"We bought tents and we asked local farmers to give us permission to erect them on their fields. Each summer we created a huge tent city surrounded by the sweetest smelling pine forests. Imagine, Ania, most of these children had never seen a forest or a lake. They had such a great time and never laughed so much. I couldn't imagine doing anything more important."

He paused. I heard some static on the line and glanced up at my wall clock. It read 11 p.m. Just as I thought we were about to say good night, he spoke up.

"You know Carl, don't you, Ania?"

"The short grey-haired guy in your building with the pinkish chubby face?"

"Yes," he said, "he was one of my campers."

I couldn't bring up the image of Carl as a child, but I began to understand why he always looked up to my father. Forty years before, my father had been his beloved SKIF camp leader.

He resumed and I think he still held the picture of young Carl as he continued.

"The 1939 Children's Republic was the last one. It was July and dark clouds were already gathering for the catastrophe, which was soon to befall us. We counsellors sensed a war with Germany approaching. The mood in the country was ominous. We saw Polish soldiers on manoeuvres preparing for the impending war, but the children were carefree and quite unaware of what was coming. They had a great summer. For many it was the last summer of their lives. For others, it was a shining memory that helped them survive in hiding, squeezed in dank basements for months on end, if they were lucky. Anyway, that's what Carl told me when I met him years after the war. It was the hope he had stored up from the camp that helped him survive. Hidden in an attic, he hung on to the belief that he would one day see those stately pines and plunge into our lake to swim with abandon.

"Soon after we returned from camp, on September first 1939, the greatest disaster of the century unfolded for our people and for so many others. The world would never be the same ..." His voice trailed off.

Chapter Three

1986

Tinek waved a travel brochure excitedly. "*Gib a kuk*, Ania, look at this. How would you like to join me on a trip to the Southwest? Las Vegas." Though he was approaching his eightieth birthday, his spirit remained as young as ever. He still thirsted to go places and see things, to experience new adventures. And he wouldn't travel alone. Since my mother died I had been his companion on nearly all his trips abroad.

"But why Vegas?"

"The neon lights," he said, as if it should be obvious. He loved light in all its incarnations and the Vegas strip promised to dazzle us with illumination that surpassed even his beloved New York. "Besides, Las Vegas will tell me much about America."

I must have looked doubtful.

"And people say it's a lot of fun too." And then he waited, leafing through the brochure, whistling "Good Day Sunshine." He loved all Beatles tunes.

Our tourist bus had been rolling on dusty Nevada roads for many hours. Unlike our previous trips where airplanes whisked us through the clouds and deposited us in busy cities, on this trip we were seeing the country as it unfolded in three dimensions. The bustling eastern megalopolis gave way to rolling farms, green valleys, and eventually to Nevada's dramatic windswept plateaus dotted with twisted pine trees, blue-grey mountains silhouetted against an endless sky. The members of our tour group were tired. Many were dozing in the recliner seats with their hats pulled over their eyes. A few were reading, but Tinek sat upright with his nose pressed to the window observing the landscape. Every now and then he would call my attention to an oddly shaped rock outcropping or an enormous cactus.

It was close to noon when the driver announced that soon we would arrive at our destination—the MGM Grand. Within half an hour we pulled to a stop on Las Vegas Boulevard. The guide announced a special treat, courtesy of the travel agency. "Since you are about to go to a beautiful new casino, I will distribute rolls of coins. Each of you will receive $20 to get started." Immediately, whistles and a chatter of excited voices filled the bus. "Okay. Good luck, group. Remember we will meet back at the bus in two hours. Then we are off to our stop for the night."

Chattering, we disembarked, walked across the vast parking lot to the impressive lobby. I wanted to freshen up and check out the shops. "Ania, I would rather take a look at the architecture and walk around exploring."

"Sure," I said. "I will find you later at the slots, Tinek, or else, if we miss one another, we will reconnect on the bus."

I poked around in some overpriced shops and spent a short time at the slot machines. In the end, I did not win a memorable sum, and, not finding my father at the slots, I headed back to the bus. It was filled with the animated conversation of gambling enthusiasts. The group was settling back into their seats, comparing vital information with their neighbours: "So how did you do?" "How much did you win?"

As I approached our seats, I overheard the woman seated in back of us asking my father, "And what about you? How much did you win?" My father winked at me as I sat down, turned toward the woman and replied, "I won $20." I looked down at his lap and saw him clutching the unopened roll of coins in his hand.

"Tinek," I asked concerned, "did you enjoy yourself at all?"

"Sure."

The bus roared to life, and soon the chatter subsided as our travel companions settled for the long ride ahead.

"You know," he said, as the last of the older casinos receded behind us, "I gamble only when it is necessary."

Nachman picked up speed as he exited Yankel's courtyard and hurried toward the train station. By now life on the street had returned. Many people were carrying bundles. Nachman wondered if they, too, had made the decision to get out, out as quickly as possible. Soon he would mingle with the crowd and blend in with the Poles. Nothing in his appearance would distinguish him. Whistling under his breath, he arrived at the station. He glanced at the pocket watch that had been his father's most valuable possession. He was late. The friends he hoped to meet—Adek and Regina—were nowhere to be seen. Would he have to take this journey alone?

With little choice, he boarded a train. Instead of heading directly east, toward the border, he travelled 230 miles west to Kalish in west-central Poland.

But why? I wondered, as I listened to his taped account time and again, unable to fully understand all the decisions my father made at the time. Maybe the only train he could board went to Kalish. Maybe he sat in a corner of a passenger compartment, fear churning in his belly that any minute he might be recognized as a Jew and denounced. Probably he escaped notice because of his blond, blue-eyed looks. I could only speculate. I chided myself for not having the presence of mind while he was still alive to ask him the questions that came rushing to my mind. I kept a sketchy map of his escape route in my head, gleaned from many tellings of the story over the years. I recalled how on one of my annual winter visits to Florida I was determined to get him to help me fill in some blanks. I waited till it was just the two of us on the beach in front of his condo.

He was reading *Years at the Edge of Existence*, a memoir by Frank Morgens. "Ania, you must read this, you must." He kept repeating how remarkable this account of a Jewish family's survival was. "If this Polish Catholic woman hadn't risked her life, they would have all been killed."

"Tinek, you are not supposed to give away the ending," I said.

"Okay, okay." He went back to reading.

Each time he interrupted I reread the same paragraph of *A Civil Action*, by Jonathan Harr. When I picked this book up from his bookcase he said, "That is another one not to miss." He devoured about fifty books each year and was always eager to make recommendations. The gulls overhead made a racket and the surf rose. I loved listening to these sounds. I put the book down, closed my eyes and began to line up the questions in my mind.

"Tinku."

He merely grunted, absorbed in his pages.

"I want to know about Kalish. I want to know what happened after Kalish."

He didn't even look up. "Ania, you have heard it many times. You know the whole story. What else can I possibly tell you?"

I tried to sound like the little girl I had once been, always pleading. "Plenty. You know I always have more questions!" I moved my beach chair closer to his and turned it to face him.

"Okay, oy, just let me get to the next chapter," he said.

"I want to plot your route in my mind. Did you go directly from Kalish to the eastern border?"

He closed his book in mock exasperation, stuffed it into his beach bag. "No," he said, "what gave you that idea? Nothing was so straightforward at that time. First we needed to get from Kalish to Warsaw, which by then was already occupied by the Germans. If we got very lucky and didn't arouse any suspicions that we were Jews on the run, we would get closer to Siemiatycze, where we expected to steal across to the Soviet side."

"Who is 'we'?"

"I have told you before. It was Adek, a distant cousin and his wife, Regina. I found them at the Kalish train station."

"By the time you finally made it to Warsaw, the Nazis were in control for only three months or so. What was it like?"

"You wouldn't believe what a mess! There was bombing, shooting, chaos, smoke—war in full swing. We saw poor people on the streets pushing carts with their belongings. Who knows where they were going? Everyone seemed to be rushing to find an illusive bit of safety, but also seemed pigheadedly determined to stay put in their city. The sight of them scrambling like frightened rabbits, and the sense of doom that hung over the city, made me only more determined that I would continue with my plan, no matter what."

"How did you figure out exactly where it was best to cross the border?"

A brown pelican swooped overhead, diverting our attention momentarily. We both looked up.

"I knew that the River Bug formed the border between Poland and the Soviet Union, except by that time it was no longer considered a Polish border. It was considered German. We only needed to find a local who would show us the right spot for crossing. But it wasn't as simple as just asking. We had to be very careful in whom to approach. Asking a German sympathizer would be, well ... you can imagine."

"Did you ride the train all the way to Siemiatycze?"

He laughed and looked out to the ocean. "No, by then it was impossible and even if there were a train it would have been far too risky. We walked for miles and miles, and then whenever we could, we hired farmers willing to drive us in their wagons to get us closer to the river. Most seemed eager to help us."

"Did you have to pay them, or did they do it as just—I don't know—a kindness to people escaping the war?"

"Oh, Ania, Ania, you are so naive. Of course we had to pay them. Our money was running low. We had very little to begin with but getting across the border was essential. By the time we finally got close to the river we found one farmer who told us he had some small boats tied up on the riverbank. We pooled our money to pay him to get us across the river after it turned dark."

"Were you frightened?"

"We were too preoccupied with the logistics to feel fear. It would not have helped us to focus on it anyway. Deep down, I think each of us was nervous, but also excited that soon we would be far away from the mayhem we witnessed in Warsaw. I had but a single thought in my mind—move, move, move."

"So how did it work out?"

"You know the answer."

"Yes, but I want to hear it again."

The tide began to roll in and the waves crashed loudly on the shore. An excited flock of gulls screeched overhead.

"At dusk Regina, Adek, and I piled into the wooden wagon. It squeaked under our combined weight though all three of us were thin. The farmer drove in the dark snapping the whip and calling out to the horse, "*Wio, wio*," to hurry him along. When we arrived at the place his boats were moored we clambered out of the wagon and the farmer pointed to the vessel that would take us across. A thick carpet of dry leaves rustled beneath our feet. Each step sounded loud to our ears. We got in quickly as he steadied the boat.

"When we reached the opposite riverbank, we found Soviet soldiers shooting warning rounds into the air and lighting flares. We stood for some moments in a small cove and listened. We were close enough to hear what was going on. They apprehended all those who landed before us. We heard the soldiers shouting that these people would be sent back onto the German side. It would have been useless to try and scramble onto the riverbank. The flares lit up the sky as if it were day. We whispered to the farmer that we wanted to go back to the shore from which we just came. He dipped the oars in and moved them so silently we thought we were standing still.

"Back on the other side, in the light of day, we decided to split up because it seemed that we would have a greater chance of disembarking unnoticed if we did it singly. We thought that we could reconnect in the next village, but it would be twenty years before I saw them again."

The wind picked up and the clouds thickened. I knew we'd be going home soon, but I needed to know more.

"When I was on my own, I decided to hire a different farmer, one who might try a different approach to getting me across. I asked a few locals and they pointed me toward a nearby farmstead. The second farmer seemed to be younger and smarter. When I told him about our failed attempt the night before he said he knew of a better spot for crossing, but one that was farther up river. 'I'll use a smaller, quieter rowboat,' he said.

"When night fell we got under way in his horse-drawn wagon. It was a few miles to the rowboat launching spot he had selected. He made me lie down and hide under a heap of straw in the wagon in case we were stopped by the Germans who by then were in control of the Polish side of the Bug. But the Germans didn't get us. Along the back road, we were attacked by a group of gun-wielding men. I heard them shouting in Polish. It happened so quickly that it is hard to remember the details. I do know that they stole my meagre possessions when they grabbed the satchel Rosa had packed for me. It's a wonder they didn't shoot both of us when they found me under the straw. I lost my satchel, but I had my life, so that was a good sign. We had hardly any time to regain our senses. As soon as the men were gone we continued toward the river. Neither the farmer nor I spoke of the incident.

"On my second try crossing the Bug, I already had an idea what to expect. I decided to run into the woods as soon as I clambered onto the opposite shore and then to lie quietly on the ground until the shooting died down and it appeared to be safe to continue. I got into the tiny rowboat and in total silence we pushed away from what just weeks before had been a Polish shore. I heard shots. They sounded as if they were coming from the Polish side. It must have been the Germans patrolling the area.

"Luckily for me, a cloudy day had turned into a starless night. Occasionally, flares on the opposite shore illuminated the pitch black. The boat skimmed the surface soundlessly. In my head I counted the minutes it would take us to reach the opposite bank. I knew I might be welcomed by gunfire, but freedom from the Germans beckoned, and calmed my nerves.

"Soon the boat stopped and rocked gently. The farmer whispered, 'You are here. Get out.' I looked up. All I could make out was a thicket of trees in the distance.

"'Which way?' I asked him, my heart beating as if it would fly out of my chest. In response, he extended his palm. It was clear he wanted me to pay for the information.

"'I have no money,'" I whispered and wished I hadn't wasted it on the previous crossing attempt.

"'Give me your watch,' he said. I handed it over.

"He motioned toward the left and said, 'Follow the railroad tracks. They will bring you into Siemiatycze.' At that moment I couldn't see the tracks, but hoped I would find them somewhere beyond the woods. I stepped out of the boat into the mud and could feel the cold water seeping into my shoes. I made my way up the riverbank, slipping as I advanced.

"The sounds of the shooting were a bit more distant than on our previous try, but I knew it wasn't yet safe to continue so I lay down in the woods and waited. Each time I heard the rustling of leaves I didn't know if animals or humans were on the prowl. I tried to still my breath. In my mind I just kept telling myself: *Stay still, you have made it this far. It will be over soon.* When the shooting subsided and the soldiers left, I moved along the railroad tracks toward the town, a bit of moonlight helping me find my way. I had never felt so alone."

My father paused. He looked at the waves as if he were trying to see himself in those long-ago woods. I tapped his shoulder gently and after a few moments of silence he resumed.

"As I approached the town, I heard incredible sounds. In my exhausted state I thought I was hallucinating. Those were the sounds of singing. Singing in the middle of the war? How was that possible? It turned out that this village was far enough from the border that the wartime tensions hadn't penetrated. The heavy atmosphere that was so evident in Poland hadn't yet taken hold of Siemiatycze, or Semyatich, as the Russians called it.

"Shortly, I discovered that there were many Jewish youths roaming the streets late at night. They were the ones singing. I looked at them in amazement. It was surreal. Their merry mood, so in contrast to the rest of Poland, must have reflected relief of having made it to the side held by the Russian 'liberators.'"

2006

As soon as we finished dinner I went down to our basement office to continue listening and transcribing the CDs. Every now and then I'd be stuck on a Yiddish word for which there was no satisfactory English translation, and chuckled at the unique expressions that contained so much emotion in a single word or a phrase. *A brokh! A gezunt oyf dayn kop!* No wonder my father loved Yiddish more than any language.

I recalled that late-nineties beachside conversation as I sat listening again to the story of my father's escape from Poland on the CD. I paused the narration for a moment, leaving him on that street in Semyatich. I gathered my thoughts and tried to imagine my young gregarious father, always surrounded by friends, alone and wrapped in the blanket of night trying to grasp safety. What was he thinking? Did he feel a stab of failure at his inability to persuade even a single relative to join him? Pain at leaving his Jadwiga behind? Guilt at having to separate from Adek and Regina for the crossing? Did he worry he'd fall into a trap? Did he consider turning back, even for a moment? If he was no different back then, I was pretty sure he didn't think about dying. Death never seemed on his radar screen. He was not one to share his feelings. Never was. The only telling detail, the most he could muster was "the brotherly love of Russia was a great lie." This statement contained more of his sense of betrayal and disappointment than a barrel of tears. I wanted to know exactly what events had caused him to say this. I hit the start button.

"The next day, I and other refugees—it turned out there were many of us—were taken by horse-drawn wagons on a sixty-mile journey north to the town of Bialystock. Like Semyatich, by the time I arrived, Bialystock was in Russian hands. I carried with me the address of my teacher Shlomo Ravin's brother who lived there. Although I had never met this man, I wanted to find a kindred spirit in the town where I knew no one. I hurried to his place.

"He flung the door wide open as if he were expecting me. He was a small man with a shock of grey hair and a rumpled linen rubashka. 'Come in, come in. *Vos makht a Yid?*' He greeted me cheerfully in Yiddish as soon as I mentioned I had been a student of his brother's.

"'Are you busy right now?' I asked. 'I could come by later.'

"'Nonsense, I am just making tea, join me and tell me everything.'

"I saw a big silver samovar on his table. It was the most elaborate thing in the modest room. We spoke for a long while. After several glasses of tea he finally mentioned his brother, my former teacher. I knew that he had died, but didn't know any details. I didn't want to bring up such a painful subject.

"'You do know my brother, Shlomo, was exiled from Poland after that bloody May Day demonstration in Lodz in 1924. Those fascist pigs in the government accused him of being a communist. Ridiculous.'

"'Sure, I remember it. It was just a year before my graduation. The entire school was in despair seeing him arrested. But you know, he used to write us letters when he ended up in Simferopol, on the Crimea. You could hear a pin drop as the teacher read them to us.' Ravin smiled.

"'You do know what happened to him later? Don't you?'

"'I know he died. I am so sorry.'

"'Died? Died? No, Nachman. He was murdered!' His face turned beet red and his eyes bulged. 'The Soviets accused him of being a Polish spy and executed him. Can you believe it? A Jew? A Bundist? A spy? But he wasn't the only one. They rounded up many Bundists. You know how the communists love the socialists. Wouldn't they like to wipe us all out of the way?'

"His ironic tone was an indication of the depth of his pain. He regained his composure and seemed embarrassed that he had shown so much emotion to a stranger. We were silent for a while and sat there, listening to the hissing of the samovar.

"'All right, *Khaver* Ravin, I am so glad I made your acquaintance. I hope to see you soon again.' With that we shook hands and I stepped out onto the street.

"After a week in Bialystock, I continued to the town of Kobryn, which is now a part of Belarus. Since the turn of the eighteenth century, Kobryn had been kicked like a football between Russia, Lithuania, Poland, and Germany, but in 1939 it was squarely in the hands of the Soviets and home to a huge Jewish community.

"As I had planned to do from the outset of my journey, my first order of business was to locate my teacher, Resnick. Rosa had planted that idea in my head, and I was glad she did because I had forgotten that he had moved to Kobryn. I knew that here I would meet someone who would be truly happy that I had escaped unscathed and welcome me with open arms. That's how it was between the teachers and students in my school. The closer I got to his street, the more excited I became. Meeting Shlomo's brother was nice, but not the same as meeting a teacher who had such a profound influence on me.

"I located the small house that was his address and knocked on his door. I expected the great big bear hug that was his trademark. But Resnick backed up from the door and asked, 'Nachman? Is it really you? What brings you here?' His tone was odd.

"'I am a refugee, like the hundreds you must have seen around town. How are you?' I replied.

"He looked me over from head to toe as if I were a stranger and said, 'Things aren't so easy here these days. I have work to do and have no time for visitors right now.' It was as if I had been hit by a blast of arctic air. This was not the man I knew.

"'Sorry for disturbing you,' I said.

"He looked down at his feet and said quietly, 'Good luck. Maybe next time,' then shut the door quickly.

"*Why? Why?* I kept asking myself as I turned toward the street and looked for a place to go. It dawned on me that the communists had gotten to him already. Perhaps he even joined the party. Associating with a Bundist, a socialist like me, could spell his end. He must have been frightened to meet the same fate as Ravin's brother, Shlomo. Thinking about Resnick's reaction and the change in Herr Boltz made me queasy. It seemed that the war was changing people. All they cared about was their own skin."

Another pause. I had to stop and absorb that painful insult. I imagined my father's bafflement. He always spoke of his Medem School teachers as a family. And to be rejected like a beggar at Resnick's door! I could feel the stab in the heart my father felt, he that valued *khavershaft* above all else. I shook my head and resumed listening.

"When it became evident that I couldn't make a go of it in Kobryn, I sold my only prized possession, my father's pocket watch, to scrape up the money to set myself up in the nearby town of Pinsk. The wristwatch I had given the peasant who took me across the Bug was an inexpensive piece. I am glad he didn't know I had the pocket watch on me. Still, I couldn't keep it. It proved to me you can't get too attached to material objects.

"In Pinsk, I shared lodging with a Jewish dentist named Levin. I spent a month or two trying to find work, but there was nothing. The money from the sale of the pocket watch was running out and I wondered what I'd do, but then I heard fantastic news. There was a call for Jewish Bundists to gather in the city of Vilna in Lithuania [today Vilnius]. The city was then known as the 'Jerusalem of Lithuania' because of the rich Jewish religious and secular culture that had been thriving there for centuries. The very fact that the Jewish Labor Bund had its headquarters in Vilna was a sign of its status. It was a big deal for a Jewish institution to have such a prestigious address.

"I had heard that people who made it to Vilna were able to obtain exit visas. Some managed to go to Asia—China, Japan; others went to Argentina and Brazil and a lucky few even went to America. I thought that if I could get there I, too, would stand a good chance of getting out and away from the war. It was the Hebrew Immigrant Aid Society [HIAS] in America, along with several other Jewish organizations, that had provided funding to help get Jews out of Lithuania and the Bund was one of the coordinating agencies. Rumour had it that Bundists would get priority for exit visas."

So that was the good news. I felt relieved and excited for my father. I looked up at his painting of the Kibbutz Hora hanging over my desk and imagined he felt like dancing at the news, even if it was just speculation. I imagined how very anxious my father must have been to get to Vilna once he had heard about the opportunity to leave the war zone. In my mind's eye I saw him heading there immediately, but it turned out I was still thinking like someone who did not fully understand the difficulties of moving from place to place during wartime. Soon I learned that there was a major obstacle—he would have to cross the border *again*.

"Crossing was very risky—one had to join with others who knew the ropes. I rented a room from a Jewish family in Lida. Today it is in Belarus. This town was only about twenty miles from the Lithuanian border. Now, all I had to do was to find people who knew how to get across that border safely and find an opportune moment to do it. It seemed that all of Lida was filled with Jews, like me, scheming to find ways to get across into Vilna and take advantage of the Bund's help. But by then winter was in full swing and the storms had begun. It snowed furiously, day in and day out, making plans for passage to Vilna more difficult. Still, all of us were filled with hope that one way or another we'd make it across the border. I and some other young men I had met tried time and again, but each time we attempted to cross we were rounded up by Soviet soldiers and sent back. It was quite lucky that they didn't arrest us."

The ticking of the clock on the desk, a sound I usually like, began to irritate me. I knew it was getting late and that dinner dishes still sat in the sink, but I hated to be interrupted whenever I immersed myself in the recordings. I moved the clock off the desk.

I may never understand exactly by what means my father managed to get himself from Pinsk to Lida, another ancient Belarusian town. Once Lithuanian, then Polish, then Soviet, by September 1939 the town was a magnet for Jews from the West. By the time of my father's arrival in the winter of 1940 it was like a Jewish beehive. Its population swelled with the influx of refugees from around six thousand to more than fifteen thousand, all waiting for passage to Vilna and freedom. *Could Lida have been the birthplace of my father's dream of America?* I wondered. While he lived in Poland, before the war, some of his cousins had immigrated to the New World, but he had expressed no desire to follow them. But when my father spoke of the possibility of getting an exit visa to various countries once he got to Vilna, it was the way he emphasized the word *America*, something he didn't do when saying, Brazil or Argentina, that made me think America was his secret wish. When he enumerated the potential places that might accept immigrants he said nothing of going to Palestine. Bundists did not encourage Jews to leave for Palestine. As secular internationalists, they believed that Jews should be free to remain in their countries of origin and continue building on their cultural traditions there.

My thoughts returned to my father in Lida. I tried to imagine his transitory stay in an unfamiliar city, nourished only with the hope of reaching Vilna with its promise of a safe land, maybe even the mythical America. I could see him clearly in my mind's eye—handsome, gregarious, and never discouraged. He was no more than sixty miles from the place that offered an exit from the hell about to erupt: so close and still so far. But as winter gave way to the spring of 1940, the doors to Vilna slammed shut. The Red Army marched in, took over Lithuania's sovereign territory as their own, and cut off all refugee transit. With the Vilna escape route closed, Nachman would have to find another way.

As much as I couldn't stomach or comprehend the vastness of Stalin's crimes against the Jews, I will forever be thankful that due to Soviet policies my father was gone from Lida by the summer. By June 1941, just ten months after my father's departure, the German army took control of Lida. Of the fifteen thousand Jews, only two hundred survived the butchery that ensued.

My eyes stung. How late was it? I retrieved the clock. It was 2:00 a.m. I turned off the CD player and headed up to the bedroom, my head still in Lida. I stood before the mirror to brush my teeth and looked at the red rims around my eyes. Had I been crying, or was it just eyestrain? I hoped it was the latter. I wanted to be like my father. He would not have cried. He would have been more determined to survive by any means whatsoever.

When the Soviets dashed any hopes that the Jewish refugees could escape through Russia, Nachman and his new acquaintances were at a loss. What now? One night around midnight, in the summer of 1940, after Nachman had been on the run for about eight months he awoke to the sound of banging on the door of the apartment he shared with two other Polish Jews. The pounding was so loud it seemed its wooden panels would split apart. Nachman opened it cautiously: soldiers accompanied by civilian officials.

They forced their way in and shouted, "You are all under arrest! Get moving. You are coming with us." In just a few moments they handcuffed Nachman and his new acquaintances and threw them into a van. It was cold so they had slept in their clothes, and that was lucky because they would have surely dragged them out in their skivvies. They rode in silence. The vehicle screeched to a halt and as soon as they stepped out of it soldiers with snarling dogs, straining at the leashes, surrounded them. The detainees were all taken to an old jailhouse. There were many other unshaven, bewildered men. In a cell meant to hold thirty prisoners, more than twice that number were squeezed in like cattle. It was stifling hot. Packed in so tightly, they were forced to take turns coming to the crack near the door to breathe the cool air. They spent their days in the cell speculating about their fate. There was very little to eat and no exercise at all. And complain? Never. Everyone knew that if you complained in Russia, your punishment would be that much worse.

Nachman, like the rest of the inmates, was called in for interrogations. These always took place at night, as if the captors needed cover for their activities, or maybe they knew the men would be more frightened and co-operative if they were dragged into the interrogation room just roused from sleep. Time and again, the Russians wanted to know only one thing: "Which German spy had taken you across the border from the German occupied land into Russia?" They asked Nachman this question dozens of times banging their fists on the table. Each time he gave the only answer he could: "I came by myself." The interrogators were not satisfied. They invented claims and crazy scenarios. In between the slaps they dished out, they urged him to confess he had collaborated with spies. "You'll never get out of here unless you confess," they warned him repeatedly. "All you need to do is sign this paper, then you'll be a free man." After several weeks all interrogations suddenly stopped. One day, at dawn, soldiers took the whole lot of men at gunpoint, surrounded by dogs and marched them to the train station. Nachman could see now that he was one of hundreds of prisoners. He hadn't realized that there were so many men at the jail.

At the train station he stood silently in a long line with the others. Soon they found out they were to be loaded onto cattle cars. It must have been an hour, or maybe two—time seemed to have lost its meaning. Like obedient dogs, the guards, with machine guns leaning against their shoulders, stood watching the hapless men. Escape from here was not an option. The guards were ready to shoot at the slightest movement. A cold and persistent mist penetrated Nachman's threadbare jacket. He didn't care where they were going; he just wanted to get inside the train. Once they were hustled into the cars, the men were not allowed to converse, and just stared at one another trying to infer something from a stance, the slope of the shoulders, the shadows below the eyes of their unwitting companions. Each tried to intuit who this or that person was. What had brought them to this point? Who did they leave behind? In stark contrast to the cold at the station, the train wagons sweltered with tightly packed bodies. Men began to perspire and remove their jackets, then their shirts. Even without them, it was impossible to cool off. The smell of sweat suffused the car.

The trip into the unknown took weeks. The train stopped frequently and neither Nachman nor his companions had any idea why. Perhaps their captors were getting some provisions, but the scraps of food they received were mouldy and hardly edible. But who had the choice of not eating? Nachman's stomach growled non-stop. Twice since he'd left home he had to make new holes in his belt. Occasionally the soldiers gave the men a small bucket of water when the train came to a stop. Nachman drank it greedily as if it were wine, sharing the one dented metal cup with the other men.

When they arrived at the great Volga River Nachman was amazed to see it. The silver grey waters moved swiftly and eddied around huge stones. Forests on its banks protected it like a stately fence. He was spellbound, imagining great fish swimming in it, though he couldn't see them. *Me, at the legendary river the Russians thought of as Mother Volga?* he thought. *Who would have imagined it?* He had read about the river as a schoolboy and remembered tracing its 2,500-mile course on a tattered atlas they had in class. Although he was a prisoner, the sight of the great river excited him. *What would Rosa say seeing me here*, he wondered.

Nachman thought that the group had reached the final destination when they got off the train, but he was wrong. The guards forced the men onto ships waiting for them at the pier. *To where?* he wondered. *Are they taking us there to shoot us? No, that doesn't make much sense. They wouldn't waste effort shipping us somewhere if they intended to kill us.* Still, no one knew what lay upriver and not knowing left too much space for their imaginations. The farther north they sailed the sparser the villages became. The forests loomed dark and impenetrable. *Whatever they have in store for us, it can't be good,* Nachman concluded grimly.

At last they arrived at a place called Poshekhonie Volodarsk in Yaroslavl *oblast* (province). By then they were about two hundred miles north of Moscow. Nachman had never heard of this place, nor imagined being this far north. Always good at geography, he wasn't sure where they were but he knew that the Arctic Ocean was Russia's northern border. The thought of spending the winter here froze his brain. *I have to stop thinking about it if I want to survive,* he said to himself. The men were marched to their new prison, unlike any Nachman had ever seen. It was a newly constructed gulag named Opalicha. He discovered shortly that six hundred Polish Jews and a handful of Polish Gentiles were his fellow inmates.

Nachman looked around as the guards took them toward the prison's central square for a headcount. He could see nothing but rows of crudely constructed wooden barracks and two high watchtowers that loomed over the camp. From the smell of raw wood he surmised the camp had been constructed only recently. Piles of timber were still strewn around the grounds, and layers of barbed wire encircled the entire area. On the other side, all that was visible was an endless forest, thick and dark, just like the one in Russian fairy tales. *So this is my safe house, but for how long,* he wondered.

They entered the barracks. Oil lamps with cotton wicks cast eerie shadows on the thin wooden planks that were to shelter the inmates from the elements. Each barrack had a triple layer of bunks constructed of rough-hewn wooden posts covered by splinters. Instead of mattresses, there was straw to sleep on and a burlap cover. On their first evening a tall, broad-shouldered young man whose name was Hoffman—a Jewish engineer from Warsaw—came into Nachman's barrack. He seemed to have been sent to Opalicha earlier than the rest of the group, as he did not arrive with them. He stood at the entrance and slowly surveyed the sorry lot. Then in flawless Russian he asked, "Which of you men will write me a list of surnames of everyone in this barrack?" It sounded more like an order than a question.

Silence. No one dared speak.

"How long will I wait for a volunteer?" Hoffman seemed annoyed.

Nachman didn't know what would happen if no one spoke up. Maybe the whole group would be punished. He was known to have excellent handwriting and thought, *What's the worst that could happen?*

After a while he stepped forward and said, "I can do it."

Hoffman looked satisfied. His eyes brightened and he handed Nachman a pad and a pencil. Nachman looked around trying to decide where he would begin making his list. He didn't want to miss anyone. The men stood as if they expected to be sentenced. There was nothing but terror in their eyes. They smelled of sweat and fear. Most were young and skinny, like Nachman. A few were middle-aged with a tinge of silver at their temples and bellies that were past prime. Several looked old and exhausted by the journey. All were bedraggled, in rumpled clothes and worn shoes that would surely not last through the winter.

Nachman approached each of the men, asked their names, and wrote them down as neatly as he could, given the dullness of the pencil and the scratchiness of the coarse paper. Their faces and names were familiar, like those of relatives and friends back home: Abraham, Beyrl, Dovid, Issac, Jacob, Max, Meyer, Moses, Yankel, ... the whole alphabet of Jewish

prophets and luminaries. *They are like me and like my brothers.*
The thought gave Nachman a sharp pang in the chest. He
thought of his two brothers who were now in Nazi-occupied
Poland. *Now these men will be my brothers,* he calmed himself.

Nothing much happened after this. Exhausted, the men
fell into a coma-like sleep. The next day a shrill alarm sounded
before dawn. It was time to go outside and stand at attention
for the count. Every prisoner had to present himself and be
ready to work, no matter his physical condition. Before the
guards barged into his barrack Nachman could hear them
stomping around in their boots and shouting outside. *This
place was not going to be a picnic,* he thought. *Just get through
this, one day at a time.* The thought lodged in his brain. It was
a refrain that would he would repeat to himself nightly as he
lay on his bunk.

The inmates were given some tepid, black liquid to start
their day. It did not taste like anything familiar. Nothing else.
The soldiers barked orders for them to hurry and unlocked the
camp gates once they all stood outside the barracks. They had
only arrived the night before. *Where could we be going now?*
Nachman wondered. Outside the compound there were more
soldiers on guard with guns drawn. They ordered the men to
clean up the site outside the camp. The whole place had been
hastily constructed and huge piles of debris remained in its
immediate area—logs, wires, stones—it fell to the prisoners to
organize the whole mess.

After working for a few hours Nachman's back ached. The
wire cut up his hands. There were no tools. Nachman was not
used to such demanding manual labour. Suddenly, he heard
his name being called.

"Libeskind, Nachman!"

"In Russia when you heard your name being called, it was
never a good thing," Nachman emphasized on the tape as he
did anytime he later spoke about the Soviet Union.

Not far from him, Nachman saw a tall man, ruddy, broad
shouldered, who looked exactly like Nachman's idea of a

typical Russian. Looking at his long leather coat with epaulets, Nachman surmised the man was a member of the NKVD, the Soviet secret police. The Russian approached Nachman, gave him a tap on his shoulder and said, "Let's go over to the side to have a chat." Nachman followed him. What else could he do? The Russian swept his coat to the side and sat on a nearby rock outcropping. Then he patted the spot beside him and motioned for Nachman to join him. This casual gesture made Nachman more nervous. There was no such thing as getting into a cozy tête-à-tête with a member of the NKVD. It spelled nothing but trouble. Nachman sat on the edge of the rock and turned his body to face the man on his right.

"So, tell me about your father," the Russian asked. His plain, broad face revealed nothing.

"He was a carpenter, but he is deceased," Nachman responded.

The Russian squinted and looked at Nachman closely. "Do you come from a rich family?"

"No," Nachman said, "we were very poor."

So far he had no problem with the questions. They put him at ease because he could tell the truth. Still, he could not figure out where this was going.

"Tell me about the kind of work you did in Poland and about your schooling." Nachman answered each question briefly, giving as little detail as possible. With each reply the NKVD man nodded and looked squarely into Nachman's eyes. The two were so close Nachman could see the Russian's large, white teeth and smell his breath. Then he paused the questioning abruptly for what seemed like eternity and lit a cigarette. Nachman thought the interview was over. He shifted uncomfortably trying not to slip off the rock.

Suddenly the Russian looked at Nachman again and shot out a question. "Libeskind, have you ever served as a leader?"

Oh, boy, here comes trouble, Nachman thought. Of course, he had. He was a youth leader for SKIF, but he worried about revealing this, so he said no.

The Russian paused for a few moments, ran his fingers
through his thick, brown hair and turned to Nachman looking
very serious: "Do you think you could lead people?"

"I guess I could give it a try," Nachman said.

The Russian stood up, smiled broadly and slapped
Nachman's shoulder. "*Vy budetye rukovoditelëm vtoroĭ kolonki!*"
Leader of the second column!

He motioned for Nachman to come with him. All the
other inmates in the vicinity looked stunned, as if a miracle
had taken place. The gate opened and their fellow inmate got
to leave the work site. Nachman was led through the gate,
past the guards, back onto the area occupied by the labour
camp and into the office of the camp's director, or *nachalnik*.
When the NKVD official and Nachman entered the director's
office, Hoffman was already there. He and the director were
meeting to discuss how to manage the six hundred men so
that the work goals required by the administration in Moscow
could be achieved. They sat around a simple pine table in the
small room that was almost as bare as the barracks, except
for the pot-bellied stove in the corner and a portrait of Stalin
over the desk. They leaned back in their chairs and waited for
the NKVD official to introduce Nachman and announce his
decision.

The director seemed friendly enough. He explained that
Hoffman, who was initially assigned to lead all the work
brigades, had made a proposal that since the group was very
large, it should be split into two sections of three hundred men
each. He suggested that he lead one group and Nachman, the
preparer of the neat and legible list of his barrack's inmates,
the other. He still had no idea what the work would be and
just what was expected of him. Soon Nachman learned that
the director was a Russian who himself was an inmate serving
time for crimes that he may or may not have committed.
He was one of millions who ended up in gulags at the whim
of the government. His job was to run the Opalicha prison
camp. It was so remote and located in an area that experienced

such bitter winters that to be exiled there was considered punishment enough.

My father had mentioned more than once that when the Polish refugees had been first rounded up and questioned by the Russian authorities they were given a choice: accept Russian citizenship, or decline. Most retained their Polish citizenships hoping that the war would soon be over and they would be heading home to the families they left behind. They also expected that as Russian citizens they would be conscripted into the Soviet military and sent to the front as the war progressed. A typical Russian ploy, according to my father, executed with all the deceit the Soviets could muster, unfolded. The Polish and Jewish refugees rounded up by the Soviet secret police were promptly excused after their citizenship choices were made. At the time it seemed not to matter which citizenship they chose, Polish or Russian. As soon as they were done filling out the forms they were released. It wasn't until several nights later that those who declined the Russian citizenship were rounded up again and declared enemies of the state. This explained why my father was arrested in Lida.

Though he was deprived of his freedom, somehow my mother's oft-repeated prophesy held even in the remote Soviet gulag: "No matter what, Nachman, you'll always find yourself being rescued from bad situations by lucky angels." And so it was. His designation as a leader of a column not only saved his own life, but gave him the chance to help many others. Nachman had been gone from Lodz almost nine months. He still had the image of that last morning fixed in his mind: Isser's pleading, Yankel's refusal to leave. Now he wondered about the soundness of his advice. "I would have hated to see them arrested and thrown into this place," he thought with regret, and optimism that they were all in better circumstances.

I hadn't worked at transcribing my father's narration for several days and was anxious to return to it, but the responsibilities of professional life intervened. My position as Senior Vice-President of education at the Wildlife Conservation Society had grown into something I could never have envisioned when I accepted the instructor's position more than three decades before. I relished spearheading wildlife conservation programs in hundreds of schools in the United States and in remote parts of the world: China, Papua New Guinea, Cuba, Belize, India, and Bhutan. By now I oversaw a staff of dozens of employees: instructors, teacher trainers, curriculum developers, animal supervisors in the Children's Zoo, and education curators at the society's three other zoos and the New York Aquarium. It was an awesome responsibility, but I felt as if I had won the lottery. Filled with births of exotic animals, the excited chatter of children on zoo outings, travel to areas where nature was still pristine, mine felt like the best job in the world.

That evening I had to finalize all of my employees' annual performance evaluations. This was one part of my job I did not enjoy. *If I get these done, listening to my father's story will be my reward*, I promised myself. I pored over each evaluation and scanned the ratings time and again. One level up or down could make a difference in the employees' raises. They all worked hard and were underpaid, a tradition in not-for-profit educational institutions. I'd have given them all an across the board salary increase if I could.

By the time I began transcribing it was past 10:30 p.m. I made myself a silent promise to head upstairs to bed by midnight, but I knew it wouldn't happen. Once I clicked the play button, I would be immersed in the Second World War and along with my father on his journey. Rummaging in the drawers for a new pen, I came across a stack of elongated notepapers with my father's handwriting. What's this? One glance and I remembered. My father was an inveterate list maker. These were lists of books he had read since the mid-1990s: scanning the record I saw he had read every new Holocaust memoir and related scholarly tomes featuring data from recently opened archives. I was familiar with those volumes. Their hard-bound spines in a rainbow of colours still stood on his wall unit, crafted according to my father's design by a Russian cabinetmaker, an immigrant like us.

The house was blissfully quiet. I was familiar with the general outlines of this story, but wanted to catch every nuance in my father's voice. His arrival in the frigid Russian unknown had me spellbound. I clicked the play button, and Tinek's voice filled the room. I was mesmerized by his melodious tone, his easy conversational pace. It didn't sound as if he were reading a written account. He was a storyteller, not a story writer. It was casual, like a conversation between us—easy and mellow. Despite the nature of the events there was no tension or anxiety in his voice. And the accent ... how I loved hearing his Yiddish-inflected English and the sections he narrated in Yiddish. So few Yiddish speakers today and all of them ancient. One rarely hears it in New York anymore. I miss it, miss it badly.

"Hoffman filled me in on my responsibilities. My job was to see that each morning all the inmates showed up promptly for the outside work assignments. It made no difference if they were unskilled, old, sick, or injured. They had to work no matter what. On site at the camp, I was to ensure that the workshops all functioned properly—the tailors, the shoemakers, the bath-house, the kitchen and the laundry. If any of these work sites were not performing as expected, it would be taken out on my skin. The workdays would be from dawn to dusk and the pay-ment would be a ration of bread. If the work quota, or *norma*, wasn't met the bread ration would be decreased accordingly.

"We divided the workforce into brigades; each headed by a brigadier. There were about thirty brigades of twenty men each. Every morning and evening there was a call to muster, when all inmates had to present themselves for inspection.

During this time each of the two column leaders, Hoffman and I had to give a report to the director.

"Based on the information supplied by the brigadiers, we reported on how many men showed up for work, how many were sick, and how many were under arrest. There was a brig in the camp, a small wooden structure with barred windows that held those that refused to go to work. The guards at the brig were also inmates. I found it very amusing that these were Jewish boys from Poland, with absolutely no clue as to how to perform this kind of duty.

"Once we were settled in I discovered that the camp had a rather large aggregation of Bundists, like me. They came from Warsaw, Lida, Baranovitch, and other small towns. None came from Lodz, so I didn't know any of them, but I knew that we shared a philosophy and that cheered me up a bit. Maybe because they had a similar political outlook, the men in my brigades got along very well and selected our division cooks from among themselves. In a place where food was scarce and worth its weight in gold, being a cook was a major privilege. In this community it was much better than being elected as mayor, or a column leader like me.

"I was glad for the cooks' good fortune and their ability to get adequate food rations for themselves, but I knew that I would not take advantage of my rank as the leader. The principles of fairness I had learned at the Medem School were etched in my brain. I would do nothing to violate them, no matter what. Despite the luck that had befallen me in being selected as a division leader, I would strive to be equal with all the other men in camp. I felt a heavy responsibility, despite the role I had been assigned, to behave like a mensch.

"The first opportunity to live my principles happened the very first week. In the morning after the wake-up alarm sounded, the prisoners were given the black liquid that by now I knew was coffee. When it was available, we also received a treat—a small ration of dry bread. On this morning it was just coffee. After 'breakfast' the men had to go outside to be counted. I was responsible to see that they showed up in full force and on time. It didn't matter if it was hot or frigid, rain or snow. We had to be outside by five each morning on the camp's main square looking ready for work.

"It was my particular job to see to it that every single man in my brigade reported for the headcount. But there were men who were obviously sick. Most of us had been on the run for months and those who were older or whose health wasn't great to begin with were not in good shape, certainly not good enough to do exhausting physical labour outdoors. These guys wanted to hide under their bunks or in dark corners to avoid being sent out for the fourteen-hour shifts. Who was I to notice them? I turned a blind eye and didn't see them.

"My men and I went outside and stood at attention waiting for the inspection by the director, then I read off the report. He shouted, 'We are behind schedule. If you louts don't buckle down and do real work, I'll have you all thrown into the brig. Here are your work orders, take them and don't look so sour. You are helping a great nation.' All the jobs assigned to us were for hard labour for which none of the men were physically prepared: chopping down huge trees, moving logs and soil, digging trenches and removing boulders. I could see that the frail among my men would not be able to manage. The brigades were escorted to work at gunpoint.

"It wasn't until a few weeks later that I discovered that Hoffman's strategy for getting the men in his division out for the head count was very different from mine. When he noticed a man missing, he searched the bunks and under them, in every dark corner, in the latrines. He shouted their names, he threatened. Unlike Hoffman, I didn't explore every possible hiding place. At worst, I thought, if my 'oversight' were discovered, I would be relieved of my duties as leader and thrown in the brig. But Hoffman was a true bureaucrat. He did exactly as he had been told. He dragged out every last man, no matter how ill, and sent him to work. As a Jew, I was ashamed that he didn't have it in him to show kindness to his fellow inmates. He made me think of Resnick and even Boltz: I hated the way this war was turning people into creatures that were less than human."

I paused to reflect on his thought. How my father would have hated the way the 9/11 attack has changed some people into fearful beings. How sad! I took a sip of tea, but it was already cold. The office had gotten too chilly. I stood up and walked over to the thermostat to raise it and my father's words rang in my head. How like my father to be so understated. From my research and comments from my father's former fellow prisoners whom I met in Israel, I learned that if the camp commander had discovered that Dad had been sheltering inmates unwilling or unable to work he would surely have been *executed*.

In the time my father was imprisoned in the Opalicha camp, he was one of more than 2 million prisoners sent to Russia's remotest and most inaccessible regions. Such placement was not accidental. The Soviets wanted to colonize these areas, but first massive construction projects needed to be carried out. My father and the others were free labour.

I sat down again and turned on the CD, but it crackled. I cringed hoping I wasn't missing any words. Annoyed, I shut it off for the night and picked up a photo of my father that stood on my desk. He was sitting in a kayak, wearing a life jacket over his white cardigan and smiling like a kid with a new toy. It was taken in Disney World on his eightieth birthday. As he grew older, he grew more daring. "I would like to ride in this boat," he had said when we passed the lagoon.

"But Tinek, you can't swim. What if this thing turns over?" I asked. A non-swimmer myself, I was concerned and it was January. The water would be very cold.

"What's to worry?" he said with a huge smile. "You worry too much, Ania. I will wear a life saver."

"It's a life jacket, Dad."

"*Ot azoy, di kats kumt ibern vaser*" That's how the cat gets across the water, he quipped.

I put the photo down, packed my work papers into a large manila envelope and headed upstairs. On my way I still thought about the extreme inaccessibility of the Opalicha gulag. The remoteness had served another purpose: it minimized the likelihood of prisoners escaping. In their weakened physical condition, it wasn't likely any could survive an escape attempt, but each camp was also equipped with trained tracking dogs. My father did not say much about this. As was the case his entire life, he made a kind of peace with whatever situation he found himself in. It was as if he made an inner bargain with his soul: *I won't lament, I won't complain, and I will survive this period, this place, this situation. And if I survive, I will not complain, but I will never forget.*

One weekend in 1992, it must have been April because the quince in front of our Larchmont home was already in bloom, my father and I sat on the porch that David had just finished renovating. *"Dayn Dovid hot goldene hent."* Your David has golden hands. "Is there anything he cannot do?" My father admired David's handiwork, looking up at the new skylights installed a couple of weeks before.

"Isn't he something?" I chimed in. "Look at those snazzy track lights." I was tickled that the project had finally been completed. Our 1926 Cape Cod with its intricate tapestry brick now stood fresher and more confident, like a woman with a facelift. But the porch with its cedar panelling and floor-to-ceiling windows wrapping around three sides at the front of the house was the pièce de résistance.

"Look, Tinek, the venetian blinds are sandwiched between two panes of glass. Isn't that amazing?"

"Ahh, America. They will never have this in Russia," my father said and twisted the handle trying to operate this marvel of American ingenuity. I brought out a tray with all the fixings for tea and we settled in for one of our discussions.

I plumped the couch cushions and sat opposite my father who always liked the big corner chair that resembled a throne.

"Tinek, I want to know more about the Soviet gulag."

"More, more, more. You always want more," he said and smiled so I knew he was amenable to talk about it.

"Do you remember what kind of work you and your men had to do in Opalicha?"

"Sure," he said. "How could anyone forget this kind of experience?"

"So, go on. Tell me about it."

"One of the assignments was for our carpenters to build a bridge."

"Why a bridge? It couldn't have been across the Volga, was it?"

"No," he laughed. "It was something quite different and amazing, in a way. To this day I can't believe that I participated in this project. I didn't know it at the time, but I learned later that the entire area was to be flooded in order to create the world's largest man-made inland sea—the Rybinskoye Morye—the Rybinsk Sea, 100 feet deep and covering 1,770 square miles."

"A sea? How can people create a sea?"

"Well, it's not easy and actually very destructive. The areas to be flooded were not all virgin forests. There were villages there where people had lived for centuries. The Russians forced the peasants who occupied these houses to abandon them. Entire populations, more than 150,000 people, had to be resettled. Just imagine, over six hundred ancient villages had to be totally destroyed in preparation for the flooding.

"We dismantled hundreds of wooden houses that stood in a huge area near the town of Rybinsk. Our job was to break the structures down into the smallest sections and load them onto wagons and trucks. We were clearing the area that would become the approach to the bridge. It was heartbreaking to see these beautiful old buildings destroyed. If not disturbed, they could have stood there for hundreds of years more, but the Soviets were desperate for building materials to be used elsewhere and wanted to salvage all the wood they possibly could."

The noise of David's lawnmower interrupted our conversation. I picked up the teapot absentmindedly, trying to envision the destruction of homes ordered by the Russians. I poured both of us strong cups of tea, and thought about the huge devastation of homes in Texas just a few months before caused by the El Niño floods.

"So your brigades did all this work? It seems like a monumental effort."

"Oh, no. As we continued with this backbreaking work, we learned that there were a huge number of slave labour camps in the area—sometimes we spotted brigades from other gulags doing similar work. The work was so physically demanding and endless that it seemed the project would never be completed, but when we were finally released from the camp, we travelled by ship over this very area that was by then flooded to create the inland sea. But, the miracle was not in our building this engineering marvel; it was our survival.

"The situation became more difficult as the time went on. When a five-month winter came with temperatures that plummeted to as low as minus forty degrees Fahrenheit, many died of hypothermia, pneumonia, and various respiratory infections. Frostbite was as commonplace as the cold. Adding to the misery was the rampant corruption in the ranks of the camp's director, his wife, and their cronies.

"The director's wife had been appointed as the camp's doctor. As a political appointee, she gave herself licence to 'buy' things from the inmates, whatever possessions they had—jackets, shoes, watches—that still had some value. She then sold these to villagers in the area and lined her pockets. Bread was the currency of the camp. The inmates were willing to sell their belongings for a loaf of bread. They were even willing to settle for half a loaf. The sons of well-to-do families had more to sell, but they seemed to need the extra bread more than others. Unaccustomed to hard physical labour and to starvation, they weakened first and were desperate for every extra piece of bread they could get. They could not endure the heavy digging, lifting, or construction work. They fell like flies. In just a couple of months, sixteen of the young men in my group died out of sheer exhaustion. Never mind the ones who died from disease."

"Dad, I've researched this. You are a master of under-statement. In the 1941 to 1943 period well over half a million gulag inmates died from starvation and disease."

"I can only speak to what I saw."

"You saw plenty."

We sipped the tea and picked at the raisins and dates I had laid out.

Dad continued, "The normal bread allotment for the day was two hundred grams of dry, black bread, or about seven ounces. But it was given out only in exchange for the completion of the *norma*. The fulfillment of a *norma* had to be verified by a kind of an overseer, a *diesiatnik*. For example, if the assignment was to dig a hole six feet by three feet, that might be the *norma* for a given period of time. If the *diesiatnik* measured it and found that an inmate completed only half a *norma*, he would allow only half of the bread allotment. A man performing physical labour could not survive on this meagre ration. The director of the camp and his wife continued 'buying' the meagre leftover possessions from inmates who still had them, to obtain foodstuffs for themselves, while we were fed watery soup garnished with small herring, a *silotka*, so salty you couldn't swallow it. If we were lucky, the entire cauldron of soup may have had one rotten potato or carrot. It didn't do much to mollify our constant hunger. After a while, the sight of corpses being carried out of the barracks on stretchers became a daily occurrence.

"As bad as our lives were, we tried to keep our spirits up by singing, telling stories of our former lives and thinking about all those we had left behind. Most of the men were really nice people. I was glad to have met them and thought that had we met under normal circumstances we could become good friends. Among us there was one Jewish guy, named Weinstock, whom I would have likely never associated with and not only because he came from Warsaw but because of his trade. By his own admission he had been a professional thief. He was tall, healthy-looking, and handsome with perfectly arched brows. He sang beautifully, too. To hear him sing, one could never have imagined him to be a petty criminal.

"When the soldiers threw him on a stretcher to take him to the brig and shouted, 'Why aren't you going to work?' he always replied. 'Let Stalin do this work, not me.' You could tell by his crooked little smile that he thought the soldiers agreed with him."

My father shifted toward one of the new windows and fiddled with its handle opening it a crack. A gust of air smelling of freshly mown grass filled the porch. I inhaled a lungful. "It's getting a little warm here, Ania," he said.

"Okay, leave it open, Dad, but go on and finish the story. Don't leave me hanging."

"Well, Weinstock was quite an operator, but a good-natured one. One time when he was under arrest in the tiny brig he begged me, 'Libeskind, please let me sleep in the barrack tonight. Please, there is hardly any space in the cell for me to stretch out and it's even colder here than in the barracks.'

"And I said, 'How could I? If this is discovered by the soldiers on their rounds, I'll be sent to solitary, or worse.'

"'Libeskind, you know I'm a man of my word. I swear, let me out and not a hair on your head will be harmed.'

"Reluctantly I opened the brig door and allowed him to sneak out to sleep in the bunk, and then I went to my barrack to catch some sleep too. A while later I was awakened to the sound of Russian voices. I knew it was the NKVD checking on the individuals confined to the brig. *That's it,* I thought. *Now I'll be arrested.* I hopped out of my bunk and walked over to the brig. To my surprise Weinstock was fast asleep in it. I have no idea how he knew, or when he slipped out of the barrack and returned to the brig. He sure had a knack of knowing better than others how to tweak the system."

"As you did."

"Well, maybe so. But I refused to take advantage of my appointed position in Opalicha. Men there were so hungry they used to sneak into the kitchens at night searching for scraps of food in the garbage. I suppose I could have asked the cooks for some extra food for myself. I would have surely received it because they knew of my role, but I never, ever could ask for what others could not."

David opened the new French entry door and came in with grass stuck to his jeans and boots.

"How are you guys? Can I have some tea?" he asked.

"Of course you can, but don't track that grass all over the house," I said.

"David, after the tea let's take a walk to Manor Park," my father said.

"Sure Nachman, it's a gorgeous day, let's not waste it." David flashed him a smile.

The private park, about a mile from our house, was a jewel of Westchester County. Sitting on the edge of Long Island Sound, the park had scenic water vistas and landscaped, winding paths, and gazebos. It had been my mother's most favourite spot in the world and we never tired of walking to it.

David went inside to clean up and my father resumed the story.

"The sweltering summer months gave way to the winds of fall and plummeting temperatures. It was freezing cold. The barracks were drafty, with big spaces between the poorly assembled boards that rendered the burlap blankets useless. There was no heat because the cabal of the director, his wife, and their Russian cronies used any available funds for themselves. Our clothing was so inadequate that we shivered constantly, slapped our hands and wrapped our arms around our thin bodies to feel warmer, but to no avail. Among all the many awful conditions, lice made a feast of our bodies. We were being eaten alive by lice. The barracks were filthy, the roofs leaked, and water dripped in with even the mildest rain.

"Time dragged on and everyone was dispirited. We dreaded the approach of the snows. There seemed to be no end to our captivity. No one had told us what our crime had been, or what the period of incarceration would be so it was impossible to envision an end to the nightmare. We had no news whatsoever about the world outside the camp's perimeter. We were a desert island. As the deaths mounted and conditions worsened daily, the atmosphere of the camp became grim.

"The men began to rebel. Partly as a result of urging by the Bundists in the group, partly due to my support, we started to plan a strike. We weren't optimistic about its result, but the situation had reached a point where we were literally unable to work because almost everyone was so weakened from starvation and many were seriously ill. The camp's doctor had neither the skill nor the medicines to help. She was preoccupied with her and her husband's survival.

"Night after night we would whisper our plans in Yiddish until we resolved what to do. We had one inmate, Levin, an educated young man who spoke Russian well. We decided that he would be the best spokesman to the Soviet authorities on our behalf. In addition to Levin, Weinstock became one of the key individuals in the strike because of his immense chutzpah. We needed all the help we could muster. First, we wrote a long letter describing our conditions addressed to the chief of the NKVD (the secret police, officially known as the People's Commissariat for Internal Affairs) in Moscow. In it we described the corruption of the director, our mistreatment and listed the deaths that had resulted from it. Levin translated what we dictated and wrote in his scratchy hand, but it was good enough. We then entrusted the letter to one of the Russian soldiers who seemed to have a sympathetic attitude toward us, and asked him to mail it for us. Anxious weeks passed. We had no idea if the letter was ever mailed, and if it did arrive at its destination whether it would infuriate the authorities. In the meantime we initiated a work stoppage.

"When the inmates were called out in the morning for muster and given their work assignments, everyone refused to budge. No one went to work that day. The soldiers guarding us must have been shocked. They began shooting rounds into the air. That seemed to change the minds of the carpenter brigades. For the first two days of our strike, they were the only ones who went to work. They were big men. They needed their full rations of food. The rest of us got nothing to eat. After the first two days, the carpenters joined us and also refused to work.

"In the meantime, those who worked in the management office were sending reports to the headquarters that all was well; that all the *normas* were being achieved. Of course, these were all lies. We continued with the strike and spent the days lying on the bunks dreaming of bread, too weak to do anything. But neither the director nor the soldiers could do much either. The brig wasn't big enough to hold more than several men. It didn't take more than a few weeks and to our amazement, one day we heard the roar of several vehicles. Those who had the strength walked outside to see who had arrived. Word quickly spread through the camp that a commission had arrived from Moscow to investigate our claims.

"Eight NKVD members dressed in leather coats had arrived at the camp. One of them was a woman. They called a general meeting of all the inmates. They also ordered that the director, his wife, and other assistants appear at this meeting. There was an expectant hush in the barrack as the NKVD officials seated themselves at the table. The director, his wife, and the assistants filed in with their heads down, avoiding our glare. Levin, our chosen spokesman, described all that was going on. He asked us to lift up our shirts to show our skin bitten by the lice and ribs sticking out. He pointed at the leaky ceiling. Then he provided the numbers of the dead, the sick, and those incarcerated in isolation. The face of the head of the commission turned red. He banged his fist on the table and shouted at the camp director, 'What have you done to these people? Speak up! What?' When no answer was forthcoming, he bellowed his question again. I was incredulous that a Soviet official was taking our side. He issued an order that we no longer had to go to work and that we were all to be given full food rations immediately.

"A week later a second commission arrived. This time it was a medical commission that checked the health status of each inmate. They divided us into three groups. One group consisted of men who were so weakened they could barely move. We were told they would be transferred to another camp where they didn't have to work until they regained strength. The second group was composed of men who were in a weakened physical state, but deemed to be able to do some work. They were to do only 50 per cent of the *norma*, but were to be given 100 per cent of the food ration. The last group consisted of men who did not have such physically demanding assignments—the tailors, the cobblers, those who worked in the office and the *nachalniks*, like myself. We were sent along with a group of Russian prisoners to a new camp called Lapushka.

"On the day we were to be transferred out of Opalicha there was a mood of unrest at the coming changes. People were saying their parting words to one another, hugging, kissing, exchanging words of advice, and sharing promises of reunion after the war. All the men came to say goodbye to me, we hugged and we cried. But as for Hoffman, people yelled at him, called him names, some spit on him. They were so angry at the way he had been complicit.

"Those of us in the third group were transferred by ship toward our new destination. I was amazed that the body of water we had crossed was the very one which we'd built. It was the Rybinsk Sea that swallowed all those ancient villages we helped dismantle. Later they loaded us onto trains taking us to another camp whose mission seemed to be more detention than labour. We arrived late and I fell into exhausted sleep, folding my pants up and using them as a pillow. When I awoke in the morning, my pants were gone. Someone had stolen them right out from beneath my head. I knew right then that this new place was not going to be a big improvement.

"But I was luckier than most because I had a friend. In short order Weinstock became the 'big man' in Lapushka. He knew how to throw his weight around. Though conditions in Lapushka were a bit better than in our previous incarceration, we were still hungry most of the time. On some nights Weinstock used to wake me at night and say, 'Here, Libeskind, I brought you a piece of sausage.' Sometimes he brought me a roll. One time he even brought me a pair of slippers so I wouldn't have to walk around with shoes that were falling apart. Whenever I told him he would get into trouble for pilfering food and smuggling it to me, he would say, 'Nachman, this is nothing. You risked much more for me.'

"In June of 1941 the Russians had entered the war against Germany. The camp administration did not want the Polish Jews mixing with the other prisoners because they didn't want us trading information and spreading rumours about the German advance. We were separated in the camp by a barbed-wire fence. I believe that by then the administrators knew that we would be released in the not too distant future, so they started treating us a bit better. We no longer had to work and whiled away the dreary days singing and speculating on the progress of the war and our prospects for release.

"A short time later, General Sikorski, the Polish prime minister in exile, signed an agreement with the Soviet Union that eventually led to my freedom. There was to be amnesty for the over 1 million Polish prisoners. Sikorski's intent was for the released Poles to join the army of General Anders who formed and commanded the Second Polish Corps to fight along the Western Allies. But the Soviets didn't keep their end of the bargain and released only 100,000 inmates. I was among them. Those who had been soldiers attempted to make it to the front, but the NKVD stymied their progress and very few made it. Most died en route.

"Upon our release, in the fall of 1941, my new buddies, Jack and Mendel, and I had to plan our next move quickly. War raged to the west and north of us, and the frozen wasteland of Siberia loomed on the east. There were not many choices. We had no money and no possessions except the rags on our back. We decided to hitch rides on freight trains and wagons and walk as far south as we could get. We would have given anything to warm up so anyplace south seemed like the Promised Land."

Chapter Four

Like Depression-era hobos, Nachman, Jack, and Mendel had no recourse but to steal onto boxcars, hoping they were empty for fear of being crushed by shifting cargo. It was more congenial to travel with his new friends from Lapushka. Nachman liked these two: Jack, skinny and tall like a lamp pole; and squat Mendel with his shock of black hair. They climbed atop trains, balanced on platforms between train cars, and hitched rides on the rickety carts of kind peasants. For many days the only means of locomotion available was their blistered feet. They were headed to the southernmost reaches of the Soviet Union with unwavering determination, days on end, then weeks. Often they would have to disembark when it became obvious that a train was not going to continue south, or that it was being cleared of cargo and passengers to make room for soldiers heading toward the front. They would look for odd jobs, find places to sleep in crowded shelters, abandoned barns, or sometimes farmsteads where work was available. And they waited—sometimes for days—until another train materialized. The few rubles they had been given when the Lapushka labour camp was disbanded lasted only long enough to keep them alive for a couple of weeks. The hunger they endured in the camps still haunted them, but they were free. That alone gave them the strength to continue trying to find some safety and respite from two years on the move.

Nachman thought of the family and friends he left behind. Their faces floated before him constantly and he wondered what had become of them. He struggled to push away visions of the dead men he saw on the killing field near Lodz and those who died in Opalicha. He didn't want the images of his loved ones to merge with the inert expressions of the dead.

How could he have known that already by May 1940 the hermetically sealed Lodz ghetto teemed with 160,000 inhabitants? In the fall of 1941, thousands more Jews deported from Austria, Germany, Luxembourg, and Czechoslovakia would swell the population so dramatically that seven persons living per room was the new normal.

Dark forests gave way to open, foreign-looking fields whose crops they could only imagine. The rushing train blended smudges of yellows, greens, reds, and ochres into a kaleido-scopic mosaic punctuated by quaint farmhouses, birches, and flocks of sheep. The train ride was a lesson in geography, history and architecture. *How much better it would have been, if it were a trip of choice*, Nachman thought. As they moved farther south, Kazakhstan's endless fields gave way to a desert-like landscape none of them had seen before. Desolate and wind-swept earth as far as the eye could see gave wing to visions of ancient caravans laden with precious cargo.

In Uzbekistan, Central Asian architecture greeted them. In Bukhara, they had time to admire the brilliant blues of the mosaics and tile works of the Ismail Samani Mausoleum. They learned from a passerby that it was the resting place of a Persian emir who had ruled the city in the ninth century. Each time they approached a stranger they picked up another tidbit about what they were seeing. It was thrilling for the men to learn history they'd never studied in school. The numerous mosques and madrasas of the city would forever remain sharp in Nachman's mind. None of them had ever seen minarets and there was a forest of them, some rising to 150 feet in the air; it was the first they had seen of Muslims. They soon learned that a significant number of Jews had lived here for centuries as well, but so different they were from their brethren in Eastern Europe. Cut off from the rest of the Jewish world for 2,500 years, they had preserved their Jewish heritage as well as developed their own distinct culture with unique dress, music, language, and dishes. The colours and smells of Bokhara were such a dramatic change from the greyness of Opalicha and Lapushka. They inspired hope that a new beginning lay just ahead. If these Jews could make it in this strange land, surely Nachman and his friends could too.

As they approached Tashkent, the capital of Uzbekistan, all that Nachman could think of was a book he had read in school: *Tashkent: The City of Bread*, by Aleksandr Neverov. Perhaps it was the hunger twisting his guts, or the memory of the book's young protagonist Mishka Dodonov's exhausting search for bread that provided hope. Maybe in his mind, Nachman thought of himself as Mishka, who triumphed in the end. To a modern traveller, Tashkent, populated by the Uzbek people, is a rich centre of Islamic culture whose bazaars overflow with local delicacies and flat breads called *lepyoshkas*, but during the war, party bigwigs would have appropriated most of it for their families.

Samarkand, the gem of the East, greeted Nachman in all of its glory, making him momentarily oblivious of his wretched condition. Dating to the same period as Rome and Athens, Samarkand dazzled with its majestic architecture: buildings with beamed roofs supported by exquisitely carved gilded columns, ornamental wood carvings and magnificent paintings in blindingly brilliant colours. The turrets atop Prince Romanov's palace looked like something out of a fairy tale. Described by Marco Polo as large and splendid, Samarkand awed Nachman who had never been out of Poland before the war.

There was so much that vied for his attention but none more than the blue, cantaloupe shaped dome of the Gur-Emir mausoleum and the jade marble tomb of the ancient Asian conqueror, Tamerlane. But the ancient monuments of the fabled city were not the only buildings Nachman noticed. The advancing Nazi front caused the Russians to move factories here from the Western regions to protect vital industries. Their smokestacks sat in uneasy alliance with the city's numerous minarets and glistening cupolas.

Nachman was captivated by the beauty, as the smoke from the lamb shashlik on the spit in the market stung his eyes and its aroma made him woozy. The odd musical instruments, bamboo flutes and strange drums, emitted ancient oriental folk music all new to his ears and it tugged at his heart. Paradise, replete with bread, seemed to be within grasp, just around the next bend in the road. He held tight to this belief. It was his talisman; no one could take it from him.

Whenever we talked about this otherworldly journey in his later years, I would ask my father to describe in greater detail what he saw so I could experience these exotic places vicariously. He would only say, "Something so beautiful is beyond description. Words would not do it justice. Anyway, I was so hungry all the time on this journey that my empty stomach consumed most of my attention." After the colourless monotony of Lodz, and after prison, the sights of these ancient, bejeweled cities contributed to my father's sense that something positive would result from his decision to flee Lodz.

Nachman and his friends settled in Samarkand in a city-sponsored shelter during the winter of 1942. They still had a few rubles, which kept them from completely starving to death, but they were hungry all the time. Thinking of food overrode every other concern. It was on their minds day and night.

Luscious platters of steaming food appeared regularly in their dreams and they exchanged them as if they were sharing restaurant reviews. They knew that if they didn't find some work soon, they would end up dead, like many of their friends in Opalicha. Women were on their minds too. They had been celibate for years. One day in March, Mendel walked into the room they shared with an air of excitement and an uncharacteristic grin.

"Aren't you looking happy," Nachman said.

"Did you get the shoes you were dreaming about?" asked Jack, thinking that Mendel had stopped at the refugee assistance centre. But he looked at Mendel's feet and could see that he was still wearing the same old holey shoes.

"What's come over you? Are you going to tell us?" Nachman inquired again.

"You won't believe what I discovered." Mendel kept his companions in suspense as he paced the room.

"*Nu, nu zog epys!*" So, so, say something already! they urged him in unison.

"Girls!" Mendel exclaimed.

"What about girls? Stop being so cryptic."

"There is a group of young women in the village who recently arrived from a Siberian gulag," Mendel said, running his hand against the stubble on his face, as if he were thinking of shaving.

"I bet they can't wait to warm up," said Jack, whose grin seemed wider than his face.

Nachman, Jack, and Mendel took turns showering under the rusty spigot in the shared bath down the hall. "Hurry up," Mendel shouted knocking on the door, "There will be no water by the time it's my turn." Nachman wiped the fog off the small mirror over the sink and carefully combed his thinning hair. He wrapped a towel around his hips and returned to the room. He rummaged for his cleanest shirt, tucked it in neatly, and smoothed his pants. Then he fished out an old rag from the box under his cot and polished his worn brown boots. He was known for his spit-buffed shoes among his pre-war friends. For now this was the best he could do.

The three arrived at the dusty alley on which the women shared a small ground-floor apartment. Open sewers on either side of the road emitted a sour smell, and some raggedy children tossed a ball along its length, dropping it into the effluent and arguing noisily about the method for its retrieval. The squat brick building had a severe, industrial look. With the huge numbers of refugees flooding Samarkand, living quarters were cramped and barely adequate everywhere. Nachman stepped forward and knocked on the door. His companions stood expectantly behind him.

"Come in, the door is open," a woman's voice called out. They entered the modest room. A sense of sudden shyness stopped Nachman near the entrance and he stood for a moment surveying the scene.

"We don't bite, you can come in," a woman with dark brown hair and large hazel eyes said. "My name is Dora," she said, and then pointed to her roommates, Rachela and Itka, who sat coyly on metal cots under the windows. Though the place was small, it had the feel of home with its gauzy white curtains fluttering at the slightly cracked windows and an oriental-looking cloth on the centre table. The teapot and thin slices of bread on a tray indicated the women were ready for guests. After awkward introductions and handshakes, Itka popped off the cot and invited everyone to join her at the table. She filled an assortment of chipped china cups with tea and pointed to the bread, "Please, serve yourselves, I just toasted them on the stove burners." The men's eyes were glued to the tray. Bread! The browned edges of the toast made Nachman's mouth water and the smell of burned bread tickled his nostrils.

"We pooled our ration coupons," Dora answered the question that hung in the air.

It had been a long time since the men could snack on bread as if it were cake. *This is good*, thought Nachman. *These women know how to live.*

After a while they felt more at ease. Laughter and smiles came more easily. Stories new and old tumbled out of them. The men were wound up like a trio of barrel organs. Nachman discovered that Dora had fled south with Itka and Rachela after their release from the Stantsiya Yaya gulag near Novosibirsk, Siberia. Rachela, a friend whom Dora had known from her native Warsaw, had become as close as a sister. The two supported one another in gulag conditions even harsher than those Nachman had endured in Opalicha. Dora told them how Rachela scrounged for discarded paper and collected it for Dora to wrap around her feet, tie with string and keep her toes from frostbite. Dora's shoes had been stolen and the guards chased the women through deep Siberian snows to their worksites.

"You embarrass me with those stories, Dora," Rachela said quietly and her cheeks reddened. "You did plenty to help me." Nachman noticed deep shadows beneath Rachela's dark eyes. She was taller than her two friends and frailer. Whenever she coughed he could see she was doing her best to be discreet, but even the handkerchief pressed to her lips could not stifle the noise.

Through the evening Rachela got up every once in a while and added a few lumps of coal to the cast iron stove to heat more water for tea. *This one is not much of a talker*, Nachman concluded, *but a doer*. He did enjoy watching the steam rise from the cups she refilled. It added a touch of familial comfort he hadn't felt since he left Rosa in their Lodz apartment. The wall clock above the corner bureau showed it was late, but none of them wanted the evening to end. When they discovered that they knew many of the same Yiddish songs Nachman said, "We have enough for an a cappella group." They sang till a full silver moon rose in the sky and the wind picked up blowing the windows wide open.

"We'll freeze tonight," Dora said, and stood up to close them. Rachela glanced at the nearly empty coal bin and sighed. "I am afraid I was a little too enthusiastic with the coal. Sorry."

That was a sign that it was time to go. It was not Nachman's way to be pushy or to listen in on people's arguments. Besides, all the bread slices were gone, including the crumbs that Jack had scooped up and tried to sneak in his mouth inconspicuously.

In a short time the men became quite taken with the women and their stories of survival in Siberia. Mendel was attracted to Itka. Jack pursued Rachela, who seemed less than enthusiastic about his silly antics and ill-timed jokes. And Nachman became a regular visitor in the women's shared quarters, seeking out Dora's company each evening. The men wooed the women with all the zeal of penniless, rag-clad refugees, bringing saved up *lepyoshkas*, as if they were bouquets of roses. Their favourite activity was sitting over endless cups of tea and sharing stories of home.

After only a couple of weeks Nachman had become a regular and walked down the alleyway to Dora's apartment with a bounce in his step and a whistle on his lips. One Friday night when Nachman came calling Dora opened the door after his first knock. She wore a navy, form-fitting dress with a fancy white embroidered collar. It was worn, but neatly pressed. Her hair was coiffed in an upswept style that highlighted her high cheekbones. Dora looked regal and worldly. There was an air of mystery about her. It struck him how different she was from Jadwiga whose round, pale face and pouty lips made her look younger than her years and whose arched eyebrows gave her a look of perpetual surprise.

The mud floor was neatly swept, two lit candles stood on the table and the teapot was on. Dora's friends usually made themselves scarce during Nachman's visits. They puttered around the stove, or sat with their noses buried in mending. This Friday they were out.

Dora sat on the cot, kicked off her shoes, and tucked her slender legs under.

"The tea isn't brewed yet," she said. "Come sit here." She patted the space next to her.

"Tell me about your family," Nachman said. "Are they Orthodox? Because nothing about you, except these candles, suggests that."

"Oh, the candles, it's just tradition," Dora said and waved her hand as if to dismiss the question.

"So what about your parents?" Nachman pressed on.

"Well, they were appalled when I left home at eighteen and opened up my own shop in Warsaw. Right on the main street."

Nachman's eyes widened. He had never heard of someone so young going into business, on a glamorous street in the capital, no less. *She's a rebel, this one!*

"What about you?" she asked, looking out the window at three boys tossing sticks at one another.

"I come from a family of Bundists. At least my brothers and I belong."

"Oh, so, you are a joiner. I'm more of a lone wolf," she said laughing and her eyes narrowed producing crinkles around them. To Nachman she looked more exotic than any of the women he had known back home.

"I am passionate about the Bund's ideals," Nachman said, peeved at such a quick assessment.

"Political ideals. I like that," she said and shifted to face him.

"And their fight to legitimize Yiddish as the language of our people," he added, so she would see that he did not have a one-track mind.

"Do you know any other Yiddish songs?" Dora asked after a pause. "I really enjoyed the ones we sang that first night." A twinkle danced in her hazel eyes.

"Ah, songs, music, that's my real love," he said. Instantly, he felt her gaze upon him and her posture seemed to thaw.

"Sure, go ahead! Yiddish songs are the pure soul of our people," she said in a way that surprised Nachman. She spoke assertively, yet her thin figure betrayed a certain undefined vulnerability.

"Do you know 'Oyfn Pripetchik'?" he asked. "On the Cooking Stove," with its warm evocation of a rabbi teaching young children the Hebrew A, B, Cs ends with references to the tragedies of Jews. Suddenly, Nachman was not sure it was a good choice.

"Who doesn't?" Dora's face blossomed into a smile.

Nachman's resonant voice filled the room. Dora's eyes filled with tears. To Nachman they looked like jewels.

"I wonder where he is now?" she whispered softly, as if her question were not meant to be heard, or answered.

"Who are you thinking about, Dora?"

"My brother, Nechemiah. He was the best student at the *cheder*. Where is he now? Where are they all, my mother and my little sisters?"

"We are all thinking of those we left behind, Dora, the ones we could not persuade to join us. Who knows? Maybe they had better luck than we," he said.

They fell silent. Nachman imagined his family seated at the dinner table bantering, the children giggling. No, that couldn't be right. His mind swung to a scene of their arrest, perhaps as unexpected as his: rifle butts banging at the door, German shepherds straining on leashes, Balcia's screams, little Esther's frightened face. He shook his head in an attempt to chase the image from his mind and tried to come up with the merriest song in his encyclopedic repertoire to lighten the mood, but they were so under the spell of memories, neither of them could bear it any longer.

Dora stood up unexpectedly from the cot, smoothed its thin calico cover and plumped the indentation in the mattress where she'd been sitting. She walked over to the dresser and pulled a shawl from the drawer.

"Let's go for a walk," she suggested.

Just then Nachman answered a knock at the door and Rachela walked in bringing with her a whiff of spring.

"What are you two up to?" she asked.

"We are going for a walk. Why don't you join us, Rachela?" Nachman asked, but she barely shrugged. She walked over to her cot and sat there silent, staring at the distant snow-capped mountains and fields of red poppies growing in their shadow. She was in another of her dark moods. Nachman noticed that with him in the picture, the women clearly struggled to come to terms with the new dynamic.

After a long while she said, "You two go. I prefer to be alone."

They hesitated. "Come, it's stuffy here. The fresh air will make you feel better," Dora said. "It's me, Rachela, you don't have to feel strange."

"No, I will be fine. I have already been out. Now I need to collect my thoughts. You won't change my mind," she added not even turning her face toward them.

Four months later Nachman and Dora found their own tiny room in a nearby building on the same street. There was a kitchen shared by several families down a long corridor and past it, a washroom with an ancient stone sink. The outhouse stood behind the building. Just a mattress on the floor and some boards for shelving was all it took to make a home. That and a couple of mismatched chairs they found discarded by the side of the road. A wonder they weren't used for firewood! By now it was nearly summer and the room was stifling, but they barely noticed the discomfort. Now that they had one another every hardship seemed more tolerable. The only thing Dora would never get used to was the outhouse.

Each evening they took long walks along the canals, catching the other up on their lives until the moment they met. The breezes that swept through the valley were like a balm to nerves frayed by not knowing anything about events to the West. Though they never spoke of it directly, each knew that the other was constantly thinking of the families in Poland. The non-stop conversation distracted them from their rumbling stomachs and painful ruminations. Nachman never ceased to be amazed by the breadth of Dora's knowledge in many areas, especially philosophy and literature, as if she had graduated from a university. She hadn't, but she read widely and attended every free lecture she could find in Warsaw, many sponsored by Jewish cultural organizations.

One night they were discussing books and Dora said, "Knut Hamsun's *Hunger* is one of my favourites. Do you know it?"

"Yes, you mean the Norwegian author? I read it in school and never knew that we would be destined to experience the main character's struggle to find nourishment."

"I was most fascinated by his desire to write. That's what made him a hero to me," Dora said. "And I was glad that he left the city at the end. Do you remember that, Nachman?"

"Not really, I'd have to reread it one day, but who can find books here? We barely find bread. What about music, Dora? I know you love Yiddish songs, but what else?"

"That's easy. Grieg is my favourite composer. I can listen to 'Solveig's Song' forever. It's the one from *Peer Gynt*."

"Ah, the Norwegians have captured you," Nachman laughed. "They are too brooding for me."

Things started to look up when Dora found a job as a teacher in a Polish school, established pursuant to a treaty between the Polish government in exile and the Soviets. She worked in a one-room wooden schoolhouse with raggedy refugee children whose noses ran perpetually and whose croupy coughs caused her worry. Each day she marvelled at their energy and inquisitiveness, but could not imagine herself being a mother. She found their innocent noises, so oblivious to the hardships of adults, both delicious and a bit annoying. But these schools were a short-lived experiment. They closed for lack of funds and Dora resumed her perpetual search for work. It surprised her a little that she missed the chirping of the children.

With so many Russian men at the front, the refugees' hands were needed to work the cotton fields during the fall harvest. Dora, Nachman, Rachela, and their whole group were ordered by the Soviet government to move a few miles south of Uzbekistan to Uch-Korgon, a village in the Batken province of Kyrgyzstan. This former Soviet Republic was all but unknown to Westerners until 2001 when the United States placed an air base in Manas from which to carry out missions into Afghanistan. Nestled between Tajikistan to the southwest, Uzbekistan to the west, Kazakhstan to the north, and China to the east, present-day Kyrgyzstan is a Turkic independent state in a landlocked mountainous region.

Here, as in the gulags, they were expected to make the *norma*, the daily quota if they wanted to eat. The slave labour in the gulags had hardened their hands and calloused their fingers, but they were still city people unused to stooping for hours over rows of plants with heavy cotton sacks slung over their shoulders. There was no mechanical equipment—all work had to be done by hand. The prickly, razor-sharp thorns of the bolls made pulling the cotton fluffs painful. Without gloves, their fingers bled, their arms were scratched raw. Who could have imagined that soft cotton garments had their origins in these wicked armoured pods?

After the harvest, they were assigned to work on building canals and had to wake up at three in the morning in order to be transported to the work site to toil endless hours, moving rocks, and digging with spades their weary arms could hardly lift at the end of the shift. Men, women, and even children had to do this work. The wages were one *lepyoshka*, or small pita, per day. They had to guard it very carefully; pitas were regularly stolen. Dora and Nachman tried to save their pita allotment to eat in small increments throughout the day, to make it last as long as possible, but this was very risky. Cycles of marginal part-time jobs alternated with total joblessness making each evening a guessing game for what would be required of them the next day.

Rachela wasn't well. Her cough became worse each day, and the lack of food didn't help her frail state. They were always hungry and so malnourished that an extra slice of black bread felt like a feast. A whole piece of potato in a soup made them swoon. They craved the taste of protein—any kind—but it was beyond their ability to purchase and even if they could, wartime rationing was so strict that even the local Uzbeks couldn't obtain it. And the few kopecks they earned always ran out. The menial jobs were scarce and there were long stretches of nothingness—no work, no food, no joy, no prospect of improvement. They were forced to eat dry *makukh*, poppy-seed pods *after* the oil had been pressed out of them. The pods were hard and bitter. The new lovers broke their teeth. Hunger was the overriding concern. Sometimes they spent days just lying on their cots trying to remain motionless as not to use up unnecessary energy and hoping to diminish the hunger pangs. There were thousands of refugees in the area, but each morning when they went outside they realized that people they had met just days before were no longer living.

When there was nothing at all to eat, they walked along the dusty roads and picked wild weeds to boil. They drank the *kipyatok*—hot water infused with the unpleasant taste of the bitter plants—and tried to convince themselves that it was an exotic tea. They urged Rachela to drink it in small sips. There was no prospect of medical help for her, but her friends did all they could. A few times they even managed to prevail on their Uzbek neighbours to provide a small amount of koumiss, fermented mare's milk. It was a local elixir said to have curative properties.

Even though she should have been accustomed to death—it was a daily occurrence in the camps—Dora was devastated when Rachela died a few months later. There was no money for a proper burial. Nachman, Dora, Mendel, Itka, and Jack carried her limp body on a wooden cart out toward the desert. The men dug her grave while Dora and Itka stood with tears rolling down their sunken cheeks, making no sound. They buried Rachela in a lonely, windswept plateau, marked only by a large stone they found nearby. For a while they all stood around the small mound in silence, the wind whistling a mournful song. When the *oohu-oohu* call of a distant eagle owl punctured the silence Mendel said, "It will be dark very soon. Let's go."

Shortly after the burial Dora fell ill. She coughed and vomited non-stop. By nightfall Nachman's hand burned when he touched it to her forehead. She lay silent on the bed moaning quietly. The cold water compresses he applied dried in moments. Nachman resolved that she would not meet Rachela's fate, not if he could help it. He woke Jack and Mendel in the adjoining room. "You have got to help me get Dora to a hospital."

"A hospital? You must be hallucinating. There is no hospital here," said Mendel rubbing the sleep off his eyes.

"After Rachela died the charcoal man said there is some sort of a clinic in the area. I don't know exactly where it is but we must look for it," Nachman said urgently.

"But there is no way for us to get there," Mendel said. "How do you think we can get her out of here even if there is a clinic?"

"Jack, please go to the Uzbek's and borrow that cart," Nachman took charge.

"The one we used for Rachela? You can't be serious."

"Yes. Go now, please Jack."

The men trudged for hours pushing the cart over rutted, unpaved roads. They lifted the cart up as gently as they could whenever they came to a deep rut. Dora's thin frame lay listless on the cart. The cart was a grim reminder of a day just several weeks before, and of Rachela's face. Nachman felt a pang each time Dora's small body bounced as they hit stones. Privately, each of the men swore to him that they would get her to the clinic even if they had to walk night and day. Finally, in the dark of night, they spotted it, a small building with a few lights glowing in the distance.

By next morning Nachman found out from the stout Kyrgyz nurse what was the trouble with Dora. "*Ana imeet sypnoĭ tif.*" She has typhus, the woman announced. "*Ana ochen' plokho.*" She is in a very bad shape.

"Please, may I come in to see her?" Nachman asked.

"*Nyet!*" exclaimed the nurse as if she were shocked that anyone would be stupid enough to enter a room of a patient harbouring a deadly infectious disease. That is when he found out Dora would be kept in isolation. "*Poydite damoy,*" the nurse added in a softened tone. "Go home, it'll be a long time before she is better, if ever ... " Her voice trailed off.

That was the exact moment Nachman realized he loved Dora. By day he slept under a tree below the window of the room in which they held her. It was one storey up and he serenaded her with the Yiddish folk songs he knew she loved best: "Tumbalalayka," "Oyfn veg shteyt a boym," and others. He had no way of knowing if she could hear him, but it made him more hopeful that she would recover. He had to let her know how he felt about her. *Maybe if she knew how strong his feelings for her were she would hang on to life*, he thought. All he could see now through the strange liquid welling in his eyes was her face flushed with fever and the stillness of her body as they ferried her here. He had not shed a single tear since he left home and now this?

The nurses were adamant the next day too. No admittance. Then he had an idea. He would write her a note and declare the feelings that until now he had not revealed. But paper was scarce and it wouldn't work for the strategy he conjured up. Nachman walked the five miles back to his home and cut up a bed sheet into small squares. It was old and yellowed anyway, he reasoned. He could do without it. He used a pen to write a love note on the scrap of fabric then wrapped it around a small stone to give it heft and tied it with a string.

He sat under the hospital window until he saw it open then tossed his note up gently. He heard the ping as it dropped to the floor and hoped that eventually it would be noticed by the attendants and given to Dora. He prayed that his note would be the first thing she would see upon opening her eyes. The prospect of them together made Nachman giddy and suddenly he realized the truth of an old Jewish proverb: "You can't hide a cough, poverty, or love."

Dora was unlike any of his girlfriends from before. He had separated the events of his life into segments of time he thought of simply as *before* and *after*. Before: everything that lived in his memory prior to 1 September 1939 when the German war machine ripped Poland apart; and after: the future—and he had no doubt it would be good, especially now that he was free and Dora was in his life.

With her olive complexion, high cheekbones, and blazing hazel eyes, Dora's physical appearance suggested she belonged in this part of the world, yet her heart yearned for the sophistication of her native Warsaw. She was urbane, politically minded, and schooled in literature. No one could have imagined her growing up in a stiflingly strict Orthodox home. Dora was a feminist when few women even considered the concept. Though the philosophy of the Jewish Labor Bund advocated for women's rights, Nachman never heard the young women in his circle of friends speak of marriage as an institution akin to slavery, the way Dora did. He doubted she ever contemplated being married and this made her more alluring and a challenge. He knew that with her keen intelligence, great business acumen, and biting humour, Dora could make it in a man's world, but he needed her.

Despite the minimal medical care and inadequate facilities of a rural hospital, slowly Dora made progress. As she gained strength she bantered with the Russian nurse a bit more each day. The nurse, fascinated by this woman, brought Dora extra portions of thin soup and some evenings snuck in a slice of bread in the pocket of her apron.

"Here, take it, take it," she urged Dora, who always replied, "I'm not hungry. Take it home for your child."

Still extremely frail, Dora became more open to Nachman's entreaties. He was becoming a real friend and she knew that if it weren't for him she might not have survived the typhus. She was captivated by his voice and his willingness to be her troubadour at a time when there was nothing to distract them from their wretched hunger. His Yiddish songs brought images of her childhood and the world in Warsaw that seemed like something out of another lifetime. Soon she fell under the spell of his charm and realized that she loved him as much as his singing. Despite her resolve to be a woman free of a man and his needs, Dora could not resist Nachman's piercing blue eyes and his beautiful voice.

When Dora agreed to marry him in the early spring of 1942, Nachman was ecstatic. Each of them longed to share the good news with family in Poland, but there were no means of communication. War still raged. Now Mexico declared war on the Axis, General Eisenhower arrived in London ready to assume his post as commander of the American forces in Europe, the siege of Leningrad continued, and news began to reach the West that Hitler was using gas to exterminate the Jews deported to the East. But none of this information penetrated to the remote reaches of Central Asia, where they remained insulated from news as a remote tribe.

Though Nachman was away from family and suffering all the indignities of a refugee, he felt that his union with Dora would augur an end to the misery, or that at least with her at his side he could tolerate just about anything. Except that Dora would never be a traditional wife. He didn't want that, either. He wanted her to be exactly what she was already—a spiritual companion and an equal partner.

The early-June wedding day dawned with promising brilliance. Even before they set out to the administrative office the temperature had risen to eighty degrees, but it was dry and a strong wind from the Fergana Valley carried the scent of grasses and smoke. The groom and bride dressed carefully in their least-worn clothes, but there was little to choose from. They hadn't bought anything except a couple of ill-fitting, used garments at the bazaar. Nachman borrowed an iron to press his shirt. It was so heavy he could barely lift it when the landlady filled it with hot charcoal. Dora wore the navy dress Nachman liked so much when they had first met. She looked in the mirror and noticed that her hair was thinning. How could that be? It had been luxurious back home. She sighed and tucked in two small tortoise shell combs, her only luxury, on either side of her head. Her cheeks were sunken, but she pinched them trying for a healthy look.

They hurried before the temperature rose into the high nineties as it had been for several days. Along the dusty road they squeezed to the side as donkeys and dromedary camels laden with cargo passed them. Roadside food stands emitted the smell of mutton fat. Uzbeks tending the grills stood enveloped in sweet, pungent smoke of local cigarettes. Nachman spotted a late-blooming poppy by the roadside and picked it for his bride. With unmistakable pleasure she tucked it into a buttonhole—it was her only adornment.

Neither of them had envisioned their wedding as a fancy affair; there was no money for a even glass of wine. Never mind the wine, there was no glass! But they did not imagine a bureaucratic proceeding so devoid of emotion as the one that awaited them. A corpulent Kyrgyz official, seated under Stalin's mustachioed face and all-seeing gaze, performed the ceremony. Her fleshy torso was wrapped in a shawl, even on this hot day, and black leather boots reached her knees. She barely looked at them and stuck out her pudgy hand, "Here, complete this form," she said stiffly. Nachman filled in their names in his best handwriting and presented it to the clerk.

"That will be five rubles," she uttered with all the authority of the Soviet state. Then she stamped a piece of tissue thin paper and that was that—they were officially married. They couldn't wait to leave the small wooden building reeking of mildew.

Shortly after their wedding Nachman and Dora's journey brought them still farther south; the distance from their homes in Poland grew to nearly three thousand miles. They moved to Kyzyl Kiya, a town south of Uch Kurgon, sitting on the eastern edge of the Fergana Valley, when they heard that it was a larger population centre. They hoped that a place with more developed infrastructure and factories would hold greater prospects of employment, but it had few real amenities. They had no idea that Kyzyl Kiya became designated as a city only five years earlier. Coal mining was its biggest industry and uranium extraction had just begun. When they first arrived, after hours on a rickety horse-drawn cart, Kyzyl Kiya, fifty miles from China's western border, seemed as remote as a lunar colony. Today, one would have to spend *five* days riding by train from Moscow to Bishkek, the capital of Kyrgyzstan. Then another nine hours of bumping along mountainous terrain would bring the traveller to Kyzyl Kiya. Though Nachman had hiked as a younger man in the Polish Alps, here the 25,000-foot peaks of the Tian Shan Range dwarfed the Tatra Mountains. Only the exceptional circumstances of a world war could hurl two Europeans to a place they could not have conjured in their wildest imaginations. But for Nachman and Dora in 1943 this forgotten corner of Central Asia was a retreat from mayhem and imprisonment.

At last, fortune smiled upon Nachman just as he hoped. In Kyzyl Kya, he found a job as a clerk in the firebrick factory, Kirpichny Zavod, and the state-owned company provided them with a room at their compound. The pay was minimal, but the small ground-floor room in a low brick building was free. Its most noticeable feature was a tall tile stove that nearly reached the ceiling. Dora applied her design sensibility to make the place cheerful: a cloth she found at the market adorned the rickety table and the meagre belongings were always neatly stacked in the one wooden chest under the window. The best thing about the place was the spectacular view of majestic snow-capped mountains.

Before the couple could settle into a routine they discovered that Dora was pregnant. A child! What an unexpected miracle in this god-forsaken place. Nachman could hardly contain his joy. The first thing he said to Dora was, "I hope it's a girl!"

"A girl? What makes you say that, Nachman?" Dora's eyes widened in surprise. Men always seemed to want sons first.

"I ... I ... don't know, but I think it would be wonderful to raise a girl, smart, just like you, or a singer like my sister, Rosa."

"I hope we find a midwife first," Dora laughed. "And we'll have to get a cradle for the baby."

"Don't worry, I'll think of something," Nachman said, looking around the spare room. A moment later he ran over to the chest, pulled out a drawer, emptied it and placed it at Dora's feet.

"Here, all you have to do is line it with a blanket and we have a sleeping place for the baby."

In September 1943, Dora bore a child. Nachman wanted to dance with the tiny bundle when the old Russian midwife handed it to him wrapped in a flannel cloth cut from an old nightgown. "*Ana krasavitsa!*" She's a beauty! the midwife exclaimed.

Dora was exhausted, but she couldn't help smiling as Nachman counted the baby's fingers and toes and kept repeating, "*A meidele, a meidele.*" A little girl, a little girl. He placed the baby gingerly on Dora's stomach and said, "We have to name our girl." They were so preoccupied getting ready for the birth that they hadn't given it any thought.

When the midwife left, Nachman sat near Dora stroking her damp forehead.

"I have an idea for a name, Dora, and I hope you'll like it," he said.

"I bet you'll want to name her after your mother," Dora said, trying to position the baby at her breast.

"No, I have a different idea. I want to honour the memory of a brave Bund leader."

Dora was stupefied. "You want to give this child a man's name?"

"No, no," he laughed a deep belly laugh. "Anna Rosenthal was one of our heroes and she was executed by the Soviets."

"Shh ... Nachman. Have you forgotten where we are?" Dora chastised him for his carelessness, but nothing could pierce his bubble. Not on this day.

"Well, I'm not familiar with this woman, but I like the fact that she was a leader," Dora said weakly and closed her eyes.

"So you agree?" Nachman was anxious for Dora's approval.

"Yes, but let's change the name a little. How about Anetka, like little Anna?"

Nachman's eyes glistened. *"Dos iz aza min guter nomen."* That is such a good name.

When Nachman and Dora's friends learned about the baby they were as excited as if they had jointly given birth to this child. Jack, Mendel, and Itka piled into the small room to ooh and aah over the baby and even brought along some new friends, Pantl and Genia. They brought good wishes and small market trinkets.

"I found this rattle," Jack was pleased with his find. The bazaars had little more than fruit and vegetables, if one could afford them.

"And I carved this bird," said Mendel, trying to put it in the baby's tiny clenched fist.

Nachman laughed. "Wait, wait, she's too young for that yet."

Itka, uncomfortable at being empty-handed, offered her babysitting services not knowing that neither Nachman nor Dora would leave their daughter with anyone.

Anetka, who would become Annette when she reached her teenage years, was the bright star in Nachman and Dora's four years of life spent in darkness. Nachman saw Rosa's face in his little girl and dreamed of the day he could present his daughter to his sister. What a wonderful aunt she would be. Of course, Pola would love her little niece too, but she'd be more serious. And his brothers would make great uncles. "She will be surrounded by love as soon as we return to Lodz," he told Dora time and again.

"Wait a minute, Nachman, what if I want to move to Warsaw and let Anetka be with my mother, her grandma?"

"Don't worry, we'll figure out these details when we are back on our home turf," he reassured her.

But for now there was no going home. War had not abated. Furious battles were fought. It seemed as if the whole world was engulfed in flames. From Guadalcanal in the Western Pacific to the deserts of North Africa, throughout Europe and east to Stalingrad, armies were killing one another and millions of civilians. By the time of his daughter's birth already more than seventy thousand Jews from the Lodz ghetto were exterminated in the Chelmno death camps. But Nachman did not know about these tragedies. He only knew from sketchy third-hand rumours that it was not yet safe to return to Poland.

Her little girl squirmed in the dented metal tub and splashed water all over the table. Gurgles of joy issued from her rosebud mouth. Dora could barely hold on to the small slippery limbs popping out of the water like silvery fish. Giving the child a bath was as exhilarating as it was exhausting. Dora had never experienced parenthood and its pleasures took her by surprise. It was a precious thing and she delighted in it each day as if the little girl were a gift of the gods. She knew that Nachman shared this feeling by the way he always jumped in to help with the baby.

Their one-room apartment wasn't much, but they had enough happiness to fill it to the brim. Neither of them had been concerned with material possessions so the few pieces of rickety furniture did not bother them. The small room had barely enough space for the baby's cradle that Mendel assembled from some discarded boards, but for now it was their whole universe. If they could only find enough nourishment for themselves and the baby and go home everything would be well.

The coal to heat the place was doled out lump by small lump, so keeping warm wasn't easy when the winter winds howled. Food was rationed and they rarely went to bed with their stomachs filled, but Dora kept the room in immaculate condition. She scrubbed the wooden floor so often she worried it would wear out. When it was still warm, she picked wildflowers along the long road to the town market and put them on the windowsill. She loved to see them against the purple shadows of the mountains. The kettle was always on. The steam gave the room a homey feel and the hot liquid lessened the hunger. After their daily struggle to survive in Uch Kurgon, their lives in Kyzyl Kiya were a definite improvement. Dora was reassured by Nachman's steadfast belief this was a sign that things would be looking up soon, perhaps even this year.

Outside the apartment there were no trees or shrubs. The entire area wore a harsh industrial look. Gravel and asphalt covered the ground. The only thing of interest was a narrow-gauge train track that carried small wagons of coal directly to the factory's furnace. Its movement gave the place more life, Dora thought, and she got used to its clanging. Her only concern was that it not wake Anetka. How she loved looking at her asleep! Nothing in their miserable existence as refugees prepared them for something so divine. When Dora first beheld the squirming bundle of energy that emerged from her emaciated body she could not speak. Nine months of carrying the baby and she still couldn't get used to the idea that a new being, unsullied by all that had gone on in the previous three years, could come into her life. And every time she looked into Nachman's eyes she knew that he, too, considered Anetka's birth an unlikely miracle.

Like Nachman, Dora couldn't wait to get back to the family she left behind. She knew her sisters and mother would shower Anetka with love. But what she did not know was that 400,000 Jews had been kicked out of their Warsaw homes and squeezed into a 1.3-square-mile ghetto surrounded by electrified barbed-wire fence. And by the summer of 1942, the Nazis had sent 254,000 ghetto residents to the Treblinka death camp.

Whenever she bathed the baby in the tub centred on the dining table, Nachman was an essential assistant.

"Quick, Nachman, do your trick. The bath water is getting cold." He knew how to get Anetka to lift up her head so Dora could wash her neck.

"*Vi iz di zayf?*" Where is the soap? Nachman asked the child in a singsong. Immediately, she picked her head up and looked at the top of the high tile stove where a precious bar of the yellowish soap lay drying. Nachman was pleased that at twelve months his daughter could understand Yiddish. He tickled her chin and Dora scolded him. "I wasn't done yet."

"Let me play with Anetka," he pleaded, then picked up the striped towel. Dora handed him the child and he swaddled her to get her dry. She gurgled and cooed to his delight.

Dora was now completely immersed in motherhood, a role she never believed would quite suit her independent spirit. Before the war she travelled alone to distant, even dangerous places like Palestine, was a theatre regular, and loved nothing more than to sit in Warsaw cafés arguing about the ideas of Nietzsche, Wittgenstein, or Heidegger with her wide circle of friends. But Anetka's arrival allowed her to see another side of herself, a discovery that caught her off-guard each time she held the little girl in her arms, or combed her silky hair. When she stopped to think about it, she was startled by the body's ability to rejuvenate itself and to bear fruit after all it had been through in Siberia, the starvation in Uch Kurgon, and the typhus. Now she spent much of her time strategizing for how to obtain enough to eat, especially for the baby.

They would pool all their meagre ration coupons and Dora would walk to the market to buy whatever nutritious food items she could find for Anetka: a bit of sugar, some milk, and the rarest commodity of all—meat. She didn't fret over shopping for herself and Nachman—they would get by on some vegetables. Every single time she handed the old Uzbek grocer all her coupons for a few ounces of meat he would ask, "You going to eat like a bird?"

"No, it's for the baby. I need to make her some soup."

"Always the baby, the baby, the baby. Don't you and your husband eat?"

"*Ne bespokoits'ia.*" Don't worry, she would tell him.

"*Vy umerete, i vash muzh umeret i vasha malenkaia devushka budet sirotskoĭ.*" Each time he made the same pronouncement: You will die and your husband will die and your little girl will become an orphan.

Despite the difficult conditions and the lives lived in isolation from everything that had been dear to them, Dora felt the days rushing by. The child was growing so quickly before her very eyes. She would have slowed it down if she could. She had no camera to record the milestones and hated losing the tiniest details to the passage of time. She knew she would never forget these priceless observations of her child's development, but hated the thought that with time the edges of the pictures in her mind might became frayed, or the images themselves dimmed.

I could hardly listen to my father's CDs without thinking about my mother. She had been such a strong and influential presence in our lives that even after she was long gone I carried on an ongoing dialogue with her in my mind. As I rewound the parts of my father's story of my early life in Kyzyl Kiya, I remembered a conversation I had with my mother when she visited us for a weekend in Larchmont.

We sat in our back yard in her favourite spot under the lilac tree. She adored its fragrance and I'd always send her home with armfuls of blooms. How they intoxicated her! It must have been Mother's Day because we reminisced about when my children were young and then I asked her, "Mom, was I the first baby you ever came in contact with?"

She wrinkled her brow, thinking way back. "Yes, I suppose, you were," she said.

"So you mean you had no idea at all how to handle me as a newborn?"

"Well, the midwife gave me some tips, but yes, it was rather a challenge bathing a slippery baby. I prayed I wouldn't drown you!"

"And you didn't have any neighbours or friends who had children?"

"Not right when you were born. I didn't meet Genia until later," she said. "But wait, wait. I remembered something. I took care of a boy, named Rysio, in Poland."

"I never heard of him. Was he a child in our family?" I asked.

"No, not at all," she said. "I wonder what ever became of him. He'd be middle-aged by now ... if he survived."

She went on to tell me that for a short while she worked as a governess for a wealthy family whose only child, Rysio, was a spoiled six-year-old brat who threw frequent temper tantrums and refused to wear the beautiful new clothes his parents bought him regularly. "This is not mine," he'd scream, throw the new garment at his young governess and try to bite her if she attempted to persuade him.

"After Rysio, I swore you'd have to be crazy to have children," my mother laughed. "You were such a delightful surprise."

"Why don't you write all these stories down, Mom?"

"Who has time?" was her answer every time.

So it was an enormous shock to discover after her passing a few scattered pages from what had apparently been a memoir she'd been writing. My father found a page from her notebook in which she spoke of a manuscript she threw in the incinerator. "Who will want to read all of this private nonsense?" she wrote. "I have kept it all in through the years, why spill my guts now?" The note pained and angered me. It was as if she were committing suicide. What had she kept hidden all these years?

I knew she thirsted to be a writer, but writing in Polish, her most fluent language, wouldn't do. She had written in Polish as a teenager and even won the coveted Janusz Korczak writing prize before the war. But in America she insisted on writing in English, though her only knowledge of it came from the evening classes she took in a local high school at night and from studying the dictionary. "English is a much richer language. It's the one that can truly express a range of emotion," she'd say, and urge me to find for her ever newer editions of Polish–English dictionaries. In the end, my father and I found several loose pages of her manuscript in various drawers and stuffed into folders. They were filled with philosophical musings that we later self-published in a small booklet. I couldn't fathom when she found time to write. Working in a sweatshop nine hours a day, then trudging home an hour on the subway and making dinner for the family didn't leave much time for anything else. I did remember that she was a very poor sleeper. Did she write all those nights we heard her on her nocturnal rounds of the kitchen?

By the time Anetka was two, she would skip the short distance down the gravel path to her father's office. Dora barely kept up with her. The nausea of her second pregnancy made her uncomfortable and tired. She had to keep a keen eye on the child as the path ran along the train track on which the clay for the firebricks was delivered in wagons to the loading dock before it was swallowed by the perpetually fired-up kilns. The sight of the little girl in this grimy industrial setting never ceased to amaze Dora. With the big red bow in her hair she was just as unexpected here as the delicate large tulip that bloomed in the dry foothills of the Tian Shan Mountains.

Anetka was fascinated by the wagons rolling with a great racket along the tracks. The only way to distract her was to say, "Your daddy is waiting." And with that she would sprint ahead like a rabbit into his office and onto his lap. It was amazing how much like him she looked, right down to her little nose and blue eyes. *Where did I get this light-haired, blue-eyed angel*, Dora wondered, for Anetka looked nothing like her.

The sight of her own little girl always reminded Dora of her three youngest sisters in Warsaw. The images of them crowding around her own mother teaching them to sew and crochet were still fresh in her mind. *Where are they now?* she wondered and hoped they and her mother were safe somewhere. But in her heart of hearts there was a deeply submerged sense of doom. *Weren't the pogroms in smaller Polish cities in 1937 and 1938 harbingers of persecution to come? Wasn't that why I chose to run from Poland*, she asked herself. Then, she'd marshal all her energy to banish the negative thought and turn her attention to Anetka who never failed to put a smile on Dora's face.

Dora entered Nachman's office. He was bent over the small desk reviewing coal delivery receipts. For just a brief moment she glimpsed the expression of disgust on his face. She knew how he felt about the Soviet ways of doing business— perpetual five-year plans, production quotas, those nasty *normas*, corruption in the senior ranks, and the dreadful monotony of his job. He was a creative man, her Nachman. She knew this wasn't his kind of place, but they needed a source of income. Most of all, she knew how he hated looking at the row of photos of the Communist Party luminaries. They graced every office and kept a perpetual watch on everyone who entered the space.

Anetka jumped into his lap and Dora saw his face light up. He pointed to a portrait above the desk.

"Who is this?" he asked the child.

"Lenin," she said beaming.

Nachman smiled with satisfaction.

"And this?"

Anetka paused and knitted her little brows. Her nose crinkled in deep thought.

"Here, look, I'll give you a hint." Nachman curved the fingers of both his hands to touch his thumbs and made circles. He lifted the simulation of glasses to his eyes.

"Kalinin!" Anetka exclaimed, naming a member of Stalin's inner circle. She then put her little fist to her chin mimicking the man's small pointy beard.

He always ended the game after she identified Stalin's image, then he spun her around in the chair and her giggles pierced the stifling atmosphere. Dora admired the game and its subtle reduction of these evil characters to child's toys. She looked out the door to see that no one was coming, for if Nachman was ever observed to be ridiculing the masters of the state, his fate would be worse than Opalicha.

Few members of their tiny community of Jewish refugees had a job as steady as Nachman's. He couldn't do anything to jeopardize it. Sometimes looking at the narrow-eyed looks and whispers, Dora felt that a few resented his relative success, but that feeling was far outweighed by the closeness they developed with some refugee families. And it was the children who helped cement a bond between families. For Mita and Yola, the eight- and ten-year-old daughters of the Yoffe's, Anetka was a constant source of amusement.

Genia Yoffe, their mother, was a woman after Dora's heart. Like Dora, a native of Warsaw, she was sophisticated and well read. The two women found a common language. Genia was the only one in their small group of friends who was not a Bundist and in their mutual lack of the socialist youth mores they were closer in spirit than with the others. For a brief time Genia's husband, Antek, was the representative of the Polish government in exile. His exalted title was *dovierenny polskovo pasolstva* (trusted representative of the Polish mission), quite an unexpected advancement for a young dentist from Warsaw. He was the one who asked Nachman to become the secretary at the mission. Many such small missions grew like mushrooms in all the little villages and towns that had significant numbers of Jewish refugees from Poland, recently released from labour camps. And it was each mission's job to oversee the distribution of the American aid to the refugees.

What odd form the aid had taken: yarn; safety pins; shoes fit for dandies; hats that would make them into clowns; and mismatched used items of clothing, sometimes in sizes so huge they imagined giants had worn them. None of the skinny refugees could use them, but they could be repurposed for smaller items, skirts, child's clothing, or bartered at the bazaar for fruit and vegetables. Some individuals who were adept in business matters were able to exchange these goods for eggs and bread. Some even traded for gold. Others travelled to where they could obtain vodka, then exchanged it for salt and other necessities. Nachman was completely inept in this sphere, but Dora's business acumen came in handy. On a few occasions he accompanied Dora to the market and she was able to get some badly needed food in exchange for the items that were their share of the American packages. One time she even managed to exchange some shoes for a moth-eaten fur coat, which she then sold to a Russian official. This short-lived period of relief came to an abrupt halt when Wanda Wasilewska, a Polish communist, became the head the Association of Polish Patriots in Russia. Appointed to this position on Stalin's personal orders, she disbanded the missions and attempted to reconstruct them as communist organs because her association was under the control of the Soviet regime. When the Americans learned of the change, they immediately stopped sending aid.

The most common topic of conversation when Dora and Nachman got together with their friends was the progress of the war. They exchanged bits and pieces of information mixed with gossip they had picked up here and there. No one knew the truth.

Nachman, Dora, Mendel, Itka; and their newer friends, Genia, Antek, and Kersh were gathered in the Yoffe's apartment. Theirs was somewhat larger than the single rooms they all occupied. Genia called her daughters, Mita and Yola, "Can you play with Anetka for a while? We grown-ups need to talk."

"Yes, Mama," they said in unison, as if they'd been waiting for this all along, and ran off to chase after the toddler.

Antek was first to bring up wartime news. "I've heard the Home Army in Warsaw has mounted a stiff resistance against the Germans. They are hoping for help from the Red Army, but the Russians have yet to cross the Vistula," he said. No one contradicted him. Because of his post as the representative of the Polish mission, the gathered gave more credence to his words.

"*Mentshen zogn zs di royte armey hot bazigt Rumenye.*" People say the Red Army has occupied Romania, Mendel said. They spoke Yiddish among themselves, which gave their get-together more taste of home than anything else.

"*S' iz nisht geshtoygn, nisht gefloygn. Mentshn dertseyln plyotkes.*" There is no basis for it, people circulate rumours, Genia dismissed him, and proceeded to recount the assorted war stories exchanged at the market, none of which had the ring of truth. The war had gone on so long it became a way of life and as much as they dreamed of it ending, they couldn't quite believe the Allies were gaining the upper hand.

"Let's not argue about that now," Dora said. "Let's stop talking about the war for a few hours and just enjoy each other's company."

"*Rikhtig.*" Correct, Nachman said, and with that he clapped his hands and broke out into everyone's favourite song, "Romenye, Romenye." Now, instead of dwelling on Romania's political situation, they listened to the beautiful land it used to be with its Jewish delicacies from *mamalyga* to pastrami and wine. Nachman's voice rang clear and strong as if by merely mentioning these foods they'd materialize on the table in front of them. Soon they were all tapping their feet so enthusiastically the girls came running to join the fun.

Since the spring of 1945 there was much talk that an end was near. Those whispers alone created excitement and everyone seemed to be floating buoyed by the air of anticipation. Rumours about the slaughter of Jews in Europe also began to spread, but no one believed them. Very rarely someone received a letter that had been posted months before and it was a sensation that it had actually made it to the farthest southern outpost of Soviet Central Asia. By May, the Soviet Union was victorious but devastated. The bloodthirsty war was over, but its aftermath would make both citizens and refugees miserable for years to come.

Families began to make plans for return home. But travelling when no trains ran on normal schedules was not for the faint of heart, especially not for Dora, in her third trimester of pregnancy in the early spring of 1946. And toting a small child from boxcar to boxcar and enduring the interminable delays in unknown cities along the three-thousand-mile route made it seem like a crazy idea. As soon as the news of Soviet victory filtered down to their corner of Kyrgyzstan, Dora and Nachman decided that they would start for home. With Dora malnourished and feeling so poorly, they put it off time and again but knew they would have to leave by March at the latest in order to get to Poland in time for Dora to give birth. The best they could count on were the sporadic cargo trains, as they could not wait until passenger trains were running again. Nachman wanted this child to be born in his own country, and Dora agreed. Poland—the land of their ancestors.

Their minds were now fixed on the future. They itched to get out of the communist, straitjacketed existence though they were keenly aware that if it hadn't been for their incarceration in the gulags they might have been dead by now. But there would be one more reason why they couldn't wait to leave this place, never to return. The ever-present secret police, the NKVD (later replaced by the KGB) was always searching for spies and traitors to the regime. People had to be careful what they said to whom and in what tone. Imprisonment in remote Siberian gulags was regularly dished out on the basis of rumours. Kangaroo courts issued swift and lethal sentences.

When some of his Bundist friends began to speak quite openly about socialist ideas, Nachman became alarmed. He still felt a deep kinship with their ideology, but was keenly aware of the dangers. Now he had a child and would do nothing to risk entanglement with the notorious NKVD. Time and again he warned his friends that NKVD agents were watching, but they acted as if they were back in pre-war Lodz.

They held meetings and a memorial rally for Bundist leaders Henryk Ehrlich and Wiktor Alter who were killed by Stalin. They seemed to be asking for trouble. Sure enough, the first in their circle to be arrested was Nachman's friend Kersh. With the prospect of home so near, Nachman became more concerned daily and tried to stay away from wagging tongues indiscriminately flaunting socialist ideas. Could he just get by without any trouble before he left this repressive regime? Nachman vowed to keep a low profile and avoid attracting any attention.

One day as Nachman sat in his office at the factory he noticed two NKVD agents peeking in the door. He knew well who they were. It was a small enough town to know all of the secret police. No way they happened to be there by chance. Sure enough, at the end of the workday, Nachman's boss called him. *"Zdrastvyïte, tovarishch."* Hello, comrade, he said, looking him in the eye.

"Chego ja mogu sdelat dla vas?" What can I do for you? Nachman asked.

"Take this envelope and drop off this letter for me at the NKVD headquarters. It's on your way home." With that he handed Nachman a sealed envelope. Nachman could not refuse his boss's request.

"No problem, I'll drop it off," he said obligingly and left the office.

Outside he felt queasy. On his way to deliver the letter, Nachman stopped at home where Dora tended to Anetka. "Look Dora, my boss has sent me on a strange mission. He wants me to deliver this to the NKVD office when it's on his way home too."

"That *is* odd," Dora said and gave Anetka a stuffed rag doll she had sewn to keep her occupied. Nachman wondered if Dora noticed the apprehension in the corners of his mouth.

"What do you think this could be about?" he asked his wife. He knew she was wise and valued her counsel.

"Come over here. I have an idea." She motioned for him to come close to the kerosene lamp that lit up their one-room apartment. "And bring over the envelope," she added.

Together they held up the envelope to the kerosene lamp and tried to discern its contents. What they saw only deepened the mystery. There was no sheet of letter paper inside. Instead, they noticed it contained small pieces of paper and various cuttings of newsprint. Nachman broke out in a sweat. A strange sensation grew in the pit of his stomach. He'd never been so frightened before. Not when hoodlums threatened him in a dark alley, not when they threw him into the Gdanska Street prison in Lodz, not when they arrested him and sent him to Opalicha. Now he had a family. He breathed in deeply and tried to shake off his sense of doom, but his usually dry hands felt moist.

"You are being set up," Dora said. Her cheeks flamed crimson. She touched his hand and he felt how cold her fingers were, frozen with unspoken fear.

"Nah, it's the usual—Soviet games. They are just testing if I'll carry out the boss's orders," Nachman said.

Clearly, there was no letter as he had been told. He knew they were trying to entrap him in something, but he couldn't think of a single idea why. *Well, these people don't need much of a reason,* he thought. "Look, Dora, I have no choice. I must hurry there now, before they wonder where I was detained," he said resolutely in a steady voice. Dora did not respond, but she followed him with her eyes as he went over to Anetka and gave a hug so long and tender as if it would be his last.

Outside, it was dusk. Soon, near total blackness would envelop the compound. *Why did the Soviets always choose the dark hours to carry out their schemes?* he wondered. On this day even the stars seemed to co-operate with them. The NKVD headquarters were not very far. A guard ushered him inside the lobby.

"State your business here," he said with formality.

"I am here to drop off an envelope from my boss at Kirpichny Zavod."

"Sit down and wait," the man said gruffly and pointed to a wooden bench.

"Can I just leave it with you?"

"No. I said already, wait."

A half hour passed and no one emerged from behind the main office door to see him. Nachman glanced nervously at the wall clock, then cautioned himself not to appear too eager to leave. His anxiety grew with each jerk of the minute hand on the clock. *Dora must be sick with worry by now*, he thought. Five more minutes and he would have been waiting an hour. No one walked through the lobby so Nachman gave up hope that Anetka would be awake for her bath by time he returned home. But at that moment the doors to the NKVD official's office opened a crack. Inside, Nachman noticed the two NKVD agents whom he had seen earlier in the day. "He is here," they announced.

"You may enter the office now," the guard pointed toward the door.

The elegance and size of the space startled Nachman. A carved desk stood in the centre of the room and behind it red-velvet curtains swept down to the carpeted floor. Compared to the dreary governmental offices everywhere else he had seen in the Soviet Union, this was something else. These people have clout and power, he surmised even before they exchanged a single word.

"I understand you have a letter for me from your boss," the man behind the ornate desk said casually.

"Yes. Here it is." Nachman handed him the envelope. The man tore it open and pieces of newspaper fell out on his desk. He looked shocked, his pleasant expression changed into a grimace. He slammed his fist on the desk and swore. "*Yob tvoiu mat!*" Fuck your mother! he said "*Gde pis'mo?*" Where is the letter that was handed to you by the boss at the factory?

"*Tovarishch*, comrade, I know nothing about the contents. I am handing you the same sealed envelope that was given to me."

"Oh, no," he said. "We know better. You have given the letter to a spy you met on the way here." The two agents nodded, smiling smugly.

"I didn't meet anyone along the road. I tell you, this is the very envelope I was given to deliver to you. I swear," Nachman replied trying to make his voice sound as authoritative and even as possible.

"Better confess now," the official growled. "Spill the beans, if you know what's good for you." But Nachman did the only thing he could—he repeated what he had just said. Time passed and the unproductive interrogation continued. So did the curses and insults. When they couldn't get a confession out of him the two agents took to their fists. They punched him in the stomach and on his jaw, then the stomach again and again. Every now and then a kick to his groin made the other pain seem mild. But his jaw and belly ached so fiercely Nachman lost count of the blows.

"Are you going to tell us the truth now, or do you want some more, you scum?" they asked with each successive punch. After a while Nachman was near to blacking out. He stopped bothering to reply.

Later that night he was thrown into a dank cell at the end of a long, narrow corridor. Nachman figured that his questioner was frustrated and furious that the interrogation yielded nothing. He felt certain that the ordeal would resume in the morning. *No, maybe the next night*, he concluded on second thought. That's the time for their dirty business. He wanted to think of a strategy, but exhaustion and nausea hijacked his brain. Every part of him throbbed. He curled up on the cement floor and fell into a deep sleep.

In the morning, he was led back into the NKVD boss's office. A small package sat on the desk. It was wrapped in brown paper and tied with string. To Nachman's surprise, the man assumed a friendlier tone. "This is a package from your wife. She dropped it off for you today." Nachman wasn't sure if this was another of their tricks. Did Dora bring him something to eat? It was possible. He knew just how worried she must have been when he didn't return home in the evening. Then again, would they have allowed a package to be delivered here? He stared at the bundle. Nachman didn't respond fast enough. What was there to say?

"See this package?" The NKVD man pointed to it. "If you want it, confess now and you can take it and go."

"But I already told you yesterday. There is nothing to confess. I brought you the envelope I was given."

"Let me ask you this." The interrogator leaned back in his chair. "Do you want to see your wife and child again?"

"Yes. Yes, of course I do," Nachman said with a fierceness that he worried was excessive.

"Well then, you know what you must do. I won't say it again." Then he shouted to the guard, "Take him to his cell. Let him think."

Just as they wanted him to do, Nachman spent his time in the cell trying to figure things out. Who may have fingered him and for what? He couldn't imagine any of his friends as informers and besides, there was nothing to inform about. He had been scrupulous in his work. It must have been his known status as a Bundist, a socialist. What if he confessed to something he did not do? What then? Would they let him go? Certainly not; he knew such a confession would seal his fate. He resolved to remain silent. And then a horrible thought overwhelmed him: I can't trust anyone. But it was against his nature and every nerve in his body vibrated with this painful thought.

By noon he heard the clanking of metal. Maybe they were bringing tea, or some soup, Nachman thought. The gurgling of his empty intestines and dull ache in his belly were familiar sensations from Opalicha. He didn't care how bitter the tea or watery the soup. He shivered—hot liquid would help him figure this out. But no such luck. The guard opened the cell and said, "Let's go."

The guard led him back to the office of the NKVD boss who had given him the ultimatum that morning. Nachman thought, *What else could they possibly want? Another chance to brutalize me? To break my spirit? Well, they don't know me!* An unexpected calm came over him.

The NKVD official had an odd look on his face. "You are a quiet one, aren't you?" he said as the guard ushered Nachman in.

"I have nothing to add to what I have already told you."

"Well, I have something to tell you then." He shifted in his chair and put his chin in his cupped hand leaning menacingly toward Nachman. His tone softened somewhat but the sly, narrow-eyed look on his face belied the new sound. "From this day forward you must observe the activities of your Bundist friends and report to us. We'll call on you. Remember what I said about your wife and child? *Panyemayesh?*" Do you understand?

Nachman looked at him without a word and lowered his head. The official took it as a yes, but Nachman simply wanted to avert his eyes from the face that had transformed into the devil. *His family's future was in this monster's hands,* Nachman thought with bile gathering in his throat. The notion that he would have to betray his friends to save his family was more than he could contemplate. *Never, never. I will never do such a thing. It would destroy my soul. Best to alert them.* His thoughts turned to something practical because snitching could never be an option.

Immediately after his joyful reunion with Dora and Anetka, Nachman rushed out to warn his friends. In his Lodz inflected Yiddish he told them of his experience. "Remember what I had told you about continuing your Bundist meetings?" he said to skinny Wawer and the ever-rotund Pantl. The men sat at the table smoking cigarettes and seemed surprised by Nachman's agitation. It wasn't like him to get excited. They looked at one another quizzically. Nachman liked both of these men, but he worried that they would fall into the hands of the NKVD. In fact, after his ordeal he considered it a strong possibility.

"What of it? What's the big deal?" they asked.

"Haven't you heard the rumours about the purges? Don't be so naive. The NKVD is watching *all* of us. Don't give them any reasons to suspect you."

"*Vos? Az mir redn az Stalin ken kushn undz in tukhes?*" What? That we say Stalin can kiss our ass?"

"See? It's just what I mean. If you keep this up you'll end up in Siberia," Nachman paused and then added, "But only if you are very lucky. Don't forget what they did to Shlomo Ravin."

The men seemed sobered by the reminder of the execution. Their faces lost some of the what-of-it look. Frowns and knitted eyebrows replaced the bravado they displayed moments before.

"And one more thing. Don't expect me at any Bundist gatherings."

"Nachman, but you are a committed socialist."

"Yes, but I'm a husband and a father now too."

He declined the tea they offered him and left feeling frustrated by their careless behaviour in the face of real danger, especially now that he had brushed up against what could be their fate. He didn't want them to be ensnared and even more, he wanted to avoid being pulled in deeper into this ugly business. A few weeks later Wawer was arrested. Nachman was called in to see the NKVD boss. Just entering the lobby sent a shiver down his spine. "So, tell us about your friend Wawer," was the first thing the man said.

Nachman raised his hand to stop him.

"I barely know the man. I can't tell you anything about him except that he is skinny." Nachman's posture and tone conveyed a certain assuredness that seemed at odds with his small stature.

"Isn't he a Bundist?"

"I have no idea. Ask him." Nachman felt empowered by the disappointed look on his questioner's face. Like a broken record, the man asked him the same questions over and over again and Nachman replied in kind. Finally, making no progress, the official dismissed Nachman with a warning, "You'll be seeing us again."

Indeed, each week leading up the family's departure for Poland, Nachman was called in, interrogated and threatened for hours. He remained mute and developed a style that walked a thin line between co-operation and insolence. They got nothing out of him, but in utter frustration they called him one last time before he left. The NKVD boss leaned back in his chair with the now-familiar squinty-eyed look and said, "Remember, you may be going back to Poland, but you are never, ever to divulge the interrogations to anyone, not even to the minister of home police in Poland." Nachman nodded in agreement and walked out one last time feeling as if he were floating.

Part 2

Purgatory

Chapter Five

Return to his beloved city and a joyous reunion with his loved ones was an image that lit up behind Nachman's eyelids each and every single night throughout his seven years on the run. The nights he had curled up in cold, dusty barns, or tossed on bug-infested bunks in Opalicha and Lapushka with hunger twisting his guts, on moonless nights made darker by the prospect of a knock by the NKVD on the door—through all those long nights one thought kept him going: *This will end one day and a better day will come.*

Thoughts of home often turned way back to his days with friends at the Medem School: making stage sets for plays, rehearsing the musical program, and later attending political rallies. The teachers who were like family came to mind too, especially Liza Holtzman and that unforgettable letter she sent from Paris. Sometimes he wondered if ever there would come a time when he could pick up a brush and paint, but the idea seemed so farfetched that it embarrassed him to even think it.

Letters had always been a source of excitement for Nachman. Each unopened envelope carried a whiff of romance, news of births, weddings, visits by friends from distant cities. He always held a letter an extra moment before opening it trying to imagine the good tidings inside. So when the postman knocked on his door in Kyzyl Kyia shortly before his and Dora's departure from the Soviet Union, Nachman was thrilled. All those years without any news of family and now they found him!

And what an embarrassment of riches: not one letter, but three and four postcards!

"*Spasiba, spasiba*," Nachman thanked the postman profusely. The two men stood for a moment looking at one another, Nachman overwhelmed, the postman watching the reaction caused by his delivery. Nachman shuffled through the cards and noted that one was dated 9 June 1940. It was in Natan's familiar tiny handwriting, each letter like a tiny black insect trying to stand up on its hind legs. Another was from Jadwiga. His heart leaped. How many nights have I dreamed about her in Opalicha?

"Why did it take six years to get this correspondence to me?" Nachman stopped scanning the package of mail and spoke to the man.

The postman laughed. "Did you think they'd give you your mail in the gulag? You were lucky if they gave you a piece of bread." So that's why he hadn't heard from anyone all these years, he reflected. How strange that someone even bothered to forward this mail to him now.

"But how did they know where I am?" Nachman mused out loud.

"The NKVD knows everything," the postman said, then he hoisted the mail sack onto his shoulder and left, leaving a trail of insinuation behind. *For all I know he is an NKVD agent himself*, Nachman thought and went inside to revel in his treasure. First, he scanned Natan's card from Warsaw. It was good to know that at least back then Natan was well, if a bit bored. Nachman's friends had relayed information to his family about his whereabouts in the Soviet Union. He could not provide an address given how frequently he moved from place to place before his arrest, but was glad the information had travelled back to Poland via the refugee network. The most interesting news was that Rosa had finally married, a man named Benjamin whom Nachman had yet to meet. The couple was living in the Lodz ghetto.

Nachman set the postcards aside. There would be plenty of time to read and digest them all later. He decided to focus his attention on Rosa's letters because she was the most detailed communicator in the family. He'd instantly recognized her exquisite handwriting so different from Natan's. *So they are all fine? Why have I worried so all these years,* he thought. From the postmark he saw Rosa was writing from his beloved Lodz. Nachman was glad Dora and Anetka were still at the market. He wanted to savour this long-awaited moment without any interruptions. He pulled the chair closer toward the window where it was brighter and carefully slit open the first envelope.

The letter, written on 2 February 1945, was shocking in its brevity. A few words about how desperately she was trying to find him, and then:

> I must inform you that after a one year confinement in a punishing concentration camp I have returned to our country. I am alone, without a husband, brothers, sister—no one is left. I only have you. I could write much about myself, about what I have lived through over the past six years, but it is difficult to write about it and there is more than one thing I would like to forget.

Nachman swallowed hard. *What does she mean by "alone"? Why? Where are the rest of them? What is it she wants to forget?* His heart thumped furiously. Small beads of sweat formed on his forehead. He wiped them with a handkerchief and reached for the second letter. It was dated 6 November 1945.

> My dearest Niemele:
>
> I am the only one who returned from the camps: Oswiecim [Auschwitz], Rawensbruck, Malchow, and Leipzig. I returned to our native city in Poland, after spending three months in a hospital in Germany (Muhlberg) n/Elba. There is a great deal to be said about

me. I made a successful escape on the 10th of April of
this year. I was a living cadaver. I had nothing to lose.
But what good is it to survive so alone? I had to sacrifice
everyone I loved. It is so difficult to live alone. I speak
to myself and I reply to my own questions. Alone like
a lone fence post.

Benjamin and I were deported to Oswiecim [Ausch-
witz] on September 30, 1944. I was with him until the
death march of Janu-ary 18, 1945. I used to see him
through the barbed wire. But on the 18th of January,
this year, they chased us on foot to Germany—men and
women separately. That's when I said goodbye to him.
And I know nothing more about his fate. I know only
one thing—after my miserable wondering, I returned to
the country, but Benjamin did not. I was 100% certain
he would return. Some of his friends returned to Lodz,
but they could tell me nothing about him ...

Nachman's hands shook. Like slow-acting poison, Rosa's
anguish seeped out of the thin typewritten page and lodged
in his stomach before it reached his brain. *What does she mean
by "I had to sacrifice everyone I loved?"* he mumbled to himself.
Why hasn't she mentioned what happened to the rest of them:
Yankel and Balcia, their children, Pola, and her family? And
what about Natan and Dorka in Warsaw? He had written that
postcard early on in the war. Surely, she must have found him
by now, so why does she feel so alone? Maybe he had emigrated abroad. Nachman had heard that people were doing
that now.

He steeled himself for Rosa's third letter, swallowed
hard, and opened the next envelope. The date, 4 February
1946, made it clear that she hadn't given up. She wrote him
letters every few months in the hope that eventually at least
one would get to him. But the words swam before his eyes.
He could hardly make sense of what he was reading. Unlike
Rosa's crystal-clear writing in their pre-war correspondence—
how he loved getting her letters while he led the SKIF summer
camps—this letter was disjointed. Jumbled paragraphs,

clipped sentences, ellipsis—everything pointed to her rattled state of mind. What he saw was impossible. He had to read it again and again and again.

> Dear Nachman, our dearest ones are not alive ... they are lost ... we lost everyone. It is so difficult for me to write about this. As I write it, I am living through the Gehenna of the Lodz ghetto over again.
> Our Yankel died a natural death, from starvation ... in 1941...

At first, Nachman couldn't comprehend how being starved to death could be called "natural." Then he remembered how emaciated men in Opalicha fell daily and later, starving, sick refugees in Uch Kurgon. Yes, I suppose in war we must change our definition of normalcy, he thought and read on, more prepared now for what was to come.

> Isser was sent out after the death of his father. He couldn't bear the hunger and looked so bad by then. He was rounded up in an action on the street and reported for the deportation selection himself.... Little Esther, Yankel's youngest, died in 1944 before we were deported to Auschwitz. She couldn't grow ... we didn't have any fats to feed her. Of course, you must know there was great hunger in the ghetto ...

For a brief moment Nachman thought there would be a reprieve to the carnage when Rosa wrote:

> Yankel's wife, Balcia, our dear sister-in-law, and their little Chaskele remained. He worked with me in the Leather and Saddle Works section. He was just ten years old and what a smart child. He took so much after our brother, Natan. I tried to help them as best I could ...

But then another blow:

Balcia and Chaskele were sent out in August. They were killed together ...

And the dirge went on mercilessly:

Our Pola and her little Reniusia were deported on March 31, 1942. Who could have imagined they would be destroyed? Until the last moment none of us knew about the existence of the crematoria. We all thought we were being sent to labour camps. They were sent close to Lodz, to Chelmno. I remember it as if it were today. I walked Pola and Reniusia to the collection point. Benjamin worked hard to get them some food for the road. Reniusia was so sweet and very sleepy and she asked to carry her own little knapsack. No one expected anything.... Even I, who was deported as late as August 30, 1944, didn't know the fate that awaited us. There was no opposition at all in the ghetto because we were so ignorant about what was to happen to us ...

Nachman's tears flooded his face and dripped onto his shirt. His nose became so clogged he couldn't breathe. A dense fog enveloped his head and his hands shook making the words jump all over the onion-skin pages. He tried to stem the torrent with the back of his hand and said, "No, no! What ... what is this? It can't be." He read and reread the letter again and again, making a vain attempt to squeeze the news into his brain, but it just would not register.

By the time Nachman learned that Natan and his Dorka were killed, he had only one thing to ease the crushing pain in his chest. Rosa informed him that Natan had been one of the leaders of the Warsaw ghetto uprising and both he and his wife were mentioned in a recently published book, *The Ghetto Resists. Good, at least he went down fighting,* Nachman consoled himself. After these deaths he hardly wanted to continue reading Rosa's long missive, but it occurred to him that it was his sacred duty to face these atrocities, to memorize them, to expose them to light so no one would ever forget.

Soon he learned that many of his aunts, uncles, cousins, and friends met a similar fate. Poor Rosa, she was left to be the bearer of this impossible message of carnage. No wonder she could barely write about it. About her own fate, Rosa was telegraphic. She married Benjamin, a man she loved, gave birth to a boy in the ghetto, suffered a terrible breast infection that lasted for months and nearly killed her, lost the six-week-old son and then her husband. Benjamin was shot as he attempted to escape the death march from Auschwitz to Germany just three months before liberation. How could one human being bear so much, encapsulate so much heartache into a few sentences? But as Nachman neared the last page of the letter a ray of hope:

> When I returned to Lodz, I found a job as a Polish typist at the Central Jewish Historical Commission on Narutowicza Street #25.... I had been managing by myself and living alone. I expected that this is how I would end my life. But fate demanded otherwise. I was working with a man, Abraham, from Krakow. He was the Yiddish typist here, in my place of employment, and he fell in love with me. I did not believe that I could be happy ever again ...
>
> We love each other and we were married on December 12, 1945. He is a decent man and has a noble soul. He is a copy of my Benjamin. I am happy with him. He respects me. He is young—36 years old. Everyone in the office likes him. He has many friends.
>
> Abraham wants to leave [Poland] but I am holding it up. I want to see you, your beloved wife and your little girl. Your friend, Rzezak, said that you have a beautiful child. Krybus, another of your friends who already returned from the Soviet Union, also said the same thing.
>
> Please live well and be happy my dears and write to me. In the next letter I will send you our photos.
>
> We must forget about everything. Now we have a new life, we are starting over ...

Nachman stared at the coal wagons outside the window and dropped the pages. They drifted down and scattered on the floor beneath the chair.

How long have I been sitting here? Nachman asked himself after what seemed like hours. Dora must have gone to visit Genia, he thought. Good. She doesn't need to see me like this. Then a thought floated into his consciousness: Rosa is alive! She's alive! We must leave immediately and get to Lodz before her new husband convinces her to leave.

By the time Dora came home Nachman was more composed, but she sensed immediately that something awful had happened. The red rims and puffiness around his eyes suggested the rumours that had been circulating recently might have been true. When Anetka climbed into his lap, he didn't bounce her in the usual horsy ride and his face showed only the faintest hint of a smile.

"Yes, they are gone, all of them, except for my sister, Rosa. You will like her," Nachman confirmed Dora's suspicions without ceremony and listed his murdered relatives in a flat voice Dora hardly recognized.

"Oh, Nachman ... what can I say?" She embraced him and held him for a long while. "Life has become so cheap, so ephemeral," she added.

"No, it isn't ... it didn't have to be this way," he said. "Let's go back as soon as we can. Maybe we'll find some of your relatives."

In the days that followed, Nachman couldn't shake the devastating blow. It crushed his insides and suffocated his dreams of a joyful family reunion. At the most unlikely times the phrases he'd memorized—"alone like a fencepost," "we must forget everything"—tortured him like the refrain of a song one cannot forget. They frayed his nerves and took away his sleep. Images of his brothers, sisters, nieces, and nephews swirled before his eyes and he wasn't sure if he was sleeping or awake. He heard Isser's pleas to run with him and Yankel's refusal to let him go. "Whatever happens, we'll stay together as a family. We will live together, or die together."

A bitter lump choked Nachman's throat each time their parting scene came to his mind. Where did that thinking get them? If only I had had more time … if only I had been more persuasive … at least Isser would have been saved. He could not imagine this, a world without his family and friends. It was too terrible to contemplate and impossible not to. As he went to sleep, waves of guilt washed over him and threatened to overwhelm him. His heart pounded trying to break out of his chest. His hands were sweaty. He had wanted so much to share with all of them his happiness with Dora and Anetka and the baby on the way. Yes, he resolved, they must rush to Lodz to find Rosa and search for the remnants of his wide circle of friends. *Maybe others are safe,* he thought, *they couldn't all be gone, wiped out as if they never existed.* A compulsion to search for them overcame him. *Perhaps they were lost in the confusion of war,* he thought, remembering how they had lost and found Bloyfarb on their march toward Warsaw.

Nachman envisioned the meetings with his school chums. They would bump into one another unexpectedly on the street. He would be walking Piotrkowska Street with a stroller and the new baby and he would see Janek coming toward him from around a corner sporting his navy beret, slanted at a jaunty angle. He would whistle their traditional greeting. Janek would run toward him and they would hug, a long bear hug—something they never did before. Bundists didn't hug; it seemed too bourgeois then, but now? Now things would be different.

Dora jostled his arm and snapped him out of his daydream. "Nachman, the train seems to be coming to a stop. Get the teapot and be ready to jump down and catch the drippings off the locomotive." She was thankful for this trickle of warm water. Without it she could not wash Anetka on the interminable boxcar journey to Poland. It was all but impossible to get seats on passenger trains deluged by the displaced. There were no regular train schedules. The war had left equipment and rail lines damaged, even destroyed. Troops returning from the front occupied the few trains still running.

Dora's belly, swollen with late pregnancy, made it hard
to move. They slept on the floor of the boxcar. Seeing Dora's
delicate state, others in the car let them take the quieter
corner, away from the cracks in the boards that let in wind,
light, and rain. The five weeks of the journey felt as if it were
months. Word that they were nearing their first stop in
Poland, Auschwitz, sickened Dora. The very name of the town
featured in most rumours, gave her chills, but she felt the baby
moving and knew that it wouldn't be long before the child
pushed its way into the world. Giving birth in the cattle car
would be unthinkable. *But not here, please not here,* she prayed.
Nachman knew they'd have to change trains at the Auschwitz
stop as the tracks past the border were of a different gauge.

When she wasn't thinking of feeding Anetka or how they
would manage with the new baby, Dora was thinking about
her mother and three sisters in Warsaw. *What had become of
them?* She hadn't received any news and maybe that was good.
She pushed aside any idea that they had met the same fate as
Nachman's family. She couldn't wait to get to Warsaw, just as
soon as she gave birth, to look for hers.

For now her destination in Poland would be Lodz,
Nachman's city. Dora had never been there and didn't relish
the thought. She knew no one there. All she knew about it
was that the place was as smog-filled with the effluents of the
factory chimneys as Manchester, England. She hadn't been
there either, but it was what folks said. It was strange to hear
Nachman speak of his city; he loved it with a passion. It was
hard for her to understand why. The only reason to go there
when they arrived in Poland would be to stay with Rosa,
Nachman's lucky sister who had survived hell on earth. But
then Dora reminded herself that her sister-in-law was not
fortunate at all. She had lost not only her husband, but also
her baby. *If that happened to me,* Dora thought, *I wouldn't want
to live.*

༄

Anetka woke up on her first morning in Lodz confused and on the verge of tears. The harsh wool blanket rubbed against her sweaty cheek and chafed it raw. She was not in the boxcar anymore and not in her familiar home in Kyzyl Kyia either. It was that place where her auntie Rosa was supposed to be but wasn't.

She sat up on the cot and rubbed her eyes with her fists. "Mama, Mama where are you?" she called out, but then she turned her head and found Mama sitting doubled over on the rickety chair next to the pot-bellied stove. It was all starting to come into focus. Anetka remembered how the night before they arrived at curfew in Lodz and how the lady who looked like an old witch slammed the door in their faces and said Auntie Rosa didn't live there anymore. Then Mama found this huge lady with a rifle on her shoulder and she was kind and let them spend the night in the guardhouse on her little metal cot.

"Mama, why are you moaning?" Anetka wanted to climb into Mama's lap and put her arms around her neck.

"Not now, Anetka, give me a few minutes. I'll feel better soon," Mama said in a strange voice as if she couldn't breathe, then she let out a loud scream. Anetka started to cry. The Soviet guard opened the door and immediately saw what was happening.

"*Vash mladenets prikhodit!*" Your baby is coming!

"I have no idea ... where to go," Dora managed to utter between contractions.

"There is a shelter nearby for Jewish refugees. There is an infirmary there."

Anetka's Mama moaned and shut her eyes.

"*Gde vash muzh?*" Where is your husband? the guard asked.

"He stayed behind at the Auschwitz station trying to get on the train with our sack of salt. It's all we brought with us."

The matron raised her eyebrows.

"They wouldn't let him on the passenger train with us. The trains are too —" The explanation was drowned out by another scream. "… too crowded. He only managed to get me and my girl on." The tiny guardhouse seemed as if it would explode with the poor woman's agony and the wailing of the little girl.

Shortly, Anetka found herself in a large room filled with cots. They stretched from one end where a narrow metal bed was jammed right under the tall window, all the way to the other side where a thick door had slammed before and where Mama had disappeared. It seemed strange that so many people would sleep in one room. A woman sat at the edge of Anetka's cot and stroked her hair. "Here is a hankie, wipe your eyes, little one," she said in a friendly voice.

"I want my mama." Anetka pushed away the woman's arm because she looked scary with those red rims around her eyes. "Where is she? Where is she?" Anetka's questions became more insistent and high pitched. Her lower lip trembled. The flood of tears was about to begin anew. The woman stood up and smoothed her dress. Like a yoke, the weight of the war sat on her sloping shoulders.

"Wait just one minute. I have something for you."

Walking to her own cot and reaching into her knapsack, the woman pulled out a tattered rabbit whose only sign of a former happy life were pinkish grey ears. The woman stood for a minute holding the toy, hesitating. "Here, you can play with this. It used to be my daughter's," she said.

"Where is she?" Anetka looked around, but couldn't see any little girls nearby. The woman squeezed her eyes shut, then turned around abruptly, spoke to an old woman lying on a nearby cot with a compress on her head: "Keep an eye on this child. Her mother is in the infirmary giving birth. I have to get some fresh air."

"What a bad time to bring a child into this world," the old woman said. In a few minutes Anetka curled up with the rabbit and fell asleep. Little sighs issued from her small chest as if she were still remembering her Mama's screams.

∽

Nachman was overcome with guilt, but what could he have done? Leave the salt? It was all they owned. He had hoped to sell it to have a few zloty before he found some work. And now what? He felt like an utter failure. No conductor would allow him to board the packed trains. He had heard that now Poles, not Germans, were killing Jews, especially on the trains. One had to be careful.

In the end, he left the sack leaning against the side of the train station. He had to get to Lodz as fast as humanly possible. He hadn't wanted to leave Dora alone, but she was so close to giving birth! He found the building at 4 Narutowicza Street where Rosa was supposed to be, but discovered that she was gone. Where can Dora and Anetka be now? It boggled his mind to think they had found no shelter with Rosa. A cold sweat covered his forehead. Where? Where are they? He walked out dazed into the street and met some people, talked with them briefly and was directed to the Jewish shelter. Everyone but he seemed to know where it was.

The shelter building was a beehive of activity. Raggedy children with dirty faces and runny noses chased one another and ran up and down the stairs. A woman in a long grey apron swept the landing, pushing the dust into the stairwell. As Nachman ascended the staircase he could smell the overpowering odour of cabbage. Though he had had nothing to eat, the smell made him woozy. He heard cries and sounds of loud voices coming from the second floor. He bumped into a man running down the stairs. "It's getting too crowded here," the man yelled. Nachman had heard that huge numbers of surviving Jews were streaming back into the city because now Lodz functioned as the de facto capital of Poland. Unlike Warsaw, the Germans had not levelled it; they used it as their base of operations.

Nachman heard people saying that the American Joint Distribution Committee was providing assistance to returning Jews. Most likely they were supporting this shelter. *Bless the Americans*, Nachman thought and climbed up two stairs at a time. A woman in a nurse's uniform sat at the desk in the hallway of the second floor.

"Do you need a bed?" she asked.

"Well, no, not right now. I am looking for my wife and daughter. The name is Libeskind. Are they staying here?" The woman scanned a long register of names running her finger down the lined sheet of paper.

"Yes. The little girl is there." The woman pointed to the large door at the end of the hall.

"But my wife, where is she?" Nachman asked with alarm in his voice. There was a tight lump in his throat.

"She is in the next building."

"Why? Why isn't she with my daughter?" The woman gave Nachman a quizzical look.

"Don't you know?"

"What, what? What happened?" Beads of sweat formed on Nachman's forehead and he wiped them with the back of his hand. The woman started laughing.

"She gave birth this morning. Congratulations. You have a son," she said breezily and it was clear that she would have nothing more to say.

Nachman stood there speechless. It wasn't a surprise that there would be a child in the near future, but now? Today? Somehow he hadn't expected that. A million thoughts at once flooded his brain, his head was spinning; his knees buckled. He imagined Dora would be upset that she had to do this alone and leave Anetka with strangers. *Will she ever forgive me? Where will we live now that Rosa is gone?* Nachman touched his empty pocket absentmindedly. *I have to register with the Jewish agency in case anyone is looking to see if I'm alive. Maybe I will find some survivors on their registers.* And then back to the immediate dilemma: *a baby, a baby, can I borrow a cradle from someone?*

What am I doing? He stopped himself and shook his head. *Have I lost my mind? I have to get Anetka, then find Dora and meet my son.* A son? He couldn't picture himself as a father of a boy. He had gotten so used to his baby girl and so thrilled with her. He had no idea what it would be like to bring up a boy. He wasn't like the men he knew. He had always wanted a daughter first and felt proud of his skills as a parent of a girl.

As soon as she spotted her father Anetka shrieked with joy and ran to him with her hands raised. He lifted her into the air and hugged her. She clung to his neck and kept chirping, "Papa, Papa where have you been? Where is Mama?"

"We are going to see her right now and your baby brother too."

"I don't have a brother," she said and scrunched her nose. "You are funny, Papa," she said and continued holding on to his neck. He felt her warm breath on his skin. Fortunately the May day had been unusually warm. He didn't need to waste time looking for her coat. They could walk out right away and hurry to see Dora. Nachman carried Anetka to the building across the courtyard. As soon as he stepped inside he could smell the disinfectant. *Well, at least it's clean*, he thought. He walked down a long hallway to the desk with a young nurse wearing a surprisingly white uniform.

"A new father?" she asked cheerfully. "Follow me."

When they arrived at a small window she said, "Wait right here. Someone will bring out the baby in a moment." Anetka tugged at his arm. "Papa, where is Mama? I want to see her now."

"Just a moment, first we'll see your brother." The window opened and a heavy-set nurse held up a baby, packaged tightly in a white blanket.

"Here is your son. He's a feisty one," she commented as the baby wailed. Only his head was visible. He looked angry. His little cheeks were puffed out and his mouth stretched in a piercing cry.

"Papa, why is he screaming?"

"Maybe he is hungry."

"Give him back. I don't want him. His face is too red," Anetka said, a final opinion that could not be reversed.

"That's not nice," Nachman said and turned to the nurse who was rocking the baby in a futile effort to calm him. "Where is my wife?"

"Turn left at the end of the hall. It's the first room on the right."

He floated down the hall. *What will we do? We have no place to live. Where will I take Dora and the children?* He was so preoccupied with his impossible situation that he couldn't hear Anetka's words. He opened the door and saw Dora lying in bed with her eyes closed. She looked drawn and exhausted. With her belly now flattened she looked so small. What did she weigh now? Less than 100 pounds for sure. He was glad that Anetka was quiet. He didn't want to wake Dora. He approached the bed and was startled by how crisp and white the bedding looked. They hadn't slept in a bed for five weeks. These past years had made him forget what it felt like to curl up in bed with clean bedding. He stroked Dora's forehead. She opened her eyes.

"Mama!" Anetka climbed onto the bed. Dora smiled wanly, reached for her and said in a barely audible voice, "Come here, baby." But Anetka noticed the small green apple sitting on the night table. "Mama, can I have the apple?"

"Yes. Go ahead and take it." Anetka slid off the bed and ran around it grabbing the apple and attempting to sink her tiny teeth into its unyielding skin.

"Dora, we have a son," Nachman said and kissed her forehead.

"I know," she said, but he couldn't tell if she was angry with him for his absence.

"I am sorry. I had no way to know about Rosa."

But Dora only pointed to the clock on the wall across her bed. "It's feeding time, they will be bringing the baby in a minute. Take Anetka and see if you can find a place for us. I can't … I can't go to that shelter again."

Nachman walked out into the street dazed, his mind roiling with all the pressing priorities. He had to find a home for his family, to get Dora out of that shelter and yet his thoughts kept circling to searching survivor registers. Anetka tugged at his arm wanting to play, distracting him. Her chirping got in the way of sorting things out. He wasn't even sure where he was headed when he passed the city hall.

It occurred to him that he might as well stop there to register his son's birth and obtain a birth certificate. Yes, that would be something practical, tangible and would give him time to plot his next moves. Dora had wanted to name the baby David after her father and Nachman went along with her choice. It didn't seem to make much difference, the boy would be what he was destined to be no matter what the name.

He went upstairs to the appropriate office and approached a clerk in the records department. "Good afternoon," he said to the woman seated behind a metal desk. The rows of file cabinets behind her made him wonder how many records of children who died during the war were stored there. The woman didn't look up. Nachman coughed to make his presence known. Why hadn't she noticed Anetka bouncing up and down?

The woman glanced at him, but continued shuffling some papers. "Why are you here?" she asked as if he were mistaken about the business of the office.

"I want to register the birth of my son."

"Here," she handed him a small sheaf of papers. "Fill these out in triplicate," she instructed him and pointed to a row of metal chairs against the wall. Nachman was glad that he thought to put a fountain pen in his pocket and glad that the ink hadn't leaked out.

He balanced the papers on his lap and tried to write as neatly as possible given the awkward surface of his knees. Then he approached the woman and handed her the papers. She read them with a grimace on her face. *What's wrong?* Nachman wondered. *Does she have a toothache?*

Her furrowed brow told him something was amiss. "I can't accept this," she spit out.

"Why? What's wrong? Have I made an error?"

"Certainly," she said. "I can't accept such a Jewish name. David? What were you thinking?"

"This is a name we have chosen for our son."

"I won't allow it," she said with finality that made Nachman sure it would do no good to argue. He already knew that disputing the decisions of communist functionaries could bring unwanted attention.

It was just a name! Could a name, in and of itself, be threatening? A bitter taste rose to his mouth. His temples began to pound. It was good that Anetka ran down the corridor and chatted with the cleaning woman, fascinated by the mop as it made wet swirls on the floor. Nachman contemplated his choices. I can leave and get into an argument with Dora about choosing another name, or I can come up with something similar—a name this bigot may not recognize as Jewish. Nachman stood before the desk still holding the pen in his hand, but the clerk was back at her papers and paid no attention to him.

He cleared his throat to get her attention. "What now?" she asked.

"I would like another set of forms," he said politely. She looked skeptical and handed him the papers without looking up again. Nachman sat on the chair at the back of the office and thought hard. He tried to recall all the Jewish male names that began with the letter *D*.

I must at least retain the D, he thought. Dov came to mind first. *No, that name means "bear" in Hebrew.* No one in the family was huge and hairy. *That won't work*, he thought nervously. He discarded it. Now a string of Yiddish boys' names crowded his brain. Strangely they were all animals: Hershel, "little deer"; Beyrl, another "bear"; Volf, "wolf." *No, no,* he chastised himself. *This isn't a game. I am looking for a* D. And then it came to him—Daniel. Silently, he repeated the name to himself several times and liked the sound of it. Then he thought of Daniel in the lion's den. Yes, that was a good name and it began with a *D*, *D* like his Dora and her father. His son would be brave and survive whatever obstacles life threw his way. It wasn't so much a thought as a decision.

He stood up and walked back to the clerk's desk. She took the papers from him, glanced at them and a hint of a smile passed her face ever so briefly. She stamped the documents, gave him change from the fee he paid and went back to her work. Nachman was satisfied, but he couldn't tell if she was an anti-Semite for rejecting David as his son's name. Perhaps she was even Jewish herself and had seen so many Davids murdered in the recent past that she wanted this child, born to a new age, to begin life with a name that would not immediately announce his identity to those that may want to destroy him. These days it was hard to say who was an enemy and who was a friend.

Nachman's next order of business was to visit one of the many offices set up by Jewish organizations, such as the American Joint Distribution Committee and the Central Committee of Polish Jews, to maintain registers of survivors who returned to Poland in search of relatives. He walked into the nearest one and spoke to the man in charge, an old Jew in a worn-out jacket. One by one Nachman called out the surnames of his friends. He already knew about his family.

"No, no, I am afraid this one isn't on my list either," the man said time and again. He was up to the *M*s.

"What about Malinowski, Janek?"

"Malinowski, Malinowski," the man said slowly. "Wait, wait, that one sounds familiar. He may be alive. Let me get the other list."

Nachman's hair stood up at the nape of his neck. The man seemed to have miraculous powers to declare people dead or alive. Where did he get such authority? The minutes seemed to stretch into infinity. The man licked his finger and shuffled through the pages. "Oh, here it is. He *is* alive. Here's his address," he said scribbling a note and handing Nachman a scrap of paper. "But I can't promise you he is still there," the man said. "People seem to be in transit almost daily these days. Everyone seems to want to get out of here," he added.

"Well, I just returned and have no intention of going anywhere," Nachman said. "This is my city."

"Suit yourself," the man said skeptically. "But harbour no illusions that your neighbours will be happy to see you."

No wonder Dora says I was born with a lucky caul, Nachman thought. To find a Medem School classmate alive filled him with such relief that his knees practically buckled. He couldn't even hear all this negative stuff the man was spouting. "Thank you, thank you," he said as if the man were responsible for saving Janek's life.

When Nachman rang Janek's bell and stood before him in the flesh, both men were drunk with joy. Momentarily, the fact that both were alive obliterated the miasma of death that each of them had been breathing in since their return. Anetka, the spitting image of her father, was a priceless gift in a city that had not seen living Jewish children for too many years. And a baby? A baby! Janek was thrilled out of his mind. "How lucky can a man get? First I found a place to live, then a job and now you with your angels?" Janek exclaimed. He picked up Anetka who seemed a bit wary and hugged her. "Let me go," she squirmed and Janek laughed putting her down. It had been a long time since Nachman had seen any of his friends laughing.

Janek and Sara were childless. They recently arrived in Lodz from their wartime hiding places. They wanted to get past their own ordeals, for who hadn't suffered since 1939 and who didn't dream of a better tomorrow? They had found one room at 4 Wieckowskiego Street. It was small with two tall windows that sat directly above the garbage bins in the courtyard below. It had no private toilet; a dozen families shared one at the end of a long dark hallway. Still, the apartment was near the centre of the city where Janek had been fortunate to get an office job, an amazing feat in a city where 80 per cent of the returning Jews were unemployed. Janek and Sara didn't plan to remain in Lodz for long. They only needed to scrape up enough money for passage out of Poland.

If it weren't for Janek's offer that Nachman bring his family to live with him and his wife in their one-room apartment, there was no telling what Nachman would have done. He was overwhelmed at the generosity of Janek's offer, but not surprised. All the Medem School students were as close to one another as siblings. Nachman would have done the same for him. Still, he asked Janek, "But how will we fit here, all of us? And what about a screaming baby at all hours?"

"Oy, Nachman, with the kind of crowding we experienced during the war when we were in hiding, this will be positively luxurious and the cries of a child—that will be music to our ears."

Only seven weeks after Nachman returned to Poland with his family, a new bloodbath shook every Jew's confidence in the community's safety. In the southeastern city of Kielce, some eighty miles from Lodz, Polish citizens, assisted by the local police, murdered forty-two and severely wounded another fifty Jewish Holocaust survivors on one day. Another thirty Jews were thrown to their deaths from trains, trying to leave, or to seek medical attention after the pogrom. The Kielce pogrom was not the beginning of the violence. In 1945, during a pogrom in Krakow, 345 Jews were killed at the hands of their Polish neighbours. Panic began to spread in the Jewish community. To Nachman, the brutality of the Soviet gulags began to seem insignificant. He had been spared the savagery of the Nazis, but now he was beginning to understand how the attitudes of the local population had made the realization of the Nazi plans possible.

Nachman pushed this new awareness to the back of his brain. *Those were evil people; the good ones must outnumber them*, he thought. These are the Poles with whom he decided to throw his and his family's lot. He had been on the run for seven miserable years and now he had a three-year-old and a newborn to worry about. And what about Dora? She was so frail and so depressed. And baby Daniel, sick with an ear infection, exhausted her. With no money for decent medical care, the poor child was already five months old and in constant pain, screaming non-stop. *No*, Nachman thought, *We are penniless; we can't become refugees again, wandering from country to country, town-to-town, awaiting charity and a visa to somewhere. To where? Some God- forsaken country where we are strangers again? Not now. We have no choice but to give Poland a chance.*

But Janek and Sara thought differently. None of their family members had survived, and they had no children. There was no reason to stay in a country that had been so hospitable to the Nazis. Janek and Sara dreamed of emigrating to Canada or any Western country that would let them in— and there weren't many. It seemed that the distaste for Jews who spoke that strange guttural language, wore odd black clothes, and prayed in synagogues wasn't unique to the Nazis. Janek told Nachman about his plan to escape from Poland, but stressed that leaving would not be easy. One had to have stamina, money, and contacts. Connections with smugglers and shady individuals who could secure false passports for a price were the key, but one could never tell if their promises were legitimate or brazen extortion. Chaos had become the new order. All of Lodz was a great transit camp with people flowing through it like a torrent of water.

After what should have been a glorious homecoming for those who sur-vived, Jews from parts of Poland, Germany, and the Soviet Union, streamed into Lodz. Since Lodz was one of the few cities that the Nazis hadn't destroyed, it functioned as the central point where people looked for survivors and registered their own status as living, so others might find them. Numbers in and of themselves were just cold facts devoid of emotion. But the fluctuating numbers of Jews in Lodz in the immediate post war period told a dramatic story. Just before the outbreak of the Second World War, there were 233,300 Jews living in the city, the second largest population in Poland. At the end of the war, when the Soviet military liberated it, there were only 877 living Jews remaining.

By June 1946, there were fifteen thousand Jews in Lodz, which became a temporary centre of resurgence of Jewish life in Poland. But by September 1946, horrified by the continued violence against survivors and bereft at not finding living relatives, thousands of Jews managed to make their way out of Poland. Some were smuggled to Palestine and to Greece with the assistance of the remnants of the Jewish Brigade that had been established with Churchill's approval in 1944. Others, like Rosa, exited via German displaced persons camps to go to the United States, Canada, or South America.

Saddled by a toddler and a sickly newborn, Nachman and his family were not among them.

On the day Janek and Sara left Lodz, Nachman and Dora rose early. They had no idea when they would see their dear friends again, if ever, and wanted to see them off in style. Nachman noticed that Dora put on the only outfit that could pass for dressy: an old white blouse that she soaked to get out the milk stains, starched and ironed and a pleated navy skirt she borrowed from a neighbour down the hall. Nachman shined his worn shoes to a spit shine. Dora rushed around the room, shushing Anetka, changing Daniel's diaper and looking for cups that weren't chipped. The bustle did little to cover her anxiety. Now they would lose the only friends they had in this city.

Dora offered Sara and Janek coffee and surprised them with a small pitcher of cream she'd bought on credit.

"I thought you drink tea in the morning," Sara said.

"Today is different, we want you to ... to—" Dora said quietly.

"To what? What do you mean, Dora?" Janek asked, arching his eyebrows.

"To leave knowing we are okay."

Under normal circumstances Dora was clever with words, but to Nachman today she seemed at a loss. He felt that way, too. He was not demonstrative. How could he express the gratitude in his heart?

Dora bundled up Daniel and tried to convince Anetka to put on her warm tights. "I hate them," she screamed and burst out crying.

"But don't you want to take Janek to the station?" Nachman asked. A smile lit up the scrunched up little face and put a stop to the tantrum.

"Can I hold his hand?' she asked and ran toward the door pulling Janek's arm, tear tracks still on her face. All six of them boarded the tram and made it to the train station in plenty of time. When the train began pulling out of the station, Janek raised the compartment window and stuck his head out. His few remaining hairs flew wild as the wind rearranged them. He yelled something to Nachman as the train gained speed. The chugging of the locomotive, the shouts of the crowds at the station, and the high-pitched train whistle made it difficult to make out what Janek was shouting: "Look under the mattress when you get home!"

When they returned to the one-room apartment that had belonged to their friends, but now was theirs, it seemed eerily quiet and large. The absence of people who had sheltered them and shared everything they had was palpable. Lodz was a hollow vessel.

The metal bed where Janek and Sara had slept was neatly made up with its thin blue bedspread; the depression in its centre was shaped like the bodies of its former occupants. Nachman lifted up the heavy horsehair mattress and reached under it. There was a rustling of paper. What is this? He pulled out an envelope and looked at Dora who stood silently next to him. The envelope contained cash and a brief note: "Use this to settle in. Be well! Till we see each other again." Nachman stood speechless for a moment then counted the worn-out bills: more than a month of Janek's salary!

"Just like Janek," Nachman said, tears filling his eyes. "He knew we would never accept this if they had handed it to us in person."

"I only hope they kept enough cash to get to their destination—wherever that may be," Dora said. "They both worked so hard to earn this money."

Ever since he moved Dora and the children into Janek and Sarah's place weeks ago, Nachman's most urgent concern was to find a job. Each day he walked the streets of his beloved city searching for places where he might apply for work. Businesses that had been privately owned prior to the war were mostly shuttered. The government was in the process of taking them over. With the Soviets in control of Poland, private enterprise would become practically non-existent. As he covered every inch of the familiar city centre, he struggled to recapture the feeling of comfort he had once felt walking these very streets. In his mind's eye he saw Yankel strolling down Zachodnia Street from the Wielka Synagogue, with the prayer book tucked under his arm. As Nachman approached Lipowa Street, he remembered how Jadwiga ran toward him one day in June right on that very block, her gauzy skirt lifted by the spring breeze. When he turned the corner at Cegielniana Street toward the Medem School, he could almost hear Isser shouting to his friends as they tossed a homemade ball of tightly rolled rags, tied with string. It was impossible to comprehend that they all had vanished. Even the sound of a factory whistle couldn't dispel his sense of disconnection. The air was thick and his limbs moved slowly.

He crossed Plac Kościelny (Church Square) and to his utter shock Nachman came face to face with Davidson, his former boss at the very last job he had held as the war scrambled their lives. For a moment the two men stared at one another uncomprehendingly.

"You are alive," Davidson choked out the words slowly and extended his hand.

"Yes, I am," Nachman replied. The assertiveness of his own voice surprised him. It was as if he were putting a stake in the blood soaked Polish soil and affirming his presence. "Yes, I am," he repeated.

"How did you manage ...?" Davidson didn't need to complete his question. It was something of a new greeting. Everyone began a conversation with it.

"You know I escaped to the Soviet Union, your wife must have told you. She was practically the last person I saw before I escaped."

"Nachman, I am so grateful to you. I owe my survival to you in large measure. I didn't know if I would ever have a chance to thank you."

"Why thank me? I wasn't here."

"Remember the bolts of fabrics you rescued from Boltz's grasp?"

"Sure I do," Nachman replied, smiling at the memory of his ride in the droshky, hugging the bolts so they wouldn't roll out onto the pavement.

"My wife sold them to pay for her and our daughter's escape from Lodz and for their false Polish papers. If it weren't for those silks and woollens ..." Davidson's voice trailed off.

With the essential information exchanged they got onto the present reality.

"So do you still have your shop?" Nachman asked. Davidson laughed in a sardonic way. Nachman had never seen that side of him.

"Now it's all a part of the state, but I am working. I got a job as an accountant at Centrala Tekstylna (Textile Central) on Moniushki Street. They knew I'd know how to evaluate fabrics, their cost and quality. That's why they hired me. Not many are left who know the business inside out as I do."

"Lucky for you," Nachman said genuinely glad that Davidson found employment.

"You know, Nachman, each morning a long line of job seekers forms in front of my office building. If I were you, I'd get on it. Maybe something will eventually turn up. I'll vouch for your experience in the business." Davidson gave him a wink and they parted.

Nachman knew that Centrala Tekstylna was a huge enterprise dealing with the city's enormous textile production that had blossomed at the end of the nineteenth century. Tsar Alexander I encouraged this growth when he visited in 1825 because it employed large numbers of people, many of whom became residents of the Russian Empire as a result of the 1815 Treaty of Vienna. By the end of the nineteenth century, Lodz was the fastest growing and most industrialized city in Poland. After the war, Centrala Tekstylna managed textile production branches across Poland and was responsible for sales of its products. It employed more than five thousand employees.

The day after he ran into Davidson, Nachman rose at dawn. He tried to dress quietly so as not to wake the children. Dora had barely gotten Daniel to sleep. If he woke him, the shrieking would unsettle Nachman's nerves. Today he needed to be calm. He looked around for something decent to wear. Always a natty dresser, Nachman despaired at the state of his wardrobe. His only clothes were the ones he wore when they left Kyzyl Kyia, plus a couple of rumpled shirts stuffed in the small bundle they carried. The only jacket he had was one left behind by Janek. Its sleeves were too short, but it was all Nachman could wear to give himself an air of professionalism. He glanced in the small bevelled mirror that Sara had left behind on the dresser and saw a face he hardly recognized. He combed his hair carefully and noticed how much thinner it had become since he met Dora and even then his hairline had begun to recede.

When he arrived at the large edifice on Moniushki Street the line already wound around the block. Dispirited men stood in line silently, every so often shuffling forward at a snail's pace. Whenever a man finally made it into the building, he entered full of hope that a job offer was imminent. Nachman took his place and contemplated what he would say in an interview. But by the end of the day the line hadn't become much shorter. A guard emerged from the building, giving the men in line their place numbers and instructed them to return the next day.

Each day Nachman got a bit closer to the door that led to the personnel office. On some days, he saw a man emerge from the building in the distance. People said this was the personnel director—a tall, stout man in a suit. Many rushed toward him with questions whenever he appeared. On the third day Nachman made it to the building, then through the door, then into the personnel office. He strode in and stood before the desk of the official who would decide his fate. The personnel director stared at him. He drilled his penetrating gaze into Nachman and made him very uncomfortable. Nachman felt as if he were about to undergo another NKVD interrogation. He didn't like how this was turning out. When he had finally made it into the building he'd been hopeful. Now he was nervous. *Why is he looking me over so intently?* Nachman wondered.

After what seemed like eternity, the man squinted and leaned forward, "Nachman?" he asked.

"Yes," Nachman responded slowly, growing more anxious.

"Pśia krew, cholera jasna," the man uttered a string of Polish profanities. "Don't you recognize me?"

"I'm ... I'm sorry, I don't." Nachman now looked at the man more carefully and had an itch of recognition, but it didn't amount to much.

"Who taught you semaphore signals in the prison on Gdanska Street?" the man asked and his lips upturned to form a smile.

"No, it can't be." Nachman was now the one staring.

"Yes. I think you know," the man said.

"Oh, Antoni!" Nachman exclaimed. "It's you—Antoni Russak!" He was shocked, but now he began to discern that middle-age paunch hid the skinny communist who had been his friend in prison. The salt and pepper in Antoni's jet-black hair, which by now was much thinner, made it clear that time had passed. Nachman remembered him as a skin-and-bones, chain-smoking crooner who could belt out revolutionary songs when the prison guards were not within earshot. It all started to make sense. As a communist, Antoni was now very much in favour, not like before the war when the right-wing Polish government threw him in the Gdanska Street prison.

Antoni pushed back his chair and came around the desk to hug Nachman. He embraced him like a bear. Then he put his hand on Nachman's shoulder and said, "Come with me." Together they walked in silence past a line of job applicants and down a long hallway to the office of the director general of Centrala Tekstylna. Neither man wanted to betray their connection. Antoni opened the door without knocking and announced with flourish, "This is my friend, Nachman. Give him a good job. This is a man who stands up for his beliefs. He is the kind of man we need in the new Poland."

After a brief interview, Nachman was hired as a manager at the company's headquarters. The division he was to join had an immense administrative scope. Nachman himself would be responsible for an office of one hundred employees and have at his disposal thirty typists to do the clerical work. Because it was a government job the salary was low, but compared to his status as a refugee in his own city, it was a dream come true. At that moment he felt happy and blessed, but a feeling that this couldn't last nagged him. He had become all too familiar with a communist regime in its very cradle.

Nevertheless, with a job in hand, Nachman felt like a man. He would be able to provide for his family.

In time Dora opened a tiny corset shop across the street from the apartment that was Janek and Sara's legacy. With the small amount of cash they had left and Nachman's new job, the family's economic outlook began to improve little by little. Dora hired a young woman from the countryside to look after the children with her first earnings. Now she could spend more time designing the women's undergarments that were not available in stores. Lingerie shops were non-existent in post-war Poland. The only way for women to get a decent corset or a brassiere was to have it made to measure. Dora had started her own corsetry business in Warsaw before the war, when she was just eighteen. She was an expert designer and seamstress. After the war, working in a small sublet space in a tailor's shop, she quickly built up a clientele and generated more income than Nachman.

It didn't take her long to build a loyal customer base that allowed Dora to rent her own small workshop on Jaracza Street. Her work was lonely and difficult, and she had to fight off corrupt government officials on a regular basis. Private enterprise in communist Poland was discouraged and shop owners, like Dora, were not permitted to hire employees. Her hours were long. She did everything herself: create the designs, buy the fabrics and notions, cut the patterns, take customers' measurements, schedule fittings and sew the garments. Her work was considered to be the finest in the city and her clientele included actresses from the nearby theatre and the wives of party officials. A few of her clients eventually became Dora's friends. Maria was one of them. A tall, handsome Polish woman with abundant blond hair, she had an aristocratic bearing and a love of literature that she shared with Dora. They would meet for an afternoon tea on many Sundays and spend hours talking. They never ran out of topics to discuss and confided in one another with a depth of mutual understanding that each treasured.

Dora's business success prompted relentless visits from intimidating government tax inspectors. She handled the harassment with a skill acquired from life under communism in Kyrgyzstan, but she paid a heavy toll. Migraines and ulcers plagued her daily. She would come home late, often just in time to say good night to the children and immediately lay on the bed with a compress on her head. Compared to his wife's job, Nachman's was easy. But there was one saving grace in their unequal work lives. Nachman, brought up with the Bundist principles of gender equality, did not resent Dora's success at making more money than he did. Sometimes he tried to improve Dora's disposition by joking about the wet cloth she applied to her aching head. "You look like an Indian, I should take a picture of you now," he would say.

She would growl and say, "You are an insensitive boor," but her soft tone and half smile made it clear she didn't mean it. He did worry about her bouts of pain, but was unable to cope with illness. He made light of her spells not because he didn't believe her or lacked compassion, but because it was the only way he knew how to handle them.

It is entirely likely that many of Dora's physical symptoms were a manifestation of deep psychic pain. Her search in Warsaw for the remnants of family yielded nothing. The entire city was reduced to rubble. The street where her family had lived was devoid of life, populated by ghosts. Her mother, three youngest sisters, countless aunts, uncles, and cousins were erased as though they had never existed. Nachman, by contrast, whose family had suffered a similar fate, had a font of inner resources to cope with the loss that Dora lacked. It may have been also a matter of their basic natures: Nachman was a child of the sun, while Dora was the daughter of the storm. He always saw the glass as filled with milk and honey. She saw it filled with bitter tea. And now after the humiliating experiences of the war and the losses the brew was more bitter than ever.

Since his arrival in Lodz, Nachman continued to comb registers of survivors regularly. He went from office to office to scour survivor lists: the Jewish Agency, the Displaced Persons Registers, the Central Jewish Committee, the American Jewish Joint Distribution Committee, and the Red Cross were daily stops, but no one he had known turned up, other than Janek.

He still had no word from Rosa. Though he was thrilled to find out that she had survived, now to his utter frustration he lost track of her. All he could hope for was that one day when she found a hospitable country she would contact him again.

By 1948 the family settled into a routine, which gave order to their days and helped fill the void in their souls. Their lives were becoming economically stable, but the emotional vacuum could not be filled, no matter how hard they tried to shrink their expectations to meet the new reality.

Nachman had taken to making regular visits with the children to the Jewish cemetery. It was one of the largest Jewish cemeteries in Europe. Nachman had often said his parents had the good sense to die before the Holocaust, sparing them the nightmare and pain of losing three children and six grandchildren. Their graves were still there. Nachman desperately wanted his children to know their grandparents. By showing Anetka and Daniel his parents' resting places and ways to tend their graves, he hoped to instill a sense of connection to their roots. True, they were only seven and four, but who knew what might happen later? *Better start them young*, he thought.

"Always remember that your *bubbe* Rachel Leah is here and so is your *zayde* Chaim Chaskel. I want you to promise me to always care for their graves."

"We will," they answered in unison, Daniel parroting his sister.

"When your grandmother died I made sure to have her name inscribed using the European alphabet, not just Hebrew. This way her descendants can find her headstone even if they don't know Hebrew or Yiddish. Do you understand?" The children looked at him earnestly and nodded. They weren't sure why, but they sensed this was more important to their father than anything else.

At first when they returned to Lodz, Nachman found the graves thickly overgrown with weeds, but still intact. It was a small miracle in a cemetery that became part of the Lodz ghetto. Still, many headstones had been destroyed by vandals and neglect. More than forty-three thousand Jewish victims of the Lodz ghetto were buried here in a field called Pole Gettowe (Ghetto Field).

Now whenever he brought Anetka and Daniel to the cemetery, they carried a small brush to clean the headstones and pruning clippers to cut down the weeds. It was the least they could do. Then he would take the children for a walk down the paths of the cemetery and point out the graves of Bundist leaders. An impressive one stood looking dignified, like a sculpture.

"Look, Anetka," Nachman had said. "See how this marble is shaped almost like a Polish letter *U* that has fallen sideways?"

"Yes, *Tatuś*. What is it?"

"It's the Yiddish letter *B*. And the next one, the vertical pillar, it's the Yiddish letter *U*, then there is the *N*, looking like a backwards *L* and the *D* looking like an *L* standing on its head."

Anetka laughed. Her bell-like voice carried in the silence of the cemetery, bouncing off the headstones. "And what is that *Tatuś?*"

"Together these letters spell *Bund*."

She looked at him puzzled.

"It's a group of people who fought to help working men and their families have better lives."

"I like them then," Anetka said and flitted off to pull weeds from nearby graves.

The Jewish Labor Bund's impressive pre-war strength was completely sapped. *With so many of its members and leaders dead, it cannot be revived*, Nachman thought. *Never*.

They continued their walk and Nachman stopped near a mausoleum whose temple-like majesty dwarfed the resting places of everyone else. It was erected for a famous industrialist, Poznanski, who owned one of the city's largest textile factories. Anetka looked up at the structure resembling a Greek temple, "*Tatuś*, who lives here?"

"No one. It's the burial place of a man who owned a huge factory. He was not very good to his workers."

"So he was not like the Bund?" Anetka asked wrinkling her nose. Her father smiled.

"Exactly."

"I don't like him," she said resolutely and skipped ahead.

Near the end of each visit he would take the children to look at the stone wall surrounding the cemetery and point out the hundreds of bullet holes left behind by the Nazis. The last stop always was the Ghetto Field where their relatives may have lain in unmarked graves, unless they had been reduced to ashes in crematoria elsewhere. *Who could ever know their horrific end*, Nachman always wondered, but put on a smiling face as he pointed out to Anetka and Daniel the acorns that had fallen from nearby trees. Happily, they ran to collect them until their pockets bulged.

"*Tatuś*, can we come again soon to get some more?" they asked.

The two incomes allowed the family to move to a one-bedroom apartment on Piotrkowska Street, the city's main thoroughfare. Once fashionable, it fallen into a state of neglect. Even by the standards of the day the apartment was small, but it was comfortable, with running cold water and only two flights of stairs to climb. At night, the front door still had to be secured with an outer metal door and a steel bar across it. The kitchen stove, much like the living room and bedroom stoves, had to be heated with coal. A hot-water heater was not installed until many years later. There was no proper bathtub other than a large metal bucket that had to be filled with water heated in a huge pot on the stove for the family's weekly baths. Taken in the centre of the kitchen, these baths were a ritual in which

Dora got the priority. She bathed first. Then she bathed the children quickly in the same water. But by the time Nachman's turn came the bath was lukewarm and soap scum ringed the edges of the bucket. It was too costly to use more coal to heat another pot of water. But as Dora's income increased so did the family's standard of living. They were able to hire a succession of nannies, and to rent summer cottages. As Anetka and Daniel got older, the family vacationed in Zakopane and resorts like picturesque Krynica-Zdrój, known for its therapeutic mineral waters.

Both Nachman and Dora emphasized achievement. They had instilled a love of books and music in their children from the earliest age. Anetka became a voracious reader and a top student in her class. Nachman decided early on that Daniel had an exceptional ear and that he would be the child to benefit most from musical education. He bought him the best brand of accordion and started Daniel on lessons when the boy turned six. Daniel was small for his age and the instrument almost covered him, but he took to it easily. Soon he was practising difficult classical pieces that were rarely, if ever, played on such a limited keyboard: Bach, Tchaikovsky, Mozart, and Beethoven. Nachman made sure that Daniel never missed his daily after-school practice sessions and that his son played the new pieces for him in the evenings. When Daniel played, Nachman was transported to his days of playing the bugle. Though he no longer had an instrument or time to play, Nachman was convinced that his son's ability to make music more than made up for any and all deprivations of the past. Nothing was sweeter to him than hearing the sounds of the red accordion reverberating off the walls of the small living room.

Nachman, always an extrovert, did his best to forge new relationships with coworkers in an attempt to rebuild a semblance of social life. But this was much more difficult for Dora, who was introverted and who did not like Lodz. She abhorred its greyness and lack of sparkle. She missed her sisters and longed for the culturally vibrant pre-war Warsaw. In Lodz she worked long hours and had fewer opportunities and less time to forge friendships. Maria was still her only close friend. Now even that relationship had dissolved in a pool of bitterness.

Dora and the children were spending the summer in a rented country cottage in Kolumna, fifteen miles from Lodz. Despite the inconveniences of country life, Dora wanted the children to breathe the air fragrant with pines. She loved nothing more than to lie on the blanket in the woods and look up at the tree canopy dappled with light while the children frolicked nearby. "There is no colour more beautiful than the green of nature," she would say. Nachman visited them only on weekends and always worried about Dora's and the children's safety while he stayed in the city on weekdays. He encouraged Dora to invite Maria to spend a few days in the country, and Dora was delighted when Maria decided to visit.

On the second night of her stay, drunken Poles banged on the cottage door well past midnight. The women and children awoke startled by loud and persistent pounding accompanied by shouts of obscenities. "Stinking Jews, open the door!" The threats became louder. "Open up, or we'll break down the door. We know you are in there!"

Maria jumped out of bed, crossed herself and said, "*Jezus Maria*, now I'll be killed because of these goddamn Jews." Then she clamped her hand on her mouth and stood there for a moment in her nightgown. Dora blanched. Maria's words were a stab at her heart. They had been so close and now this. Maria tried to apologize, "I ... I ... don't know what came over me. I am sorry."

Dora considered the possibility that fear chased the wicked words out of Maria's mouth, but it didn't matter. The words shattered her trust. And once trust was broken, it could not be repaired. After a while the thugs gave up and left, but Dora lay awake all night distraught much more over Maria's reaction than over the drunkards' behaviour. If such a good friend harboured an inner core of prejudice so close to the surface, what was there to say about the behaviour of indifferent Poles toward their Jewish neighbours when Nazi edicts sawed terror among the population? Did people like Maria give up her mother and her sisters? Would Maria have been one of those rare souls who hid Jews or would she have given Dora up in a minute, fearful of the Semitic look people claimed she had?

When morning came Dora asked Maria to leave. "But Dora, let me try to explain ..."

"Please, don't. I will never be able to look at you the same way. I will always see betrayal in your eyes."

Dora turned her back away from Maria. She was damned if she'd let Maria see the tears welling in her eyes.

The ugly display of anti-Semitism that lay just below the skin of many Poles did not end with the incident in the country. Just as Dora tried to bury Maria's duplicity, a source of deep psychic pain, Nachman experienced it at work. He was an excellent performer who had first-rate rapport with his supervisor, a sharp young woman, Wieslawa Olczak. She was certain that the top honours accruing to their division were due to the efficiency and smooth relationships among coworkers that Nachman encouraged and nurtured. She recommended him for a major promotion. This in itself was unusual, as few Jews employed at Centrala Tekstylna ever advanced.

The director general came into Nachman's office. Nachman looked up from his desk surprised, the old man rarely stepped out of his top-floor lair.

"To what do I owe the pleasure of your visit, sir?" Nachman set aside the folder in front of him and stood up to shake the man's hand. "Please, sit down," he added pulling out a chair.

"No, no I'm hurry, but I have good news for you, Libeskind."

"Yes?"

"You have done a stellar job. Mrs. Olczak, your supervisor, recommended that you be promoted to a director-level position."

Nachman smiled. "That is excellent news. I enjoy working with Mrs. Olczak. Please thank her and thank you for the confidence in—"

Before he could finish, the old man interrupted him. "There is one condition, however, before we can move forward."

"Oh? Please, tell me," Nachman raised his eyebrows. He couldn't imagine what it could be.

"I will come straight to the point: you must change your surname."

"My surname? But why?" Nachman uttered in total astonishment.

"It is ... ah ... it's, how shall I put it? It's unseemly to have such a Jewish-sounding name on the nameplate of a director."

"Well, I *am* a Jew."

"My point exactly."

The knot in Nachman's stomach tightened. Open displays of anti-Semitism were common in the streets among hoodlums, drunks, and indiscreet gossips. In offices and places of business such attitudes were not always so visible. Rather, they would come wrapped in euphemisms, innuendo, and false accolades: "You people are so good at managing money" was a favourite phrase. Nachman struggled to find the words to express his outrage, the direct assault on his very being rendered him nearly speechless. The boss shifted his stance uncomfortably waiting for a response.

Nachman spoke in the calmest voice: "I am sorry. Under these conditions I cannot accept the promotion." He turned toward his desk.

"Don't misunderstand, we really appreciate what you have done, we'd like to—"

"No, sir," now Nachman interrupted the boss. "Libeskind has been my name for generations. I intend for it to continue."

"Well, have it your way." The boss turned without saying goodbye and closed the door a touch too assertively.

Several months passed, but just as Nachman had given up hope of the promotion there was a change of heart somewhere in the hierarchy. Nachman received a letter advising him that the promotion had been approved. Though he had no way to know if anyone had interceded on his behalf, the incident strengthened Nachman's resolve to always be himself. Dora wondered out loud if Antoni may have had a hand in the reversal, but Nachman didn't think so. "Antoni always does things by the book," he told her.

"Except when he hired you," she laughed.

"It could have been Wieslawa," Nachman said. "I suppose we'll never know."

In truth, Antoni and his wife, Claudia, had become good friends with Nachman's family. Claudia was as broad as her husband and wore her greying hair in a distinctive upswept hairdo. A childless couple, they delighted in Anetka's and Daniel's antics. Sometimes the families vacationed together. During a rafting trip down the Dunajec River in the Pieniny Mountains, Antoni and Nachman stood teetering on the wooden raft as it went over rapids. Antoni sang at the top of his lungs the Yiddish songs Nachman had taught him in prison all those years ago. It was an unlikely duet, this huge Pole and slight Jew raising their voices on a river like a pair of Venetian gondoliers. Such friendships with the Polish people were as unusual as Nachman's complete trust in them.

As soon as he recovered from his quintuple-heart-bypass surgery in 1985, my father began discussing new travel ideas. "Ania, I would like for you to join me on a trip to Poland," he said, as we sat in Manor Park on a bench listening to the surf. He must have seen my grimace, because he stiffened and said, "I thought you liked travelling with me."

"It's not that," I said. "I really don't have any desire to return to Poland."

He couldn't comprehend my negative feelings toward Poland and we never really spoke about it, not in a way that could lead to understanding.

"But we haven't been back in twenty-eight years!" he said. The frustration and longing on his face were visible. His facial muscles tightened and he looked out into the sound as if he were already imagining himself flying over it.

"So what? There are so many places we haven't been," I said, avoiding telling him how I hated the idea.

"Ania, let me explain," he said slowly and deliberately, as if he were talking to a very difficult child. *"Ikh muz dortn gein."* I must go there, he said forcefully and I knew right then he would, no matter what.

Still, I asked, already knowing the answer, "But why?"

"All these years I have been wondering if my parents' graves have remained intact. Who will assume their care in the future if you don't even know how to find them?"

"Future," I said. "I'd have to go there more than once, then."

By now he sounded almost as if he were pleading. "Ania, these tombstones—if they are still standing—are a testimony to the existence of a once-vibrant Jewish life—our community."

I knew what he was thinking: his family's fate.

"I know, Tinek, I know. You want your parents' graves to stand for all the murdered Jews."

"Yes," he said and fell silent, staring at the water.

"I will think about it," I said.

It was unusually warm on that June day in 1956. The trees in Sienkiewicza Park were in full bloom. Nachman and Dora settled on a bench in the shade of an old oak tree and watched Daniel chasing Anetka down the manicured lanes laid out in Versailles style. It was a rare moment in which they could speak in Yiddish. Marysia, the maid who lived in their home, had the weekend off and they could communicate without resorting to the usual clipped Polish sentences, the code words, or facial expressions that might suggest they were conspiring.

Marysia was a good woman. There was no point in having her come under any suspicion just because she worked for a Jewish family. They never spoke Yiddish in front of her for fear of making her feel uncomfortable. They didn't want her thinking that they were speaking ill of her. They thought she was an exceptionally decent human being and never worried that she would report them to the authorities ever hungry for every morsel of private conversation. Their neighbours ... well, that was a different matter. People had to be highly circumspect in what they said, where, to whom, and in what tone. Even children in communist Poland knew that walls had ears.

In fact, on this Sunday, Nachman and Dora were having a conversation that would have been suspect had anyone overheard them. Every so often they swept the area around them with their eyes to make sure that no one was within earshot. "If they withdraw our permit to emigrate one more time, I'll—" Dora said.

"What? What will you do?" Nachman interrupted.

"I don't know. I can't take this game anymore," she replied.

"Look, we have to keep trying. Let's not give up. We have been through worse," Nachman reminded her.

"Maybe they heard that you refused to change your name," Dora speculated about the reason why for the fourth time the communist authorities had denied their exit application to Israel.

"Or it could be that the tax goons never find anything to hang you with. It must drive them crazy," he said and Dora began laughing.

"Why are you laughing, Dora?"

"Because if I didn't laugh, I'd cry. Our situation is so absurd," she said. "Why should we be held captive here? At least before the war one could come and go as one pleased."

"Shh," Nachman shushed her and pointed to a couple walking toward them in the distance.

Theoretically, it was possible for Jews to apply for exit visas to Israel. In practice, however, first approving, then often revoking these permits was a harassment tactic favoured by the communists. This was especially true for the handful of applicants who stood out in any way—owning a private workshop, like Dora's, or refusing to change the last name to a more acceptable Polish one, as Nachman had done. To maximize the provocation, the bureaucrats would wait until the families resigned their jobs, sold off belongings, and terminated leases on their apartments, then send out revocations in the eleventh hour.

The children ran around the park chasing the birds and each other. Dora watched them as she spoke with Nachman and admired how bright they looked in their matching sweaters and berets that Marysia had knitted. Each sweater was a complex weave of reds, greens, oranges, and blues that stood out against the grey buildings at the perimeter of the park. A pang of regret stabbed at Dora's heart. She wished she could spend more time with her children. How innocent and unsullied by the war they were! Most of all, she was tired of the repeated visa denials and starting over time and again, yet she knew Nachman was right. Eventually they had to let them out. She brightened at the thought of being reunited with her sisters and brothers in Israel, the ones who had emigrated from Poland when Palestine was still a desert wasteland in the 1920s.

Each time she and Nachman discussed the prospect of leaving Poland it was always mixed with a deep concern for the children. Daniel had become a virtuoso accordion player and it was no small honour that at age nine he'd become the youngest performer on the newly inaugurated Polish television station. Anetka brought straight-A report cards each year. How would their adjustment to a new country affect their achievements? They would likely do well, but it would not be easy for them. This was an unspoken worry for both parents. Yet Nachman and Dora desperately longed for the closeness of family and old friends, the ones that they had made as children—the kind one cannot replace. Despite their efforts to engage with a handful of friendly Poles, their lives were now empty of familial relationships, cherished old friendships, Yiddish literature and newspapers, theatre, and Jewish communal life. There was no family with whom to celebrate holidays or birthdays. No one who could truly understand the pain of their losses. The void was so vast that often it loomed like a chasm between them.

"I got tickets to see Chekhov's *Cherry Orchard* next week," Nachman said.

"I am glad. I haven't reread that play in ages," Dora said. "I am making a corset for the lead actress," she added, but by then Nachman had that faraway look in his eyes. She knew just where his mind had wandered. "Are you thinking of your performances in Ararat?"

"How did you know?"

"Haven't you told me a million times about your Yiddish acting group from before the war?"

"Sure, it was my obsession, but you know, it was mostly musicals. Nothing as serious as Chekhov."

"Still, I know how you miss it."

"Yes, that and the Yiddish newspapers we had before the war. I never thought I could start a morning without at least glancing at one," Nachman said.

"How many Yiddish newspapers did you have in Lodz?" she asked, having only been familiar with Warsaw's cultural scene.

"Oh, let me think … we had—" he counted off on one hand, then the other "—at least eighteen Jewish dailies and dozens of periodicals." Pride was written all over his face.

"What do we have now?" Dora asked.

"Does it matter? One, or two." He looked around and lowered his voice: "But they are communist rags."

They spoke of it rarely but each of them felt acutely the lack of a vibrant Jewish community. By the mid-fifties only 2 per cent of the Jewish population remained in Lodz and though the communist authorities sanctioned a limited number of Jewish activities, they were all sullied by the required propaganda and Stalinist party line. For Nachman who abhorred communism even before the war and tasted its practices in the Soviet Union any simulation of Jewish culture was distasteful.

In March 1957, Nachman and Dora obtained their long-awaited exit visas for Israel. Finally, the communist authorities had opened the door a crack! Nachman and Dora had known how the doors could slam shut at any moment so they hurried. Hastily ordered packing crates appeared in the apartment one day and soon they swallowed its contents. The children moped around the empty, echoing rooms. "Why do we have to leave, *Tata*?" Daniel asked his dad for the umpteenth time.

"Don't you remember? I already told you. We are going to the land of our ancestors—Israel. I am sure you will like it."

"But I don't have any friends there," Daniel pouted.

"Don't worry, you will make them fast."

"But you said they don't speak Polish, *Tata*?" Anetka chimed in.

"No, both of you will have to learn Hebrew."

"Hebrew? Is it similar to Polish?" Daniel asked.

"I am afraid not," Nachman replied, but thought that he and Dora wouldn't need to struggle with a new language. He expected they would be able to speak freely in Yiddish. The idea made him grin with the anticipation of it.

"*Tatuś*, where will you work when we get to that place?" Anetka's tone turned serious.

"Oh, I don't know yet, but I will get a job as soon as we get there. It's a young country; they need people to help build it."

"But you don't know how to build things," she said.

"Don't be such a worrywart. Mama and I will figure things out. All you have to do is study Hebrew and make new friends."

"I don't want new friends. I want Ala and Ania and Vita."

"Have you forgotten? They are leaving too," he said. She

sighed so deeply that for a split second he wondered if it was right to uproot the children so suddenly. But the thought passed as soon as the image of Isser, left behind in Poland, came to his mind.

"Where are they going?" she asked and he noticed tears welling in her eyes.

"I am not sure. They are probably going to Israel too." The thought of the mass exodus brought the flight from Egypt to his mind, except now there was no one to part the waters.

ও ও ও

My father and I were clearly an oddity on the Lodz-bound train: two middle-class New Yorkers in the heartland of Poland, twenty years before it joined the European Union and awoke up from its post-communist malaise. It was October 1984 and we hadn't been back for nearly thirty years. My bright fuchsia sweatshirt, my Pumas, and my father's spiffy L.L. Bean jacket contrasted sharply with the drab garb of our fellow riders and the threadbare upholstery of the train. Though years have passed, I can still feel the gentle rocking of the train and the curious glances of our neighbours in the compartment.

Our sticker-covered suitcases revealed something of our journeys to distant destinations, and attracted as much attention as the cadence of our English conversation, punctuated by phrases of fluent Polish. We shared our compartment with an elderly woman seated across from me, a world-weary middle-aged woman with a young girl seated next to her, and two uniformed train conductors. From time to time they all cast furtive glances in our direction.

Shortly after the train pulled out of the station the elderly matron lit a corner of cloth with a match and commanded the younger woman to sniff the smouldering handkerchief. Acrid odour filled the compartment.

"Take a deep whiff," she commanded. "I promise this smoke will relieve your toothache. I have used this remedy for years." The middle-aged woman dutifully inhaled the damp, smouldering cloth. If I hadn't been sure we were in Poland this alone would have convinced me. Superstitions were alive and well here. This one was innocent, but what about other, more sinister irrational beliefs? Did this woman still believe that Jews made matzo out of Christian children's blood?

The train stopped at a forlorn railway station. A few passengers got on. The two train conductors sharing our first-class compartment tipped their hats and got off. The little girl, fidgeting with her purse, snuggled up to the woman with the toothache. "Mommy, does it feel better now?"

"A little, it's hard to say."

"Give it a few more minutes," suggested the older woman.

The smoke and the rhythmic clanging of the wheels against the tracks brought to mind an image I tried to push away: crowded trains disgorging confused passengers at Auschwitz. *I can't do this*, not now, I warned myself and took a deep breath. The anxiety generated by returning to the city of my childhood gnawed at me. With each small station, with each series of fields, with each shabby-looking housing development, Lodz drew nearer. My discomfort mounted as long-forgotten station names, like Skierniewice, Koluszki, and Widzew, tripped off old switches in my head. I recalled old train journeys from Lodz to Warsaw and the last one in May 1957 that took us to Venice where we boarded the ship bound to Haifa.

Endless fields outside the train windows blended into a grey-green smudge mixed with visions of my childhood: picking mushrooms in dark forests, anti-Semitic hooligans banging on the shutters of our summer cottage, my bike rides through Sienkiewicza Park. Questions formed that perhaps should have been answered long before my departure from New York: *Why am I willingly returning to a place that holds so many unpleasant memories? Why am I risking dredging up scenes of growing up in postwar Poland, drowning in a sea of anti-Semitism?*

Surely, there must have been some pleasures growing up in Lodz. I did recall how hard my parents worked to surround us with as many niceties as zlotys could buy. Still, all the delights of childhood now lay buried under a mass of old hurts. The material possessions of my youth had done little to neutralize the constant rejection by my Polish peers or to soften a deep sense of loneliness.

Of the thousands of Jews in pre-war Lodz, only a couple of thousand remained after the war. Unable to leave, they stoically endured the communist regime until sporadic thaws allowed them to obtain exit visas. To my knowledge, my brother and I had been the only Jewish children in an apartment house of more than forty families. If there were others, they did their best to conceal their identities. In school I was one of a handful of Jewish children among several hundred students. I don't recall defining myself then particularly in terms of my Jewishness. We were not a religious family. But if my parents did not publicly emphasize our Jewish identity out of concern for our safety, everyone around me certainly did so on my behalf. Our neighbours, my parents' acquaintances, even my friends, thought of me as "the Jewish girl"—nice, well mannered, smart, yet distinctly different from them. With a brand of cruelty especially reserved for children, they pointed out my differentness. "You don't have a Christmas tree, where will you hang your ornaments?" "You have no grandparents, aunts, or uncles. Where are they?" Then they tried to console me. Often they said, "You have blue eyes, light hair, a small upturned nose—you don't look Jewish at all!" No matter how hard I tried I wasn't one of them. This was definitely not a place to which I longed to return.

Yet my father's attitude toward this trip couldn't have been more different. He was excited as a kid when I finally agreed to go and we purchased the tickets. He had been one of the few who loved his bleak hometown. He would have no disdain for its smokestacks and grey streets, for the less-than-friendly citizens, or for the aura of urban decay—a city neglected since the time of the Nazis, who spared it from destruction. To him every corner would sing of his childhood pleasures; every street name would help him reclaim a piece of his youth.

The train pulled into the Lodz station. A grim industrial centre, Lodz, the second-largest city in Poland, loomed before us. Would we recognize the city we left nearly three decades before? Had the street names changed? Would we find anyone from our former life here? Most important, would my grandparents' tombstones still stand in a recognizable condition?

A short cab ride to the Hotel Grand suggested that the changes, if any, might not be noticeable to the untrained eye. A few high-rise buildings, a few streets widened, but still the same old trams in the heart of the old city, precisely as we left them. At check-in the hotel clerk eyed us suspiciously. Americans fluent in Polish were an oddity here. She scanned our passports for a long time. "*Państwo tu kiedyś mieszkali?*" Have you ever lived here? she asked.

"*Tak,*" I answered. She raised her eyebrows and her right thumb looking at us as if we were the luckiest people on earth to have gotten out.

A tiny hotel elevator took us to our floor. Two porters, each jockeying for the gratuity, carried our scant luggage with ceremony. Creaky, endless corridors, a musty smell and very worn Persian runners accompanied us to our room. The whole place was so quiet I was beginning to wonder if we would be the only guests here. One of the porters told us that the hotel was scheduled for refurbishment in time for its upcoming centennial. As soon as the porters left our room, without bothering to take off his coat, unpack, use the restroom, or look out of the window, my father plunged into the telephone book. With a mixture of excitement and nervousness he pored over the dog-eared directory, eagerly searching for names of people from our past.

His finger paused at a name. He lifted the heavy old-fashioned receiver and made the first call. It yielded just the response I had feared. "No, Antoni Russak doesn't live here. This is his nephew. *Zmarł, siedem lat temu.*" He died seven years ago.

"What about Claudia?"

"No, his wife is not here either. *Niestety, ona zmarła w zeszłym roku.*" Sorry, she passed away last year.

My father turned away from me and I thought I saw him wiping the corner of his eye with the back of his hand. When he turned back, his crumpled expression reminded me about the special relationship he had with Antoni and what close, old friends they'd been, all the way back, before the war. Despite my own discomfort with Polish people who had tormented me for years, my father did not have such feelings. I saw the grief for Antoni etched on my father's face and I felt a tinge of embarrassment. There were many good people among them. Why wasn't that enough for me?

Chapter Six

The ancient prophetic dream had come true in 1948. Israel was a reality. Since its establishment, the central mission was to settle the new state by gathering exiled Jews strewn to all corners of the world. They came from war-ravaged Europe and North Africa: sophisticated German *fraus* with feathers in their hats and husbands in tailored tweed jackets and Moroccan wives in ornate caftans and tinkling silver earrings and husbands in white djellabas. Successive waves of immigrants flooded into the country adding to the nearly 175,000 Jews who lived in Palestine as of 1931.

In 1957, the year of Nachman and his family's arrival, Polish Jews were a tiny minority among the sea of Moroccan and Tunisian Jews. The young government scrambled to absorb the surge of humanity, but it strained the capacity of cities and villages to bursting. Hastily constructed transitional camps for new émigrés dotted the country's least habitable regions. Givat Olga, a pristine stretch of desert by the sea, was meant to be just such a holding facility for the families offloaded daily by the dozens from rickety Egged buses. Disgorged onto the hot sand, the families huddled, confused, as if they had landed on a desert island, no clue how to begin their lives anew.

This is where Nachman and family first set foot on Israeli soil. Well, perhaps not literally. First, they disembarked from the ship that had ferried them from Naples to the port of Haifa, where they were met by a gaggle of excited family members. To Nachman, these people were all strangers, but their friendly smiles bode well for his family's future in this new country. They were Dora's sisters and brothers, who had had the good fortune and sense to emigrate from Poland well before Hitler came to power. Warmest of them all were Dora's rotund sister Chava, and Nechemiah, the Orthodox brother who momentarily forgot his strict religious code and hugged Dora with enthusiasm and tenderness. They introduced themselves one by one, but it was impossible to understand the young ones because they did not speak a word of Polish or Yiddish. The Orthodox boys stuck out their little sweaty palms in a greeting. The bronzed kibbutz kids giggled and spoke to one another in Hebrew, occasionally pointing to their new cousins. Aunts and uncles whose faces neither Anetka nor Daniel had ever seen hugged them again and again and gave them playful tweaks on the cheeks.

Shortly after the exuberant greetings, Chava directed Nachman, Dora, and the children to the government-sponsored bus. "They will take you to your new home. No need to worry about where you will sleep. This is your country. Look around you, it's all yours, you are home now." She opened her plump arms wide, and ushered them all wide-eyed toward the bus.

"Wait … wait," Dora cried, confused by the sudden encounter with her loved ones, people she hadn't seen for over thirty years, and stunned that she was about to lose them again. Propelled by a swell of others streaming toward the waiting bus, she proceeded to board it with Nachman and the children in tow as if they were all trapped in some sort of a mechanical dream.

"Don't worry, we will follow the bus and see that you are properly settled in Givat Olga before we return to the kibbutz," Chava yelled. Dora craned her neck out the open bus window to speak with her sister, but then the bus sped up and all she could hear was the wind whistling in her ear. Nachman and Dora were so bewildered by their abrupt departure for Givat Olga that neither had the time to grasp fully the sense of dislocation that began to gnaw at their guts. Just ten days before they were in Lodz where everything they saw, heard and smelled was recognizable, even the occasional disdain in the faces of their neighbours. There, they were at least comfortable in their cozy apartment, if not with their countrymen. Until now they had taken this sense of instant recognition for granted.

Nachman stared at the strange street sights flickering like a foreign film outside the bus windows. His head was spinning; here nothing seemed familiar. Not the strange bronze faces, not the young soldiers. Could they really be Jewish? The vendors at the food stands sold snacks he didn't recognize, threw brown balls into the air and caught them in what looked like pockets of bread dripping with thick sauce. The signs on the businesses and streets looked vaguely like words in the prayer books that were tucked in the farthest corners of Nachman's childhood recollections. For the first time in his life Nachman could not read anything, and this distressed him more than he expected. *How will I ever navigate in this new life?* he wondered, but did not want to say it out loud and pierce Dora's bubble. She was lucky. She still had family and now she would reconnect with them and they might take him into their circle. The thought cheered him as the bus bumped along the coastal road that hugged the shore.

Nachman had never seen a body of water quite like this. This was even bigger than the Rybinsk Sea he had helped build back in the Soviet Union. The water was turquoise and tranquil, not steel grey and angry-looking like that of Rybinsk. This was the glamorous Mediterranean, the playground of the rich and famous, a vision from the weekly magazines he had read in Poland. He was mesmerized by its colour, which

seemed to go from blue to green in an instant. After an hour
of staring at the rhythmic yet monotonous waves and sand he
thought, *This is beautiful, but not as impressive as the mountains
in Poland.* He smiled remembering how he used to take the
kids mountain climbing in the Tatra Mountains. They would
begin each climb with a picnic in the verdant foothills dotted
with goats, sheep, and shepherds tending their flocks. How
the children cheered and screamed with nervous joy when
they climbed as far as their short legs could take them. He
had bought each of them mountain-climbing sticks and over
time they festooned them with metal medallions bearing
names and logos of every peak they had climbed, or hoped
to. He turned back to look at them; they were both asleep with
Daniel's head resting on his sister's shoulder and bobbing up
and down with each bump in the road. No, the sea would
never best the mountains, not for Nachman.

Givat Olga had been settled just four years before they
arrived, but it did not have the spit and polish of a new place.
A refugee settlement composed of crude barracks on Israel's
rocky Mediterranean coast, it sat directly on the beach area
of Hadera, a town situated in a swampy backwater fifty
miles south of the Lebanese border. Only sixty years before
it had consisted of fewer than ten families and four guards
to protect them from marauding gangs. Israel's first paper
mill, established in Hadera at the same time as Givat Olga,
spewed foul emissions that smelled like rotten eggs, reaching
the settlement when the winds blew toward the sea. Some
of the barracks already looked weather worn and unkempt,
and gave off an air of instability. The more established cities
of Tel Aviv and Haifa were about thirty miles from Givat
Olga—an insurmountable distance to the newly arrived, who
couldn't afford bus or train fare. Even if they did, they would
not be able to find the words to ask directions in the ancient
Semitic language that, for European Jewry, had languished
for centuries as a daily medium of communication and
remained sequestered in Hebrew prayer books. Now Hebrew
was resuscitated as the language of the new country.

Aside from row after row of barracks, there was nothing here. One could easily have wondered if these structures were dropped from the sky on a barren desert island. Save for the narrow ribbon of pockmarked road sandwiched between the shore and the rows of wooden barracks, there was nothing to remind newcomers about their former lives. It was a clean slate devoid of shops, vendors, trees, playgrounds, bushes, streets, lampposts—populated only by endless stretches of hot yellow sand. Even the lizards knew better and escaped into their burrows to avoid the scorching sun. At first glance the crude barracks reminded Nachman of Opalicha, though the weather immediately corrected this notion for it was sweltering hot and the humidity permeated every crevice of his body. He saw Dora fanning her face furiously with the Hebrew brochure they had been given. Discretely he sniffed his armpit and scrunched his nose. He desperately wanted to jump into a shower. In Poland, even the hottest summer days barely reached the high seventies and here it was only May and already in the mid-nineties.

Not understanding the group leader who guided the new arrivals in Hebrew toward the barracks, they followed as if they were migrating lemmings. They waited in line with other families who had the same kind of stunned expressions and whose young children kept saying they were thirsty. Anetka and Daniel were too hot and tired to argue and they stood there with a look of boredom, or resignation—Nachman couldn't tell. At last their turn came. A heavy-set man with greying tufts of hair pointed to a barrack and handed them a key. "For your new home," he said smiling, then reached into his pocket for a handkerchief to mop his brow. The barracks had been built high off the sand and Dora barely managed to climb up the five rickety steps. She looked as if she would collapse with heat exhaustion. A single bare light bulb hung in the middle of the space. There were four metal cots against the wall with khaki-green military blankets at the foot of each. A bare rectangular table and chairs completed the furnishings.

Against one wall stood a metal sink and a cabinet with a hot plate. "Where is the bathroom and the shower?" Nachman inquired guessing that the man would understand him. He did—he was a Polish refugee himself.

"The toilets are there," the man opened the door and motioned outside to a row of outhouses. "And the shower is right here."

"Where?"

The man pointed to a spigot outside the barrack. A piece of pipe with an on/off valve just above a concrete pad stuck out of the wall. "Don't worry, you won't need hot water here," he added cheerfully.

Nachman noticed that since their arrival in Givat Olga, Dora had hardly uttered a word. *What was she thinking? She must be appalled.* After Opalicha, he knew he could adapt to any conditions. Dora, on the other hand, was different. She had suffered conditions even worse than Opalicha in her Siberian gulag, but Nachman felt that she should not have to endure this place. In his mind she was a queen. How could he subject her to this miserable shack after the comfortable life they had made for themselves in Poland? Nachman looked around at the spartan barrack and tried to formulate a plan, to come up with something encouraging to say. After all, it had been their joint decision to leave and this wasn't supposed to be exile. This was to be homecoming.

His thoughts were interrupted by the voices outside. Moments later, Chava trundled up the stairs and stood inside. Chava and her husband, Benjamin, had followed them in a vehicle borrowed from their kibbutz. Benjamin walked in behind Chava holding a bag. "Here, we brought you some provisions so you'd feel at home," he said, and started taking them out of the bag. "There's some salt, sugar, here is bread and here are four oranges."

Nachman stood still near the table watching Benjamin, but his thoughts were racing. *I have to find a way out of this*, he thought, and looked at his daughter. She was so pale compared to the tanned cousins they had met at the port. *How quickly would she adjust?*

"Oranges?" Anetka came rushing over, excited. "Let me look at them. We never had any in Poland." She picked up an orange and smelled it inhaling deeply. "Paradise," was all she said, putting the orange back on the table and sitting down at the edge of the nearest cot. Dora sat at the cot below the small window and held her face in her hands. Her palms obscured her eyes. Daniel read a magazine he had carried with him from the ship, oblivious of the tension in the room. For what seemed like eternity no one spoke.

Chava walked over to the sink to fill a dented aluminum pot with water. The water ran brown. She stuck her hand in the stream. "It's so warm I hardly have to heat it," she laughed, then announced: "I will make tea. Benjamin, did you bring the tea?"

"No, you didn't tell me to buy any."

"Oh, well," she said.

Nachman thought she was embarrassed, but he really didn't know her enough to tell.

"Let's put away the groceries," she chirped and turned toward the cabinet above the sink. She grasped the handle to open it. "Better check for scorpions," she said casually. The handle fell off with a clunk. She looked at it as if she had never seen such an object. For a few moments she stood in the centre of the space with her hands on her hips and stared at the light bulb as if it would enlighten her how to deal with the situation. Then she regained her balance and declared in a tone befitting a judge rendering a decision, "Dora, you cannot stay here. We hadn't planned on it, but I am taking all of you to Kibbutz Gvat. Let's get out of here."

Nachman felt a rush of relief, not for himself, but for Dora.

Dora rushed to her sister and buried her face in her neck. They hugged for so long Nachman thought they were permanently glued together. He felt awkward with Chava's generous invitation. He had no job and few prospects. It made him uncomfortable to have his family pile into the kibbutz for an unspecified period of time. After all, he thought, they work hard and don't have much themselves. It was well known that freeloaders were not welcome in the kibbutz. But he knew that it would do no good to argue with Chava. Dora always said her older sister was like a cyclone. Once she got going there would be no stopping her. He imagined she must have endured conditions far worse than Givat Olga when she first came to Palestine in the 1920s. Dora told him how her sister had lived in a tent and survived malaria and other tropical diseases trying to establish a life in what had been an insect-ridden swampland. *To Chava this barracks must seem a cut far above what newcomers to Palestine accepted in exchange for being in their homeland,* he thought.

Not only did he feel embarrassed to accept Chava's generosity, Nachman felt in his bones that a kibbutz environment would rub against the grain of Dora's personality. She was intensely private, independent, and entrepreneurial. Communal life was not suited for someone like her. The shared Siberian gulag bunks and packed living quarters with families who had sheltered them in Russia had permanently soured Dora on communal living. Still, they would not have to spend the night here imagining yellow scorpions under the sheets, or tolerate the broiling heat of the khamsin that was expected the next morning. They were going north where it would be cooler.

It was dark when they arrived at the kibbutz and could see very little, but the fragrance of roses filled the night air as they walked the narrow path from the parking area. Benjamin carried their suitcases up the one flight in the low concrete-block building.

"Welcome to Kibbutz Gvat," Chava said as she pushed the door open.

"You didn't lock it?' Dora asked.

"Here? Never," she said. "Our own people are all around us. We are safe here."

Then they sat around the table exchanging pleasantries as Chava served tea and cookies.

"So much to catch up on," Dora said.

"Don't worry, we have all the years ahead to talk and talk. Tonight we are all too tired. It has been quite a day."

"Where will we sleep?" Anetka asked, looking around the one room. "Is there a bedroom for us?"

"No, this is all the space we have." Aunt Chava flashed a wide grin showing a mouthful of healthy teeth. "Your uncle and I will go to sleep in our friends' apartment, a couple of buildings away. They happen to be travelling right now. The four of you can squeeze in on this sofa."

Anetka turned to inspect the piece of furniture. It was narrow and strewn with small, embroidered throw pillows.

"Here?" she asked, her voice rising.

Chava's eyes turned to narrow slits as her cheeks bloomed into another wide smile. "Don't worry, it's a pullout sofa. See?" She bent over it and pulled out the low trundle bed from below.

"Oh," was all Anetka managed to say.

"Is it all right if I take a bath?" Nachman asked. He was desperate to dip in the tub and stay there to cool off and to think.

"Sure, but remember to squeegee the water toward the centre of the floor in the bathroom when you are done."

Nachman was puzzled.

Chava laughed. "We have no tub here, just a showerhead in the centre of the bathroom and no shower curtain either. This way it all dries faster and we get no mould. You'll get used to it." Her high cheekbones made her eyes narrow in amusement. Dora sat in a corner chair looking lost.

"Don't worry, Dora," Chava said sensing her sister's discomfort. We are allowed to have guests for ten days, after that, you will be assigned a job."

Dora's cheeks flushed. "You know, Chava, I only know how to sew corsets and brassieres. I don't know how to farm or milk cows."

"Stop worrying, we will teach you," Chava said cheerfully. "If farming is too daunting, you could always wash dishes. I am going now. See you in the morning." She turned off the light switch closest to the door and closed it gently behind her.

At long last they were alone, but too exhausted to converse. They flopped into bed shimmying close so as to avoid falling off. Nachman turned off the last light nearest the bed. Unfamiliar shadows danced on the ceiling. The only sound in the room was the ticking of the wall clock. Then Dora broke the silence. "Nachman, I can't live on a farm. I am sorry. I just can't." He could tell she was tired by the way she sighed. It wasn't like her. Normally she'd still be up unpacking, making lists, giving out instructions and organizing their lives.

"We will go Tel Aviv in a few days and I will start looking for a job," he whispered hearing the children's rhythmic breathing. They were already asleep. "I have plenty of experience and I'm ready to do just about anything. It will be fine, Dora. I promise."

The next morning her parents informed Anetka they'd be leaving her and Daniel at the kibbutz. "All by ourselves?" she asked, incredulous and tears welled in her eyes.

"Of course not! You are staying with Aunt Chava and Uncle Benjamin," Nachman said.

"But … but … what will we *do* here?" Anetka's voice was high-pitched and tremulous.

"Do? What do you mean do? You will go to school," Dora said.

"But the kids here don't speak Polish, do they?"

"Well, no. You will learn to speak Hebrew, don't worry."

Anetka sobbed and her mother consoled her. "My sister, Chava, speaks Polish. She's very kind. She will help you."

Within several months Dora had opened a corsetry workshop in their sublet apartment on Arba Aratzot Street in the fashionable new northern section of Tel Aviv. Slowly, her exquisite workmanship attracted a loyal clientele and generated just enough income so that Anetka and Daniel could return from the kibbutz where they had been living, studying, and working under Chava's guidance. But Nachman was still job hunting. Day in and day out he went out in the morning to look for work, returning with a diminished supply of pep that he managed to manufacture afresh each evening, as he scanned the want ads in the *Letzte Nayes* and other daily papers.

Eighteen months of an intensive but fruitless job search weighted Nachman down like a leaden coat. Never given to depression or brooding, not even in his darkest hours of exile and imprisonment did he have such a crushing sense of uselessness. In Poland, despite everything, he was employed, useful. He thought of Mrs. Olczak his young Polish supervisor and her intelligent face framed by a blond bob. "You should have my position instead of the other way around," she'd said.

Standing there in the once Grand Hotel in Lodz, my father flipped through the phone book, brightened, and dialled. By today's standards the 1984 voice transmission technology was poor. I could hear her at the other end—the phones were too loud: "Yes, Mrs. Olczak is here. This is she. Of course I remember you! Your voice hasn't changed a bit, Nachman," she exclaimed, her tone full of warmth and disbelief. My father held the receiver away from his ear so I could listen, though it wasn't necessary.

Half an hour later my dad's former boss, Wiesława Olczak, now an elegant grey-haired Polish lady, stood at our hotel door with a bouquet of carnations and tears in her eyes. I called the front desk and ordered coffee from room service. Their words tumbled out, the two of them trying to catch up on each other's lives, unfinished sentences, meaningful glances.

"It's so hard to make up for lost time," my father cried.

"Yes, if only you didn't have to leave Poland back then ... but I know why you had to. Those of us on your side should have been more vocal. We were complicit by our silence."

"Let's talk about our plans," my father tried to diffuse the heavy air in the room. "Ania and I are going to look for my parents' graves," he said.

"I worry about their condition," she said. "Much of the Jewish cemetery has been vandalized. My husband and I can take you. It will be safer that way."

I didn't want to intrude on their conversation so I unpacked my suitcase, browsed through some travel brochures and refilled their cups from the coffee thermos. Surreal hours. I was eager for the visit to end. I walked over to the window and said, "It's getting dark out." I think Wieslawa understood my meaning.

Before she left, my father talked with her about the current conditions in Lodz. "Any plans for renewal?" He tried to steer the conversation to the present, but Wiesława seemed intent on dwelling in the past.

"You know, Nachman, the absence of Jews has left a great void in Polish cultural life. I feel it very keenly and regret it greatly."

The next morning we awoke to a downpour. The hotel room, cavernous and depressing the day before, seemed even drearier as streams of rain rolled down the dirty windowpanes and bounced off the concrete windowsills. This hotel, once so elegant and accessible only to the very wealthy, was a sad reminder of life in pre-war Lodz. The rain coincided with my mood, but my father, who could make the best out the worst situation, was raring to go the cemetery.

The Olczaks arrived early in their tiny Fiat. The vehicle, bought after ten years of instalment payments, was their most valued possession. They decided to devote the entire morning to helping us search for the gravesites. Gasoline was rationed and we were reluctant to cut into their month's allotment, but they insisted. Their goodwill and genuine interest boosted my spirit.

As we neared the cemetery, which had once been located on the outskirts of town, we saw that now crumbling housing projects engulfed it. By some inexplicable act of mercy, it alone had escaped the bulldozers. We continued circling around it, trying to find the entrance.

"It may surprise you," Wiesława said, "but some formerly negative, or indifferent Poles have become nostalgic about the loss of Jewish culture and its customs."

I wanted to ask just what was it they missed, but decided to keep quiet.

She continued her chatter as if she wanted to protect us from the depressing scene unfolding before us. "A few of my countrymen have belatedly taken on the role of protectors of Jewish historic sites," she said.

A whole new kind of Pole seems to have been born, a philo-Semite, I thought, and wondered what my father would think of Mrs. Olczak's comment, but he was busy chatting with her husband.

In short order she informed us that intervention by these newly minted philo-Semites may have been the one reason why this cemetery hadn't been razed. In fact, she said with pride, "Recently this cemetery was declared a national treasure. It will be restored with government funds."

If only such sympathetic sentiments had emerged before the complete decimation of Lodz Jews, thousands could have been saved, I thought.

Despite their warmth, I had trouble feeling at ease in a place whose thriving pre-war Jewish community—including my family—was erased. *Only three-tenths of 1 per cent remained, three-tenths of one, three-tenths of one*, my brain seemed to be stuck and repeated that number over and over until I felt numb.

The parking garages of a housing development now abutted the cemetery's perimeter wall and almost obscured its entrance. Just steps away, we could barely make it out. The unrelenting rain made things more difficult. We unfolded ourselves from the Fiat and opened the black umbrellas. In the thick autumn fog the cemetery looked like a dreamlike apparition. I approached the gate slowly walking ahead of the seniors in our little group.

Before me a long grassy road stretched past the cemetery office to the inner entrance. So this was the last road for my grandparents. My father often said they had the good sense to die just before the war. I knew he meant that this spared them from suffering the indignities of Nazism and permitted them to have a proper Jewish burial. I couldn't believe I was actually here again. The young girl, running among the headstones three and a half decades before, seemed like a stranger. The forsaken appearance of the place made it look as if no one in the world cared for those whose journey ended in this place. In the distance I saw remnants of an imposing old building.

"Dad, what is the building ahead with the Stars of David under the eaves?" I turned back to ask him. He stood there glued to one spot looking up. Was he reliving the days of his parents' funerals?

After a moment he said slowly, "This was the mortuary where ritual preparation for burial took place."

"What's in it now?" I asked of no one in particular.

"The caretaker must live here," Mr. Olczak speculated.

Broken windowpanes on the building were a stark contrast to the lively geese grazing outside. After a few minutes I realized that Mr. Olczak might have been correct. The geese and the small farm plot located within the cemetery's gates did suggest that a family, who needed assurance of food beyond the monthly rations, was living here. The evidence of life at a cemetery seemed intrusive and awkward, yet strangely reassuring. *Imagine eternity spent listening to the honking of geese*, I thought, and mixed emotions flooded me. Was it sacrilegious or a blessing that a family has chosen to live in this odd place, caring for graves of Jews who have no next of kin left in Poland?

To help him in locating the graves, my father carried with him photographs of the gravesites taken decades before. The yellowing black-and-white snapshots showed my youthful parents and five-year-old me with long braids, against a backdrop of tombstones. A black-robed cantor stood in the background of one of the photos. I didn't know if he had been sent by the Jewish congregation to chant prayers over the abandoned gravesites. I couldn't imagine my secular father hiring him. I remembered my childhood trips to this cemetery and how diligently I swept the tombstones, how my brother collected the acorns around them.

My father had taken the photos shortly after we returned from Kyrgyzstan. Not finding any living relatives left in Poland after the war, he found a small measure of solace in visiting graves of loved ones who had died before the Holocaust. Now, years after they were first rediscovered, my father longed to find these graves once again so he could pay his respects to his parents.

The gusts made our umbrellas useless. Just a little way down the main road we could see the evidence of years of neglect. Thick weeds and thorny underbrush had engulfed even the tallest tombstones. With his short stature, my father was completely lost amid the unruly growth as he hurried down the once familiar pathways, calling "I think we are almost here." But it was hard to tell. The 105-acre cemetery contained more than 180,000 graves and was perhaps the largest Jewish cemetery in Europe. I could tell by the swooshing of the wet leaves that he was just steps away, but I couldn't see him. I was worried that he might fall, trip on the vines, or stumble on the haphazardly strewn remnants of gravestones. But, somehow, it seemed improper to shout. It was impossible for me and the Olczak's to maintain contact and to follow him, but we tried nevertheless in a frustrating, single-file march. Had I realized this would be such a tangle of vines I might have carried clippers. Now we had nothing but the umbrellas to push the growth out of the way. The thorns stuck to my coat, tore my stockings, and scratched my hands. Tiptoeing through the puddles and mud, I sensed that our mission would fail. I admired the Olczak's for their tenacity in accompanying us on this quest and wasn't sure if I would be as helpful if the situation were reversed. Wiesława caught up to me and made a feeble attempt to console me. "Perhaps tomorrow you will have better luck," she said.

"Maybe I should have knocked on the caretaker's door," I said, and looked at my watch. It was getting late.

"I don't think he is home," Mr. Olczak said. "I noticed that the lights were out and a heavy lock hung on the door."

My father, undaunted, insisted on searching. We continued. I saw many fallen tombstones, victims of time and vandalism. The perpetrators had been merciless. Many marble name plaques had been stolen, making the search infinitely more difficult. There were even a few open graves. My shoes were all muddy and the cold penetrated my parka. I was freezing and tired and wanted to get to the hotel to gulp some hot tea, but the Olczak's and my father kept moving on.

"Now that the cemetery has come under state protectorate, the perimeter fence will be closed up and guarded," Wiesława assured me with embarrassment as we tried to catch up with my father. For his sake I pushed myself to continue deeper into the cemetery, stumbling on broken stones and tree roots, trying to make out fading names on the headstones that still stood, leaning as if exhausted by what they had witnessed. In my gut, I knew we were in the wrong place. I couldn't feel my grandparents' spirits here.

Finally, I called an end to the search. It was too much for my father and we were all thoroughly soaked, scratched, muddy, and deeply disappointed. We departed in silence. The Olczak's apologized profusely when they dropped us off at the hotel. "It's not your fault," my father said. "It's just the passage of time."

That evening at the hotel Dad and I hardly ate any supper. Our soup spoons clinking on the plates of borsht echoed in the near empty dining room. The once grand space, filled with remnants of old-style furniture bereft of its glorious past, made us more depressed. We went to bed dispirited, not chatting as we usually did. I buried my head in a book, but my father kept leafing through the phone book.

Waking in the wee hours it occurred to me that we could visit the Jewish congregation and inquire about the existence of old burial records. But it was Saturday and it would certainly be closed. I had serious doubt that I would ever return if our second mission failed, but I owed it to my father, myself, and to my children, to make another effort. As soon as he was awake, I said to my father, "Listen, we can go to the Jewish congregation on Monday and see if they can help us with the exact grave locations."

"Why? I know where the graves are," he insisted. Stubborn old goat!

"Tinku, I know you know, but given the conditions we saw we'll need some help. I'm not going to the cemetery without some more guidance."

"Okay, okay," he relented, "but I want you to know that I know. Listen, Ania, Monday is our last day here. What if we end up going home with nothing?"

I was startled by the uncharacteristic lack of optimism.

As if being unemployed in his land wasn't dispiriting enough, there was another corrosive aspect to Nachman's life in Tel Aviv. A chorus of "Hebrew! Hebrew! Hebrew!" assaulted him whenever he uttered a word in Yiddish. Neighbours and family members continually reminded him to stop speaking his mother tongue. Strangers looked in shock, as if he were uttering profanities, when he spoke Yiddish to Dora in the market. "*Hebrew* is your language now." Their eyes shot poison arrows more hurtful than the kind words of his sister-in-law who said, "Nachman, really, you need to abandon the language of the Diaspora. You too, Dora. The faster you do it, the happier you will be here."

Though Nachman was no longer an active Bundist (the Polish communist government dissolved the remnants of the

Jewish Labour Bund in 1948), he still cherished the fact the Bund had fought to legitimize the Yiddish language. In pre-war Poland, the legitimacy of Yiddish had been an official part of the Bund party's platform. Yet here in the land of the Jews, it was looked upon as an abomination. The use of Yiddish as the medium of communication in daily discourse and in the arts was an essential component of the Bundist identity. *Language is the basis of a culture,* Nachman thought every time he was rebuked for the use of his mother tongue. *By delegitimizing Yiddish, the Israelis are wiping out our heritage,* he thought. Eleven million Yiddish speakers in Europe, dozens of Yiddish newspapers in Lodz alone, theatre companies, lectures, seminars, novels, poetry, humour—all of these were to be relegated to the garbage? To Nachman this tasted as bitter as gall. He remembered how before the war the Bundists were against the revival of Hebrew as a secular language and opposed to concentrating all of the world's Jews in Palestine. With a rich ancient heritage in the European countries into which they and their ancestors had been born, the Bundists saw those countries as their very own. Why depart for Palestine, which was not the cradle of their ancestors since the Middle Ages and even before? And now he was forced to speak Hebrew. No, he would never be a traitor to the language in which his mother crooned lullabies, the last words he had said to Yankel, and the lyrics he sung to Dora as she lay in the hospital in Kyzyl Kyia. *They may as well tear out my tongue, even my soul, if I have to give up my language,* he thought. And the more he thought it, the less he seemed capable of absorbing the odd guttural Hebrew words that Anetka and Daniel spewed forth like a fountain.

One day over dinner, Dora finally had an encouraging piece of news. She had heard about the possibility of a job in a lumberyard owned by none other than the father of Shimon Peres, then the director general at the Israeli Defense Ministry (since 2007 president of Israel). Mrs. Ruth Dayan, one of Dora's best clients, was her link to the most powerful Israeli politicians of the day, and had recommended Dora's shop to the senior Mrs. Peres. Nachman's attitude improved instantly. "So, tell me about it," he said with more energy in his voice, though work in a lumberyard was not his dream job.

The next morning Nachman headed out optimistically to the Peres lumberyard, but learned that the job was temporary. It was open for only a month, six weeks, at best. The manager for whom he would substitute had gone to Bulgaria on an extended lumber-purchasing trip. It was not easy to find experienced administrators like Nachman willing to work for just a few weeks, so he took the job. Even Mrs. Peres' recommendation couldn't get him steady work.

After the job finished, in June 1958, Nachman's employment situation grew more acute. He couldn't find any comfort, not even in the one country he'd thought would be the answer after the communist oppression in Poland. To him, a healthy unemployed man was an emblem of wonton indolence, someone who was lazy and unworthy of respect. He walked around the apartment among Dora's piles of half-sewn brassieres. He knew he must have looked lost by Dora's sideways glances that betrayed how broken hearted she was for him. On some days she enlisted his help in using a small hand held device that inserted eyelets into the corsets she was working on. "Nachman, do you have a minute?" she would call out from behind her sewing machine, brushing the hair off her sweaty forehead.

Of course he had time. Time was all he had. "Yes, what do you need?"

"Can you help me with the eyelets again?"

"Why not? What else do I have to do?" he would say with a sigh. This was not the kind of work he needed. He was too humiliated to ask relatives for help with the job search.

Unbeknown to Nachman, Dora had asked her kibbutznik brother-in-law, Benjamin, to help. His thin, wiry body was such a contrast to her rotund sister, but he was a generous man whom she knew from pre-war Warsaw. He had many friends in the city. Benjamin made numerous calls on Nachman's behalf and visited all his Tel Aviv acquaintances in person. At last he brought good news. There was work to be had at a corrugated-box factory, Cargill. Nachman set out to their office the next morning full of optimism. He took the bus to the outskirts of Tel Aviv. The crowds on the bus jostled him. He was worried that his jacket would become creased from the tightly squeezed-in bodies, but calmed himself with the hope that this would be it—a job he could sink his teeth into and feel like man again.

Soon he arrived at the factory, a low concrete building. Workers in overalls and heavy boots scurried around the compound's grounds. Nachman found the personnel director's office and was greeted warmly by a stocky middle-aged man in a white open-collared shirt, rings of perspiration around the armpits.

"So, my old friend, Benjamin has recommended you. His word is as good as gold. When can you start?"

"Today, if you like," Nachman replied, tension easing in his shoulder blades. And in an instant he thought, *This was too easy.*

"By the way," said the director, "you do know we can provide each applicant with work for only two weeks. We want to be fair. We have too many applicants."

Nachman exhaled and his shoulders sagged. He'd allowed himself too much hope.

The personnel director seemed to know it and said, "After several months you can try us again, we may give you a few more weeks."

It's better than nothing, Nachman thought, his heart sinking.

Nachman and Dora brought Anetka and Daniel from Kibbutz Gvat as soon as they found a place to live in Tel Aviv. By then the children spoke Hebrew nearly like the natives, or at least that's how it sounded to Nachman with all those guttural "ch" sounds. Because of her outstanding grades from Poland, Anetka was admitted to the highly regarded school, Ironit Aleph. It amazed Nachman how resilient the children were. Anetka suddenly seemed comfortable with her peers as if this had been her home since birth. He'd overheard her conversation with her girlfriend, Slawka.

"He was so gorgeous. You have never seen such green eyes!" Anetka sounded positively smitten.

"Who was this guy?" Slawka asked.

"I told you. He was this blond Turkish Jew I met on Dizengoff Street during the Independence Day celebrations."

"Oh, yes, the one with that group of boys from the neighbouring school. Did you dance with him?" Slawka remembered and now she wanted all the details.

"I did," Anetka said and closed her eyes smiling. "It was heavenly."

"Did he kiss you?"

"I'm not telling."

Nachman knew a day would come when Anetka became interested in the opposite sex, he just didn't think it would be this soon. She was only fifteen. He had so much on his mind that he couldn't consider the implications. *Not now. I'll let Dora deal with this*, he thought.

In the spring of 1972, after a cold that wouldn't go away, my mother had finally taken a day off work to visit her doctor with badly swollen glands in her neck. They had been plaguing her, on and off, for years—this time they seemed worse than ever. At first, she crumpled under the diagnosis: lymphosarcoma, a blood cancer.

I had just come over for a quick lunch—my parents lived in the Bronx, very close to my workplace—and found her sitting in her slip at the kitchen table with her face in her hands. I hadn't realized she was crying, but her hunched posture and the sight of her undressed in the kitchen at midday stopped me in my tracks.

"What's wrong, Mama?" I asked. She didn't reply. Hollow animal sounds issued from somewhere deep within her, but I hardly recognized what they were because as an adult, I had never seen her in this kind of state. I walked toward her cautiously. She was so deeply ensconced in her grief I was afraid I would intrude on a painful private moment. I put my arm over her shoulders. Her skin was cold and clammy. "Please, Mama, tell me what happened."

She sat up sharply, blew her nose and said, "Next year by this time daisies will grow over me."

What? I had no idea what she was talking about. She stood up, went to get her robe and in the few moments it took her to return to the kitchen she seemed totally composed.

She was sixty-two when the lethal diagnosis was delivered and, initially, it shook her to the very core, but a few weeks later she would say in a quite casual, offhand way, "Well, no one will have to say I died young." Outwardly, it seemed that it took her only a short time to absorb the body blow of her condition. After that, she kept the prospect of her demise at bay by sharp gallows humour, retirement from her sweatshop, and planning for trips abroad. My father was in a relatively brief state of shock when he discovered Mama's diagnosis, then he responded with his usual, unabated optimism that the infusions of poisonous drugs would eventually cure her, or that quite probably, new therapies would be discovered while she was in a temporary remission.

Now it was the fall, four months after her diagnosis. I sat with my mother, at her apartment on Gale Place, for our usual lunch of a hard-boiled eggs, toast, and tea. My father was at work and I had run over for a quick visit from my nearby office at the Bronx Zoo. Now that I knew about her condition, I tried to spend every possible moment with her. I had only recently started my job as a zoology instructor at the Bronx Zoo and begun graduate school in the evenings at a Jesuit school: Manhattan College. That day my mother enjoyed reminiscing how I'd come to that point. She was proud that I decided to pursue a professional career and a graduate degree. "You should never be reliant on a man," she said. "You need to be your own person."

"I know, Mama," I said. "That's what I'm trying to do, but my job brings in only a pittance of a salary and I can't be home for the children."

"Don't worry. Keep doing the best you can and stay at the job. Don't jump around, like some other young people do who want instant gratification. Eventually, moss grows over the stone," she said cryptically.

"What do you mean, Mom?"

"Well, stick to your job, put your nose to the grindstone, you will advance in your institution. You won't always be an instructor."

"Mom, I want to talk about something else," I said. "When is your first chemo treatment?"

"Oh, that," she waved her hand as if to dismiss my question. "Look, Ania, your lunchtime is almost over. You've got to get back to work."

I sat at my desk shuffling through an old stack of letters and documents my father had filed in a large brown manila folder. It was packed to bursting and tied with a rubber band, now stretched and crumbly. I was looking for my parents' correspondence from the time we lived in Israel to refresh my sense of our family dynamics back then. I felt very fortunate that my father had been such a pack rat. All the letters were still there, in their original envelopes. Reading the letters my mother had written to her sisters and my father's letters to Rosa, the entire Israeli interlude came into my mind's eye with unexpected freshness. I could see it all in living colour: my father hunched over, scanning the paper's help-wanted columns, my mother puttering in the kitchen, preparing his favourite soup, Daniel

practising his accordion on the terrace, and me trying to sneak
out for a date with Yom Tov, my boyfriend.

Furtively, knowing how Nachman hated to ask anyone for
favours, Dora continued to seek help from anyone who might
have job contacts in Tel Aviv. She decided to ask her half-
brother, Yitzhak, a prominent novelist, for help with a job.
Of all her relatives and friends, he was the last one she would
ask. She wasn't very close to him; he was much older and they
had grown apart after he had left Poland when she was still
young. By now he had built a cold intellectual wall between
himself and his half siblings. Yitzhak's surname had been
Blausztein when he immigrated to Israel long before World
War II, but he shed his Jewish surname in favour of a Hebrew
one. Now he was Sela, a stone, strong, massive, imposing. Dora
felt aggravated with him for abandoning her family name, but
his action wasn't unique. Along with the Yiddish language,
many Jews discarded their last names like worn-out clothes.
Names that had belonged to their fathers and grandfathers
were transformed into newly minted Hebrew names with a
mere stroke of a pen—new names for a new start. Dora knew
that this was something Nachman could neither understand
nor stomach. It made her proud that he did not forsake his
last name when it would have been such a boon to his career
in Lodz. "Never, never," he had said.

Though Yitzhak was an intellectual with airs, he liked
Nachman and his plain-spoken, direct manner. He decided
to help his brother-in-law through his contacts and spoke
to a friend, the director of the main Tel Aviv post office on
Allenby Street. The first question the director asked Yitzhak
was, "What can your brother-in-law do? Does he, for example,
have any language skills?"

"Oh, yes," replied Yitzhak enthusiastically. "He speaks
Polish, Yiddish, Russian, and some German. He is a seasoned
administrator too."

"Well, excellent, we need linguists. He can work for us as a censor. You do know that we must be careful about security and check out the communications. Don't you?"

"Yes, yes, of course," Yitzhak replied, wondering if it was really still necessary. It was true that the Arab world wished them to disappear, but he wasn't sure that snooping on mail was the way to go.

"Tell your brother-in-law to come in on Monday. I need him to start right away."

Yitzhak was delighted that at long last he succeeded in rescuing Nachman from the abyss of unemployment. This was an office job befitting Nachman's experience, a real job, nothing menial, like the Cargill job Benjamin had tried to get him. Before Yitzhak stood up to leave the post office, he and the director exchanged a few family updates. "I'll go now. I see you are very busy," Yitzhak said. "Let's get together for dinner soon," he said nearing the door.

"Wait, Yitzhak, I forgot to ask you the most important question—how old is your brother-in-law?"

"He is forty-five." Yitzhak knew Nachman was forty-eight, but he took the liberty hoping to allay any concerns about age.

"Oh, Yitzhak, I am so sorry! The regulations do not permit me to hire anyone over forty years of age." Yitzhak's face fell. He stood at the door for a moment searching for something to say. His friend looked embarrassed that he had extended the offer before settling the age issue. The director stood up from his chair, walked around the desk toward Yitzhak and touched his arm. "It's an old British rule. I can't do anything about it. Believe me." It was clear to Yitzhak that remnants of professional civil service practices introduced by the British still had some resonance.

Yitzhak was a passionate Zionist who stated loudly and often that every Jew had an obligation to live in the new state of Israel, but the episode at the post office gave him pause. It upset his long-held belief that for a Jew to leave Israel was sacrilege. The bitter aftertaste lingered long after he turned away from the profusely apologizing director and left the office. How can a family survive if a man over forty is considered too old to work? He decided to do something contrary to his nature and to his way of thinking. He chafed that he had to do it, but what choice was there?

Yitzhak arrived at Nachman and Dora's apartment to deliver the disappointing news. Dora opened the door enthusiastically. "Shalom, Yitzhak, it's so good to see you. Nachman come here," she called out. "Yitzhak has news for you." Nachman appeared from the kitchen, taking off the apron he had worn to wash the dishes. It hung limply in his hand.

"*Vos makht a Yid?*" he greeted his brother-in-law and sat on the sofa next to Dora. Yitzhak remained standing in the middle of the room. He looked uncharacteristically deflated twirling his beard hairs and looking down at his shoes. Then he said with resignation in his voice, "Well, Nachman, now you can really think about emigrating to America with a clear conscience."

Dora knew Yitzhak well enough to know how much he must have hated absolving Nachman. She wouldn't have guessed that such words would ever come from Yitzhak's mouth: heresy!

And she knew something else. After hearing what the job would have been, Dora knew that Nachman would have never accepted it.

The evening of the post office rejection, I listened with a knot in my stomach to the entire conversation through the open door to the bedroom where I was finishing my homework. I wanted to shout, "No, no, don't go to the consulate, Tinek," but I kept quiet. Even then I could tell this was not a conversation in which my opinion would have been welcome. I had fallen head over heels in love with Israel, but knew it did not love my father back. The youth and vitality of the country that thrilled me so when we first arrived had worked against him. Hit by the twin obstacles of his age and language, my father made the momentous decision right then and there.

After a long pause in the sparse conversation, he said to Yitzhak, "Tomorrow I'm going to the American consulate to get a visa application. I know my sister Rosa will try to help me."

I knew well that ever since my father rediscovered his sister through the refugee grapevine he had been dreaming of seeing her. After she left Lodz for a displaced persons camp in Germany, she had remarried, had two daughters, and settled in the eastern United States.

That night my parents continued the doomsday discussion. They must have believed Daniel and I were asleep. Guilt at eavesdropping gripped me, but I listened, rolled up tense as a ball.

"Please, Nachman, let's give it a few more months. I have a couple of new clients. I am pretty sure we can cover the rent for now," Mama said.

"No. I can't go on like this," my father replied with such finality, I knew he would not change his mind. There was steel in his voice, but gentleness too. I couldn't see them but imagined that my father held Mama's hand and looked directly into her hazel eyes filled to the brim. I knew how much Mama would miss the family she had rediscovered in Israel if we had to move to America—a place that in my mind was nothing more than a fairy tale. It was quiet for a while and I wondered if Mama was crying though I knew it wasn't her style. After a long moment I heard father's voice brighten. "I have an idea, Dora, please listen, and don't say no yet."

"Yes, what is it?"

"If your sister Chava can help us become kibbutz members, I will stay."

"You can't be serious, Nachman. You know how I feel about living such a life."

"What's wrong with it? People can be happy working the land, seeing their trees and fields bear fruit. They gather, they sing, they eat together, they celebrate the holidays together."

"Oh, yes, that and gossip together and know everyone's business and not know from week to week what their job assignment will be. Can't you see? It's Russia all over again—the masses controlled by a central committee. I want to be my own person." Mama's voice conveyed crystal clarity.

"I didn't think I could persuade you, but I tried. I'm such a fool," my father sighed.

"No, you are not a fool, but you are a creature of the Medem School—one for all and all for one, that kind of thing. A socialist through and through. I can't do it, Nachman. I am sorry. I just can't."

"Well, it's settled then we will try our luck in America. If—"

"If what?" Mama sounded alarmed.

"If they will issue entry visas for us. You know there is a very strict quota. Everyone wants to go America. It's everyone's dream."

"Yes, such a dream, to start over at fifty and learn a new language." I recognized the cynical tone that sometimes seeped out of her.

I couldn't stand to hear the rest and resolved never to leave the country I had fallen in love with. No, never! I wished fervently for the quota to have been exceeded so that no more visas would be issued, ever. I pulled the covers over my ears and tried to fall asleep, but a dark moth kept circling around my head. I tried to swat it away but it mocked me, asking over and over, which is the Promised Land? *Eretz Israel* or the *goldene medine*?

Part 3
After

Chapter Seven

People had warned Nachman that a metropolis the size of New York could dwarf a mere mortal, disorient him, and make him yearn for the place from which he came. But what did they know? he thought. From his first day in New York Nachman fell completely under its pulsating spell. Like with Dora, it was love at first sight. His pockets were empty and he had to spend his nights sleeping on lumpy cots and pullout sofas in friends' apartments, but it cost nothing to fill his lungs with the sense of freedom that radiated from the crowds on the streets rushing about, trying to fulfill their American dreams. The city's perpetual hum made it sound like a giant beehive and like bees, people here were productive, each with a task that ensured survival. He was hopeful that employment would materialize in the near future. It had to. There was so much happening in this vital city that, surely, it would take an inexhaustible stream of labour to get it all done.

Before he left Israel, family members had warned him repeatedly about the pitfalls of what they saw as an urban monster. Chava's words still rang in his head. "Where do you plan to live when you get to New York? Hotels are way too rich for your pocket. You don't want to end up homeless." Her disillusionment shone through her words. He knew that she and the rest of Dora's family saw him as a traitor to the cause of a Jewish homeland. Surely, they knew that as soon as Dora was successful in obtaining her visa, she too would leave Israel.

"I have old friends in New York," Nachman had said. "They'll put me up if necessary, if things don't work out at Rosa's."

"How long has it been since you last saw them?" Chava's eyes narrowed into two slits.

"Oh, let me see." Nachman pressed his lips together and shut one eye doing a mental count. "About twenty-five, thirty years. Hard to believe so much time has passed. I feel as if it were months, not decades."

"I hate to say it, but aren't you being a bit naive? Things change, people change—"

"Not *my* friends," Nachman responded with such conviction it was clear his world would end if he were proved wrong.

And it was a good thing that Nachman had a backup plan. He wished he could erase that first visit in his sister's home from his brain, but it made itself known when he least wanted to think of it. Oh, Rosa had been so happy to see him at the pier when he first arrived. The way she squeezed him he thought she'd never let him go. When he had arrived in her home and marvelled at its numerous bedrooms, the luxurious living room with its white shag rugs and plump plastic-covered sofas, and the kitchen outfitted with modern appliances, he knew Rosa had noticed how impressed he was. She faced him, put her hands on his shoulders and said, "Don't you worry, Nachman. You'll start saving money as soon as you get a job. In a year, you can have a home just like this." Her words felt like hyperbole, but she reassured him time and again: "In America you don't have to worry about getting a job."

But only a couple of weeks later, her second husband, the one she'd written about in the letter right after the war, who she had said was a copy of her first husband—kind and loving—slapped him on the back and with unmistakable emphasis said, "Nachman, if you do not join our synagogue and become a regular at services, you will embarrass us. Worse yet, no one in this town will hire you." Now his brother-in-law's coolness became clear: Nachman's kind of secular Jew was not welcomed in this Pennsylvania town, at least not in the Conservative Jewish community.

For him, who had been dreaming of reuniting with his sister, this was a rejection worse than any he had experienced. To Nachman's consternation, Rosa had become as deeply religious as this new husband. Join their synagogue! It was incomprehensible to Nachman that, after God had allowed the murder of their family, her husband, and her baby, she would be open to blind faith. She was never like that. Then he remembered what she had written to him in 1946: "We must forget the past." This was something he would not do. He felt it was his sacred duty to remember and to pass the knowledge to new generations. He wouldn't keep the atrocities away from his children. Though he understood the reason, the reality of her so changed ate at his gut.

Rosa had been transformed by her experiences in the Lodz ghetto and then Auschwitz. The two decades they had been apart had made a dramatic impact. Nachman wondered if she still sang spontaneously going about her days or if she smiled at anyone other than her young daughters. To him her demeanour seemed so automatic, so devoid of joy. Where was the outspoken, fun-loving, free-thinking Rosa he remembered? It was as if the persona he knew had been erased. No, he wouldn't stay here, cause trouble, disrupt their lives, subject them to the scorn of their community. He'd move to New York and take his chances there. The very next day he left and the way Rosa hugged him at the train station he knew she understood.

As soon as he arrived in New York, Nachman's old friends opened their hearts and their Bronx homes. "Don't worry about anything, you can stay with us until you get a job!" each of them said. When they all gathered to greet him in Blima's cozy living room, they vied for his attention.

"My daughter has gone off to college, you can sleep in her room, Niemele," Blima said, her eyes moist. He remembered her from first grade. She was the tallest girl in his class. She hadn't lost her thinness, like some friends who were well into middle-age spread. With her aristocratic bearing and silver threads in her hair, she looked distinguished. Nachman was touched that she called him by his childhood nickname. Niemele was the name of the child in the poem they'd read together in school. Other than these people, there was no one left who'd known him as a child, or knew this name that had been such a part of his growing up. Even Dora didn't use it. Well, Rosa did of course, but she had vowed to forget the past. An image of Blima as a schoolgirl made it hard for Nachman to accept that she had a college-age child. College—the very idea bowled him over. No one in his pre-war circle of friends had gone to college. *In America, even children of working-class people go to college*, he thought. *Maybe Ania and Daniel will get higher education too*, he thought wistfully, then chastised himself, knowing he had to get them to America first.

Jack intruded on Nachman's thoughts: "Blima, where will you put your daughter when she comes home for holidays?"

Nachman hadn't seen Jack since they parted company in Samarkand. He looked good. Already like an American!

"I don't have to worry about that now," she said. "Do I?"

"I have an idea," Jack said. "Nachman can sleep on the pullout couch in my living room. You've seen it, Blima. It's such a big room. He will be comfortable there and he won't be displacing anyone."

Blima looked peeved. "Look, Ruchcia and Shmuel and Mordechai and Hershl all want him to stay with them too, so don't be so pushy."

"Who is pushy? I just want Nachman to know he is welcome and that we will do everything we can to help him start a new life in this *goldene medine*."

The golden land! Nachman beamed. Soon he will be able to find a place for his family and the means to support them.

Entrance visas, passage on a boat, English lessons. He wished it would all happen soon because he had been gone only three months and already he missed them terribly.

"You know," he chimed in, "I can take turns, a week here, a week there, that way I won't inconvenience anyone too much." He did a quick calculation. If all of them wanted him and he rotated among them, he had about five weeks to find a job and a sublet. Should be enough. A flood of relief washed over him: his old Medem School chums did not disappoint. He was right to have counted on them.

Friends made many job inquiries on Nachman's behalf. But he didn't know a word of English and at nearly fifty it was challenging to deal with a language that could break your tongue if you weren't careful. Fortunately, Nachman had fortified himself with the conviction that in America his age would not be an obstacle and he was willing to do just about anything. He learned quickly that there would be no chance of a job if it weren't for connections, even if they were as tenuous as spider silk. It didn't matter if the potential boss was somebody's cousin thrice removed or a neighbour or even an old flame, he had to have something that in America they called an "in." *Well, maybe that is not so different from Poland or Israel*, he reflected.

A succession of job applications for blue-collar jobs where one could manage without English followed: night watchman, bakery assistant, grocery stockman, but for one reason or another they did not pan out. Still, Nachman held on to the notion that America was a golden land of opportunity. Each day he set out with a fresh supply of hope that dwindled by the evening. In a brown bag he always carried a salami sandwich and an apple packed for him by one of the friends who was hosting him. He made the rounds of the referrals, then ate his lunch on a park bench or on a concrete outcropping of a building. Just being a part of the city felt like a miracle. He pretended he was on a lunch break from a job. He would imagine the kind of apartment he would sublet. He knew he couldn't afford a real rental when Dora and the children finally joined him. It would have to be in a sublet in a walk-up, and likely on the fourth or fifth floor, but he would make sure it had lots of light coming through the windows and a television set and maybe even one of those electric floor cleaners.

After a few weeks of preliminary inquiries his friends concluded that Nachman needed to learn a trade. His administrative skills without the language were as useful as last year's snow.

"Nachman, I have a proposition for you," Blima said one day as she was setting the dinner table. She had bags under her eyes, but her voice was chipper. "In the evenings, after I come home from work, I can teach you to sew on my machine."

"Sew?" Nachman repeated the word as if he didn't know its meaning.

"Yes, sew. This way we can try for something in the garment district. You did know that the rag industry is the biggest business in New York. Didn't you?"

But all that Nachman could picture was his Dora stooped over the machine, pumping the foot pedal and guiding the delicate lace for a half-sewn brassiere under the needle. He could no more imagine himself sewing than ... what? He couldn't even think of anything as unlikely. He could deal with numbers, statistics, charts, schedules, budgets, shipping, deliveries, and if the fates were kind, with music and design, but sewing ladies garments? He just couldn't picture it. Still, if he had to ...

"Blima, can we try a few other places first?" There was timidity in his voice. He felt the burden of being a problematic, uninvited guest all over again. It wasn't anything any of them had implied. But he knew well the saying—after a few days a guest stinks like a fish. And by now they must have tried to get him interviewed in twenty or thirty places.

"Okay, Nachman, I will speak with Jack. I think he knows someone in a belt factory. These are belts for ladies' dresses, but it doesn't involve sewing."

Nachman exhaled. He hadn't realized that he was holding his breath.

That evening, Nachman read and reread letter number twelve from Dora and the children. After dinner he sat on the edge of the bed in the child's bedroom he now occupied. It struck him as funny that the room was like a miniature botanical garden. Roses climbed on the ruffled curtains, on the wallpaper, and on the very bedspread on which he sat. He fingered the blue air-mail envelope he had already read several times, but it gave him pleasure to know that when he unfolded the two thin flaps he would be hearing their voices once again. It was reassuring that an ocean away there were three people who loved him enough to give up their newly found home and come to live with him in this alien land. Still, he worried about how it would all work out. Could he make them happy here, in a land where except for Rosa there was not a single relative and where Dora did not know anyone? How would the children take to a new language and the necessity of making new friends? They were now teenagers, so it would be difficult. He forced himself to stop brooding and returned to the letter, but there was a knot in the pit of his stomach.

They were punctual in responding to one another and wrote letters daily, numbering them so they could reconstitute their written conversations easily. On the days one or the other of them had to skip writing, there were profuse apologies and good reasons for the lapse. He longed to hear their actual voices, each with its unique timbre, but calling overseas was impossible. Even his hosts could not afford such luxury and they were already part of the burgeoning American middle class.

Letter number twelve made him sadder and more vulnerable than he had felt yet. He had disillusioned Dora, because when he departed Israel they thought that Rosa would help him find a job quickly. Dora reminded him of that in every letter. And now what? He had tried to get jobs in Pennsylvania and New York for four months and nothing; no results, not even the faintest interest in any of his skills. He was sorry he'd written to Dora what Rosa told him about how quickly they could enjoy the American life he had envisioned. Now she wrote: "My dearest, Nachman, our money is running out. I am trying to sell more of our household possessions to make ends meet ..."

The words made him feel awful. He sat chewing his lip absentmindedly and recalled what Daniel, only thirteen, had written in the previous letter: "A man offered us a pittance for our brand-new fan. I am completely insulted by this idiot's offer, it's a fraction of what you paid for it." Smart kid.

Nachman smiled, but it pained him that without the fan they would swelter in the Tel Aviv heat. Dora was trying to sell their custom-made down quilts covered in blue and gold silk squares they had brought from Poland, but in the Middle East there were few takers. "I did sell the embroidered pillowcases and matching sheets," Dora wrote. "Don't worry, Nachman, I think I can make the rent this month."

Previously, Nachman had to tell Dora that in New York two people had to work outside the home in order to cover the rent for a modest two-room apartment, the gas and electric bills and to buy groceries. He wrote his budget projections: "If we could each make $40 a week we'll be set. And you would have to work only for a short while until I can get a raise, then you can be my English queen again and not have to travel two hours a day on the subway. The bad thing, though, that in all fairness I have to reveal to you, is that you will have to work in a shop for someone else. I know you have been your own boss all your life, but here it is simply not possible."

How he hated telling her that, but it was only fair to let her know the good and the bad. He had already written many times about the wonderful possibilities here: "Dora can you believe that every single one of my friends has a television, a telephone, an electric vacuum cleaner and brand-new gas stove?" But in his heart of hearts he knew that Dora was never impressed by possessions.

Nachman blinked to clear the tears in his eyes and focused on the letter again. The very act of looking at their handwriting brought them closer: Dora's barely intelligible scribbles that ran at erratic angles; Ania's plump, generous letters; and Daniel's perfectly formed tiny characters, well-engineered, standing straight and never straying from the horizontal line. *Just like their personalities*, Nachman thought. Yet this letter was different. Dora's tone was ominous.

> Nachman, you asked me in your last letter to advise you how long you should wait before you determine if we can make it in America. I will not help you with this. It was your idea to go and you are on your own with this decision. I will only say that I am willing to live with any decision you make. I just want the empty chasm between us to close as soon as possible.

The letter was like a mosquito. It buzzed non-stop and kept him awake for many nights in a row. He agonized. *How long before I give up and return to Israel with my tail between my legs? No, never. I am not giving up*, he concluded time and again, though there was a residue of loneliness and doubt lurking beneath his easygoing surface. Something was bound to turn up soon. In the meantime, he would start taking evening English classes at the local high school. He remembered how easily Russian had come to him, but then again it was a Slavic language, a cousin to Polish. English, on the other hand, was diabolical. His tongue would never be able to make those "th" sounds!

On a Sunday afternoon Nachman sat on the bed with a black-lined notebook in his lap reviewing the week's vocabulary words for the Monday quiz when the telephone rang. Blima and her husband were out and he was not in the habit of answering their phone. But it rang so insistently that he ventured out into the hallway where it sat on a little table with a seat attached and answered it. He lifted the heavy black receiver tentatively. It was not his home after all. He was relieved when he heard Jack's raspy voice. He sounded excited.

"Nachman, I have a word of an opening in a leather belt factory, but I was uncomfortable telling you about it," Jack said.

Oh, that must be the job Blima had mentioned several weeks before, Nachman remembered.

"Uncomfortable? Why?" Nachman was genuinely surprised.

"Because—"

"Because what?" Nachman pursued.

"Well, you were a big man in Poland. Blima had told me how you managed a division with hundreds of employees back in Lodz."

"So what?" Nachman said. "Work is work, there is no shame in a honest day's work."

Jack was quiet for a moment then said, "I know other immigrants, professionals, they would never consider doing factory work."

"You know me better than that, Jack. I come from the working class—the proletariat. Remember? I don't care what I do as long as I work. If I can make $40 a week, I'll be fine. I'll be able to rent an apartment."

"Okay. I will call the boss today. Tomorrow morning I want you to go to West 35th Street and see him."

At last Nachman had a job. He wouldn't have to take Blima up on her offer to teach him how to sew. The factory in the garment district was a jumble of noisy machines operated by Puerto Rican and black workers. Stacks of leather sheets lay piled on long tables. The stacks teetered precariously, ready to be cut into belts. As he took in the shop, the only familiar feature was the smell of leather. Except for the foreman, he was the only white face on the floor. He couldn't communicate with the workers but they smiled at him. He appreciated that they gave him this universal sign of welcome. Instantly, Nachman regretted that the world had abandoned Esperanto. *If we all spoke it, things would be so much easier,* he thought, as the foreman instructed him in broken Polish how to use the machine.

At the end of two weeks at the belt factory Nachman wrote to Dora:

> You see there was nothing to lose your head over. I have managed to earn $72 already. Some of my pay goes for taxes, but I am careful with spending and eat only soup for dinner at the buffet. They are so nice here and give me three slices of bread with butter instead of the two they are supposed to. I am still not paying rent. This way I'll save up enough so you and Ania can buy a couple of gently used American dresses for your trip ... when you get your visas. Remember? I showed you that thrift shop on Allenby Street before I left. I want to make sure you arrive in New York in style. But first things first. I will write Rosa again to see if she has contacted her Senators about expediting your visas.

Soon Nachman fell into the rhythm of a workingman's life. It made him happy to get up at six thirty in the morning and be out the door by seven. He walked to the subway purposefully, like an American, and already felt comfortable riding it. He knew the names of all the stops on the D line. By eight he stood at the machine that made holes in the belts. He found the work easy enough—not inspiring, but it was work! At six thirty in the evening he rushed into the subway so he could make it on time to his English class in the Bronx where he joined a mini United Nations of classmates.

"Dora," he wrote, "you would hardly believe the mix of people in my class, two Russians, three Italians, one Puerto Rican, and one French. Where but in America can you find such an interesting mix?"

The daily two-hour class was over by nine thirty and he was so tired by the time Blima opened the door and offered

him a snack that all he could do is say, "No thanks, I have just
enough energy to do my homework." Then he'd collapse into
a sleep deeper than he had known for years.

One day, after Nachman had rotated to stay with Hershl,
his host came home from work so excited he could hardly
speak: "Niemele, I think I have found you a job."

"But Hershl, I have a job already."

Hershl shook his head impatiently. "You know that I work
for a printer? Right? Well, my boss knows another printing-
shop owner, who happens to be a rabbi. He'd probably pay
you a little more than your factory boss. He needs someone to
deliver fresh reams of paper from the warehouse to his shop
and to make deliveries of print jobs to his clients. Do you think
you can do that?"

"But Hershl, how are the deliveries made? I don't drive."

"To tell you the truth, I have no idea, but if you want the
job I'll tell him tomorrow."

"Of course I want that job. It sounds more interesting than
standing at a machine all day and I can use any extra money
... that's for sure."

Nachman needn't have worried about driving. The paper
deliveries were made by hand truck. All he had to do was to
load the cartons of paper onto the truck, balance them carefully, and make sure that none slid off as he steered the heavy
stack on uneven pavement and over high curbs. Getting across
the street during rush hour and at lunchtime required acro-
batic skills. People came out of office buildings in giant waves.
They advanced like armies in tight formations, meandering
between trucks and cars making turns. If one wasn't careful
and equipped with eyes at the back of one's head, one could
be toppled in an instant. And with a load like his, Nachman
knew that it would cost him his job. He knew well what some
people would say, "Aren't you embarrassed to do such menial

labour—you, Niemele, with such a good head and so much talent?" But he was not embarrassed in the least.

His new boss was a nice man and communicated with him in Yiddish. *Ahh, what a pleasure to speak my mother tongue without anyone chastising me,* Nachman thought. After one week the boss said, "Little by little I will teach you how the photo-offset printing process works and in time you may become a stripper." Nachman was alarmed. Stripping—wasn't that something he had read about in Polish newspapers; about people who flung garments off their bodies until they stood naked as the day they were born? He couldn't for the life of him fathom what such an indecent profession had to do with printing.

"What does this job entail?" he asked cautiously, hoping he had misheard. The normally serious boss, a rabbi with a foot-long greying beard burst into a deep belly laugh.

"Stripping in my business is a process of preparing the negatives for the press. One needs a bit of design sensibility and for my jobs, a knowledge of Yiddish. As you might have noticed many of my clients are yeshivas. They need me to print many of their newsletters, books, and brochures in Yiddish. My black and Puerto Rican employees can't help me prepare those layouts. I can't expect them to know an aleph from a beit."

Doing something that entailed design, now that was something of real interest. And to use Yiddish, that was a delightful surprise. Nachman had missed reading Yiddish printed words; for the previous twenty years they had been the forbidden fruit. Who would have thought that hauling paper on the streets of Manhattan would lead down such a promising path? What would Dora think about this job?

The paycheque Nachman received that first week—$38.49 after taxes—seemed like a generous sum after eighteen months of unemployment in Israel, but he hadn't yet tried to rent an apartment or shop for groceries. The size of the paycheque mattered a lot less than the fact that he was once again earning a living and that he could walk with his head raised high. He did not know that the average American family income was around $5,000 per year in 1959. Unless both he and Dora worked, they would fall well below poverty level. Their lives would bear no resemblance to the economically comfortable existence in Poland. No summer cottages, no vacations in the mountains.

For now the most pressing concern was to find a strategy to get Dora and the children to America, because if that did not work out due to quota restrictions, everything else would be meaningless and there was no way he was going back. Of all the places in the previous twenty years, New York felt more like home than any other.

My father once told me that when he awaited our arrival in New York he measured each week by the number of minutes, not days. For him time dragged like an old man climbing a tall staircase. Our letters became more urgent. Sometimes we wrote twice a day, just so every new morsel of information would be transmitted. "By now Rosa has contacted each of her Senators and appealed to them for help in expediting your visas.... She will call their offices next week," he wrote. Each tiny advance made our departure feel imminent, but then another setback, another inoculation, another form to be submitted.

I remember how conflicted I felt. I missed my father desperately and worried we might never see him again, but a part of me didn't want the visas to come. I was as in love with Israel, as a young girl who falls head over heels for a first boyfriend: passionate, blind to reality, and nervous about potential separation. Here I felt a part of something though I wasn't exactly sure what. I didn't want to leave my blond Turkish boyfriend or my many cousins who had taken me into their family as if I were a sister, not a mere cousin. But the visas came in August 1959 and we set off for America: Me with turmoil in my stomach and my brain, Daniel with excitement, and Mama—well, it was always hard to know what she was thinking. She was a deep and dark well. I agonized: *Where would I go to school? How would I communicate? Where would we live?* After a stormy, twelve-day passage on the SS *Constitution*, we were greeted first by the Statue of Liberty then by my father and finally by his entourage of Rosa, her family, and my father's friends.

Everything looked strange: the buildings loomed dark and endless, like the Tatra peaks we could never reach. What a contrast they made to the low, pastel Bauhaus architecture of Tel Aviv. The noise was overwhelming. The air was different: it enveloped me in a hot, sticky embrace that threatened to strangle me. I felt totally lost and miserable, and if it weren't for my father's excited chatter, I'd have braved a swim back, though I didn't know how to swim.

After ten of the most unsettling months apart, when we were finally reunited life began to assume a kind of normal rhythm, but it was a new, rougher normal. We struggled with the more rapid pace of life, the brashness, the difficult language, the overwhelmingly noisy subways, the anonymity of neighbours. Still, time took off like a bird soaring on currents.

Chapter Eight

How I managed to transform myself from a diffident, Heidi-like, pigtailed Polish girl into a reasonable facsimile of an Israeli sabra with bare feet, bronzed face, and confident attitude is the essential mystery of the immigrant experience. But as this rapid change took place, neither I nor my parents could have imagined me shedding the new persona in favour of yet another. After my arrival in New York, the former Anetka, who had become an Israeli Anat, turned into Annette. I continued to excel academically at the highly selective Bronx High School of Science, where I was admitted by a sheer miracle, without a word of English. Within three months, I wrote a composition on the American Revolution and my strict, owlish history teacher gave me an A. My parents could hardly believe it. "You know so much English already, how is it possible?" Seeing them beaming I felt better about being uprooted so harshly from my beloved Israel, but I still schemed how I could go back. If it weren't for meeting David, I might have found a way to return.

David, my husband, had been a classmate at the same high school, but then I was still too reticent about my ability to speak English so I remained on the sidelines and did not engage in the school's social life as did David. I hardly interacted with anyone and never noticed David, nor he me.

We first met at a mutual friend's holiday party in our first year of college and it was love at first sight for both of us.

When I was admitted to City College of the City University of New York, the same school as David and scores of other immigrant children, I became the first person in our family to attend college. My high school guidance counsellor had assured me that City, as it was called, was a one of a kind, top-notch academic institution, that getting in was equivalent to getting a full scholarship to an Ivy League school. Were it not for City, I might not have attended college, as my parents made just enough money to cover basic necessities. Going through college with David made those years more exciting than I ever imagined they could be. We took many classes together and I doubt I would have done as well in organic chemistry and calculus if I'd studied on my own. I graduated with a bachelor of science in biology and David with a bachelor's in chemistry.

We were married in 1965, immediately after college graduation, but not before a minor battle with my father. I knew his attitude toward weddings well. It could be summed up in his oft-repeated pronouncement, "Vedding, shmedding, if you love each other vot else do you need?" He never gave much credence to official ceremonies and when it came to my wedding he gave me a hell of a hard time. As an atheist, he did not want me to be married in a synagogue. He could not believe that his only daughter, the one who was said to be his clone, would do this. "Why can't you just go to city hall and get the certificate, like me and Mama?" he pleaded.

"You two were married in Kyrgyzstan, during the war. It's no comparison."

"Oy, Ania, do you think that the mumbo jumbo from a rabbi you don't even know will improve your marriage? You need love to have a good marriage, nothing else." When I stood my ground he said, "I hope you won't expect me to wear a yarmulke to the synagogue. If I have to wear it, I'm not coming."

This attitude of his to avoid anything remotely related to religion was familiar to me, but I thought he'd relent for my

big day. Actually, neither I nor David needed a rabbi, but we
wanted to please his Orthodox Jewish paternal grandparents.
David's mother was Puerto Rican and that side of the family
certainly did not care. In the end, my mother intervened and
persuaded my father to attend the service that, fortunately,
was Reform and a yarmulke was optional. The wedding was
modest, practically a non-affair. An awkward reception in my
in-law's house followed an equally awkward ceremony in a
cavernous reformed temple that resembled a church. There
was not much to prepare for. I bought my $15 white wedding
gown in Klein's bargain basement on 14th Street. A pair of
white gloves that reached my elbows and a tiny headpiece
with a white fabric rose on top were the extravagances I
allowed myself.

One reason I believe my father relented and consented
to appear at the synagogue ceremony is that he liked David
very much. Both of my parents did. David's attendance at
the Bronx High School of Science—the only student from
his middle school who was admitted—was evidence enough
of his intelligence, but his confident, warm personality won
them over first. They marvelled at his cascade of black curls
and six-foot height. Among them and their short European
friends he looked like a giant.

"Your daughter married a real American, not a *greener*,
like us. You will be okay in America," they assured my father,
though he did not need such reassurance. He was all right
from the minute he landed in the New World.

It was my mother who was not. She was pleased with her
children's academic successes. Daniel entered the elite Bronx
High School of Science and then the Cooper Union for the
Advancement of Science and Art, one of the nation's foremost
institutions. He graduated with a degree in architecture. There
was no doubt in Dora's mind that the move to America was
beneficial for the children, but for her ... she'd never feel here
at home. My mother's grief was well armoured by a protective
coating of biting humour, most with a political bent. She
could tell jokes with professional timing and had an uncanny

ability to memorize dozens of the most barb-ridden puns. I have no such talent, but I recall one joke that she told about an interview at a Russian radio station:

Interviewer:	We hear that gulag conditions aren't as bad as some people claim.
Journalist:	You are absolutely right. A colleague went to investigate five years ago and hasn't returned. He must really like it.

When she presided over jovial chats with acquaintances over tea, no one would have guessed her inner state because the conversations were punctuated by peals of laughter. But I knew it was her means of keeping the ghosts at bay. And unlike most women in their mid-fifties, my mother enjoyed interacting with young people, my and my brother's friends. She didn't mind our music or long hair or outlandish hippy clothes. "I prefer to hear new ideas. You young people will inherit this world. I'm tired of the rehashing the past," she'd say, her cheeks and eyes aglow, even when she became ill.

In 1965, I became pregnant with our first child. I was twenty-two and terrified of giving birth. "How would something as big as a human come out of *there*?" I would ask her. She always gave me a variation on the same theme. "Look around you," she'd say. "See these hundreds of people walking around the street?"

"Yes. What about them?"

"They were all born. All their mothers gave birth! If so many women can do it, why shouldn't you be able to?" It always made me feel lighter and silly for having worried.

Within two years of our Niagara Falls honeymoon we had two blue-eyed babies: a girl, Jessica, and a boy, Jeremy. My parents were delighted beyond any expectations. When she still worked, my mother devised a route home from her job in the garment district that took her directly through the Macy's children's department and bought more little outfits than my baby girl could possibly wear. My father loved parading in Van Cortlandt Park with his granddaughter in the carriage. He took to calling Jessica "my *ponczek*"—a Polish jelly doughnut. "She's as plump and as sweet," he'd say. And just as when I was born, he was thrilled to have a female grandchild. When our son, Jeremy, was born two years later, it was another cause for joyful celebration. We need more Jewish children, was the unspoken desire of both my parents and though I never heard them say it, I saw it in their eyes every time they beheld the children, or when they told them of the lost family members when our children grew older.

I had begun my professional life as a researcher at the Sloan Kettering Cancer Center in New York, but after the children were born and past infancy, I itched to get back to work. I missed the camaraderie, and a second income would be enormously helpful. I pursued graduate studies in educational administration and eventually accepted a job at the Bronx Zoo. Here, unlike in my previous job, the work was all about life and renewal. Each day brought the thrill of observing exotic animals and devising educational programs to ensure their survival. David and the children never tired of the tales of my workday experiences. This was definitely the kind of job to bring home.

I was happy that my parents were such a large part of my children's growing up. I had never experienced the warmth of a grandparent's love and missed it more than ever seeing my parents interacting with my children. Until the mid-seventies we lived in the Bronx, only a couple of blocks away from them and could spend most Friday dinners and all holidays together. Our family was small, but we made it up in closeness. The thing I cherished most was the influence my parents had on the children. My father had few personal possessions with which to captivate his grandchildren when they were still young: no fishing rod, no woodworking tools, no collections of stamps, baseball cards, or any of the myriad objects that some people collect. When they were still in grade school, their grandfather's keyboard was still just a gleam in his eye. He didn't start playing it until they were grown and out of the house. But he did have one particular object that caused the children to examine it like a holy relic, with eyes full of wonder and amazement. One day, as he emptied his worn briefcase, looking for something he had stashed inside, a brown, wrinkled piece of paper fell out. I bent down to pick it up.

"Be careful, don't throw that out," my father said anxiously as I lifted it with two fingers.

"What is it, Dad?" I asked, feeling its silky texture and staring at what must have been a million wrinkles that formed a cryptic map-like surface.

"It's my lunch bag."

"Lunch bag?" I stared at him with a mixture of shock and pity. "Tinku, how long have you used it?"

"Why? What's wrong with it?"

"It's so, so ... I don't know, *ancient!*"

"What does its age have to do with anything? It holds my sandwich just fine."

Now, the children rushed over to eye the object under discussion.

"Careful, careful," he said. "I have used it for a few years. No sense ruining it now."

"*Zayda*, do you mean this very same bag?"

"Yes."

"How many years have you used it?" They asked almost in unison, their mouths agape.

"Oh, I don't remember exactly. Two or three."

"But why *Zayda*, why?"

"Why not? Who says you have to throw away things that still work?"

"Oh." They didn't know what to say in response to such a rational statement.

"Just think of how many trees we waste each time we throw away our lunch bags, or perfectly good cardboard boxes, or paper napkins."

My father's "waste not, want not" attitude extended far beyond lunch bags. Anytime he bought a new item of clothing, a rare event in itself, he would slip the receipt in the pocket.

"Tinek, you have already paid the bill, why are you saving that receipt?" I asked him once as he put it into the pocket of a new raincoat.

"I'll show you why." He walked over to the closet and took out a hanger with a brown sharkskin suit.

"See this suit?"

"Yes. I recognize it. You have worn it many times."

"Look," he put his hand into one of its pockets and pulled out a yellowing receipt.

"I bought it in Macy's nine years ago. I wouldn't remember that if I had thrown away the receipt." He put the hanger in front of himself and turned toward the closet mirror.

"It still looks as good as the day Mama picked it out for me. It's an old friend."

My father's behaviour anticipated the environmental movement by many years. He was a one-man reduce-reuse-recycle proponent before the term was ever coined. He didn't need studies or reports. He did what was obvious to him. It wasn't that he was cheap. Quite to the contrary, he was extremely generous. But it would never occur to him to discard anything that still had useful life. And the deprivation of the past must have been another reason for his scrupulous recycling.

As soon as I took the letter out of the mailbox on that day in December 1973, I couldn't wait to tear it open. It was from my father. His writing was distinctive, like no one else's. I slid my key along the envelope's edge. The dry glue yielded. I pulled the thin, lined sheets out without disturbing either the postmark, or the colourful "Love" stamp. The odd writing caught my eye first. It was definitely not my father's. As I looked at it more closely, it seemed almost like Arabic script. The words were encircled in an exotic, vaguely oriental border. They read: *Garden of Allah*. What on earth is this? I unfolded the other sheets. Each bore other exotic words written in a lettering style that was decidedly not my father's: *Mar del Plata, Maison Grande, The Mimosa,* and *Casablanca.* I opened the door to the house, threw my bag and coat on a chair and plopped on the sofa to unravel the mystery. The last page finally yielded the answer. "I am including as good a facsimile of the neon signs on the hotels and condos in our area as I can, so you will know when you approach our neighbourhood. I tried to reproduce them exactly as they are written. They are so bright, I'm sure you won't miss them."

So that was it. My father wanted to allay my anxiety about my first trip to Miami Beach. The trouble was that finding my way, though not my forte, was the farthest thing from my mind. I needed to prepare myself mentally to face my mother, whose body was ever more wrecked by disease. I dreaded what I might find when I got there, but this was not a sphere in which my father was capable of helping.

My father had called me from the Barcelona Hotel in Miami Beach where they had gone for a short vacation. "You won't believe it, we found a sweet little studio. We can actually afford to rent it for the entire winter," he said. He was excited as he recited the details. "We can see both the Intracoastal Waterway *and* the ocean from the terrace. You must come to visit," he said cheerfully. Nothing about Mom's condition.

"Okay, Tinek, I will come for sure, but I have to turn over some of my projects to my assistants," I said.

Since Mama's diagnosis, I had walked around in a terrified daze as if it was I who had been stricken with an incurable disease. I had spent hours in the library researching every study about the disease, no matter how obscure. I helped her find a physician who was considered to be the best in his field.

I took her to endless tests and therapy sessions. I rearranged my work and graduate school schedules to fit in the endless appointments. I didn't care if I'd lose my job or fail my exams. I feared nothing more than her death. I began to dread any cold she might catch from my young children because her immune system was grossly compromised by the treatments. I knew that for her the beach would be an irresistible lure because she loved water. Would she catch a cold on one of those crystalline blue days when the north winds whipped up the surf? Each time the phone rang in our home, especially late at night, I picked up the receiver with adrenalin coursing through my body, expecting the worst.

I was hysterical inside, but I wanted to project hope and confidence.

"The warm weather will be good for Mom," I said at the end of that call about the condo, but I couldn't disguise the image in my brain: Miami Beach as a stage whose black curtain was descending. I forced myself to shake off the grim thoughts and it came to me that my father's initiative to find the condo rental was a major breakthrough for him. It was his way of engaging with Mama's situation in a realistic way. On rereading my father's letter, I was again seized with worry about Mama in Florida. Two years had passed since her diagnosis and her remissions were shorter and shorter. How long would it be before they stopped altogether? But I had promised that I would visit and I was definitely going. Now all I needed to do was to steel myself to face this humid place where demons masqueraded as palm trees.

Brilliant sunshine was a rarity in dreary Lodz. It forced me into a more positive frame of mind on that Monday in 1984. Instinctively I knew that without it our second trip to the cemetery would be doomed. I prayed inwardly, hoping this day would bring success. It would be devastating for my father to return to New York not having located the graves. He was already seventy-five and I didn't know if he'd ever be back. More to the point, I was sure I wouldn't.

He remembered the exact location of the Jewish community office from years ago. If burial records still existed perhaps they would help us learn the precise location of the graves. It was a long shot, but we had come from so far away. We arrived at 78 Zachodnia Street around noon.

"This can't be it," I said to my father. Filthy peeling walls and an abandoned courtyard suffused with the stench of melting tar, hardly suggested that we arrived at the centre of Jewish affairs.

"Yes, this is the place," he said.

Cautiously, we entered the vestibule to the right of the dim entrance to investigate further. A brownish liquid flowed in a rivulet across the cracked pavement inside. An old man emerged from the shadows. As he approached we could see that he supported his one-legged body on crutches. He looked directly at my camera, which instantly identified us as foreigners, and suddenly addressed my father in Yiddish. "You have come from far away, haven't you? There isn't much left here. Can you spare a zloty for an old Jew?"

I reached into my purse and reflexively pressed a bill into his hand. He mumbled thanks, gave us instructions to the office upstairs and limped away.

We climbed up the dim, dank staircase. Broken steps and a potent odour of stale cabbage accompanied us to the second floor. At the top of the landing we passed through a narrow, dark hallway into a small office. Two old men were bent over small bowls eating a lunch of watery soup and bread. The older man introduced himself first. His name was Mr. Mintz. He said he was the chairman of the congregation. His cloudy eyes and tentative tapping gestures when he reached for items on the table made it evident he was nearly blind. I judged him to be well into his eighties. The younger man, perhaps in his early seventies, was Mr. Frogiel, the secretary.

We apologized for interrupting their lunch and explained why we had come. It turned out that we were not the only foreigners who found this office. Israelis, Australians, Americans, Canadians, Brazilians, and others had been making a similar pilgrimage to seek out graves of their loved ones. Our request for information, though infrequent, was not entirely unique. They weren't surprised and offered us some soup. We thanked them and told them how little time we had to accomplish our search. Since this was our last day in Lodz, Mr. Mintz agreed that we had to get to the cemetery by 3 p.m. while Mr. Kaczmarek, the caretaker, was still on duty.

Mr. Frogiel got up and emerged from behind a desk laden with dusty papers. His stooped shoulders, yellow complexion, and baggy grey suit gave him a sorrowful look of a man trapped in a tragic past. He walked out of the office with a resigned sigh. A few minutes later he returned carrying an ancient-looking metal box. Rusty at the corners and banged up, the file box of pre-war burial records was miraculously hidden throughout the war. "We managed to salvage some of the files. Perhaps your parents' cards are here," he said, opening the box. My father looked on in disbelief.

With trembling hands I rummaged through the yellowed, brittle file cards. Each was a precious relic. Each bore the history of a life and death. Few of the individuals whose names I saw on the cards would have loved ones looking for them. I read the names slowly. Somehow I felt as if just by saying their names out loud I was resurrecting them for a brief moment. Finally, I got to the end of the entries filed under the letter L. No cards for my grandparents. As if in a trance I continued to shuffle through the cards. In a moment—a miracle! I found the two cards: Ruchel Laja (Rachel Leah in English) Libeskind and Chaim Chaskel Libeskind—my paternal grandparents, misfiled.

The information was detailed and precise, right down to the burial date. It was forty-nine and fifty-seven years respectively since the Khevra Kadisha (Jewish Burial Society) clerk dutifully recorded this information. How could he have known the feelings his leaning, spidery letters would evoke more than a half century later? Just seeing these cards made my journey worthwhile. Though I had never known my grandparents, the anxious moments made me feel closer to them. I thought of my father's stories of my grandmother's pink cheeks. I could almost imagine her face now, flushed in excitement at being discovered by a grown granddaughter from America.

We left the office triumphantly and grabbed a cab to the cemetery. A chubby, friendly driver was surprised at our request. He had never before been asked to go to the old Jewish cemetery at Chrysantem Street. From the previous day's visit with the Olczaks we were already familiar with the location of the caretaker's home, the old mortuary. The geese were still there gazing and honking as two small blond girls ran among them. I approached the building hopefully and knocked at the door.

A short man emerged. Bloodshot eyes were the most prominent feature of his thin, stubble-covered face. His clothes were shabby. His breath smelled of alcohol. I would have been nervous had I met him under other circumstances, but at the moment he was our only hope. We promised to reward his efforts and he agreed to help us find the exact location of the plots. Once again we embarked on the search, but because the day had been sunny and we were armed with grave locations and an assistant, I felt encouraged. He moved quickly through the dense growth, with the confident pace of an expert and we followed. I asked him how he had become so familiar with the cemetary. He told me that his father and uncle had been caretakers here. It had become a family tradition, of sorts, to work there. He was surprisingly articulate and sympathetic. "Don't worry, I will find these graves. I'd be embarrassed to have you leave without accomplishing your mission. You have come a long way."

After he disappeared in the tangle of vines, a question hit me like a bolt of lightning. Kaczmarek was Polish! How could he possibly identify a stone nameplate inscribed in Hebrew, especially one that might have broken off and fallen some distance away from its designated site? My father, probably preoccupied with similar thoughts, returned to the cab to get the old photos that might help in identifying the headstones. I attempted to follow Mr. Kaczmarek, but kept losing sight of him as he bent over the stones to brush off the leaf litter.

Suddenly he called me. "*Pani Berkovits. Znalazłem! Jest tutaj!*" I found it! It's here! I rushed toward the sound of his voice. To my amazement I found him on his hands and knees. In one hand he held a piece of rock which he used to scrape mud and leaves off the fallen stone; his other hand was proudly pointing to the Hebrew letters: Chaim Chaskel Libeskind. "Only the name plaque remained, the bastards stole the large marble centrepiece," he said.

"How did you manage to read it?" I asked, wide-eyed.

"I taught myself some Hebrew, to help people like you," he said looking down. "We get occasional visitors from abroad. I can't have them leave unrewarded."

I called to my dad, "Forget the pictures! Mr. Kaczmarek found your father's grave!"

My father approached and silently bent over the fallen stone, staring at it, tears welling in his eyes. "Fifty per cent of the mission is accomplished. Now we must find Mother," he said calmly, and followed Mr. Kaczmarek down the path. Within a half hour the caretaker located grandmother's gravesite. Her stone, too, had fallen over and been broken at the corner, but since it had no marble plaque to steal, the vandals left it intact. There was evidence that a tree had taken root at the base of the stone, and eventually its life force pushed down the vertical section of the tombstone. I wasn't prepared to find a tree growing out of my grandmother's grave, reaching toward the sun. A great sense of relief washed over me. I wanted to hug Mr. Kaczmarek.

Slowly we walked back to his home, past once-magnificent, large mausoleums, now crumbling. We could see that the government restoration the Olczaks had mentioned was in its early stages. I wondered if the mortuary building would be part of this renewal and what would become of Mr. Kaczmarek and his family if this were the case. As we entered his home I squelched the gasp in my throat. It was poor beyond my wildest expectation. A large beaten up table stood in the centre of the cavernous space. Odd chairs in various states of disrepair looked as if someone had discarded them. There was a pot on the stove emitting an unpleasant cooking odour. There were cots against the far wall, covered by tattered blankets.

His young wife and two little blond girls looked at us expectantly. *Perhaps if we agreed to engage Kaczmarek in restoration of the tombstones, the pay would provide this family with food and comforts for months to come,* I thought. I was so relieved that he found the graves that I'd have agreed to any sum he named. He probably knew it because he quickly quoted a substantial fee. I accepted the deal instantly, paid him a deposit and asked him to send me photos of the restored stones when the job was completed the following spring.

We went to the hotel satisfied that our visit had not been in vain, though it still pained me to leave my grandparents surrounded by strangers and the honking of geese. It was odd. Before this trip I hadn't thought of my grandparents on a daily basis. Sure, I lit the memorial candles on their *yahrtzeit* dates, but my grandparents were not an ever-present concern. Now I knew I would be thinking of the gravestones and worrying about their condition.

I boarded the plane to Miami that February 1974 full of disquietude, my father's letter with the whimsical reproductions of neon signs tucked into my purse. I was grateful that my flight arrived sans turbulence, on time, and that my suitcase was the first one spit out of the luggage chute. *All good omens*, I thought. I stepped outside of the terminal and was immediately enveloped by gentle warmth. A taxi pulled up to the curb and the driver motioned for me to get in. He loaded my bag into the trunk and with a chivalrous sweep of his arm took my coat. "You won't need it here. All you need here is a bathing suit," he said. I searched my memory. *Did I pack one?* I wasn't sure. I had mostly expected to make doctor rounds here.

The taxi sped along the highway and approached the Julia Tuttle Causeway. Majestic palms lined the sides of the road, stretching across the sweeping bay, blue-green water lapping gently against the bulwark. Ahead I could see impressive condominium buildings, resembling sails of giant ships. I was struck by the aura of calm against which a large city skyline was superimposed. There was an unexpected sense of glamour and excitement that my mind was as yet unprepared for. What I saw just did not square with the images I unwittingly carried at the back of my brain.

At last we rounded the corner to the condo where my parents were staying on Indian Creek. I experienced a brief moment of anxiety at how my parents would look against my surprisingly vital first impression of Miami Beach. It had been almost four months since I last saw them. As I gathered my things and prepared to exit the cab I looked toward the building's entrance. Both my parents stood there like bronzed sentinels waiting to greet me. I ran out and practically tackled them. "How did you know exactly when I'd get here?"

"We watched from the balcony and saw the taxi pulling up to the curb," they said almost in unison.

I stepped back to look at them after the initial barrage of hugs and kisses. They were tanned to a crisp and they glowed. I hadn't seen them so happy and alive in a very long time. My mother wore a long pink terry robe with a delicate eyelet embroidered collar that set off her dark skin and gave her a healthy glow. Her cheeks had a dash of pink, like peaches that are about to ripen. No one would have guessed she was already in her late sixties. My father was a vision in blue. Despite his small stature, he looked athletic in his blue shorts and Cuban-style matching shirt. He stood up straight; his shoulders broad and strong, the load that had been piled on them nowhere to be seen.

We went upstairs and I was treated to a brief tour of the studio. Then my father gestured toward the terrace where my mother's dinner was set out on a red-checkered tablecloth. It looked like a tiny seaside bistro. The savoury smell of cooking mixed with the fragrance of the bougainvillea below. I surveyed the view from the terrace and was struck by something vaguely familiar on the building across the road. A bright red light flashed the words *Garden of Allah*.

"Dad! It's the drawing in your letter, the one on the first page," I exclaimed.

"That's why I put it first, so you'd know that you are almost here," he said, proud that his careful rendering of the sign was effective. We stood on the balcony quiet for a few moments, immersed in our thoughts. "So this is our Miami Beach," my father said as if he owned the entire city. My mother just stood there smiling, her face still turned toward the sky.

We moved to Larchmont in 1976 hoping to give our children a better school experience, but they missed their Bronx public school, their old friends, and most of all the proximity to their grandparents. My parents used to come for weekend visits and my mother adored Larchmont. It was her idea of a quaint British village and she could spend hours contemplating the water at Manor Park. But they still lived in the Bronx and worked in Manhattan: Dad at the same Stone Street print shop and Mama in the garment-district fur sweatshop. By this time they were able to upgrade their apartment little by little. My father's frugal attitude did not extend to the furnishings in their home. First, they bought a white oriental rug for their living room. Then my father splurged on the first Stressless recliner when it came on the market from Denmark. He loved its buttery leather and shiny stainless-steel frame.

He was especially fond of modern lamps. Mama and he would scour the many lighting stores on the Bowery and his face would glow like the brightest light bulb when he turned on all the globes on his 540-watt Sputnik lamp. Perhaps because for years he could not afford to be generous when it came to lighting, he wanted to make up for all the dark years. He loved light and his compulsive usage of electricity in America was his only departure from an environmental ethic. Bright light always elevated his mood, which would seem impossible in a man who was nearly always in good spirits. Now he could afford the lamps and since the rent at the Amalgamated Houses included electricity, he could illuminate his living room with largess. "Ah ... America," he would say in satisfaction each time his fingers found the switch and flipped it on.

For years I wondered how my father reconciled two opposing instincts: to save one paper bag for years, while using electricity with abandon. And then it became obvious. The paper bag and the receipts stored in the pockets of his garments were his past. Early poverty and years of deprivation had marked him in indelible ways. The light, on the other hand, represented his renewal in America. The lights stood for enlightenment and openness, for nothing hiding in dark corners. Like Lady Liberty's torch, his Sputnik lamp was America itself.

My father absorbed the news of my mother's illness like every other hardship he faced: we'll beat this thing. Ever the optimist he said, "She is getting better already," even though her flushed cheeks were the result of the drug cocktail she was taking, and not any real improvement in her condition. When she was too sick to work, she retired, and they spent more time in Miami Beach in the winters, in between the chemo series.

My mother delighted in the ocean. She adored it almost as much as she had loved the evergreen trees in Poland on our summer vacations. Though she didn't know how to swim, she'd don her bathing suit and a rubber swim cap and dunk herself into the waves with abandon, as my father watched from the shore. Never mind the cancer. Here she felt alive. He wasn't much of a beach fan back then. To him mountains were still the most beautiful natural places on earth.

By the time they decided to make the annual Florida trips, my mother had accepted her illness, but not in a way that made her a passive victim. She insisted that in periods of remission they travel more widely, using the small savings they managed to put aside each week, no matter how little money they made. Each of my parents' trips made me crazy with fear that Mama would get sick and not find access to proper treatment facilities. But she, ever the fearless adversary of her disease, took every opportunity to remind me not to worry: "Everyone has to die of something, don't they?" I hated hearing it, but she had a point. After a while it became a macabre joke between us. I was awed that she could laugh death in the face.

The first overseas trip they took was to her beloved Israel to see her sisters and brothers. It was such an emotional homecoming she almost forgot her illness, my father reported when they returned. There was only one caveat: she refused to allow him to take photos of her because she hated wearing the wig. "Russia took my teeth and the cancer my hair, I'm disappearing little by little," she said with a sense of irony, but not bitterness. My father told me this years later and he was still unsettled by her pronouncement. Trips to London, Paris, Mexico City, Buenos Aires, and Rio de Janeiro followed in subsequent years. In each city, my father's Medem School classmates, or the men who had survived the Opalicha gulag and were eager to reciprocate his kindness hosted them.

But there was one trip my mother did not want to make.

My father asked, "How would you like to visit Poland, Dora?"

She looked at him as if he'd lost his mind. "Poland?" she asked as if it were a place on the moon.

"Yes," he said. "We can go to Warsaw and then to Lodz to check on the condition of my parents' graves."

"*Far undz gants Poyln iz a beys oylem.*" All of Poland is a cemetery for us, she said and closed her eyes. "There is nothing there now for us."

For once, my father didn't try to convince her. He stood up, walked over to the wall unit put on her favourite *Peer Gynt* record and that was that.

The golden land had been good to my father. I knew he would not trade places with anyone. Until Mama became very ill and he was forced to retire to care for her, he enjoyed his job and liked his coworkers. The three hours he spent each day commuting on the subway from the Bronx to the tip of Manhattan didn't bother him, like some others who said it was exhausting and dangerous. Why were people so fearful? This is America, no one will bother you, no one will listen in on your conversations, no one will ask you for identity papers, and the police will always be on your side, he used to tell me. It didn't matter that the boss didn't pay for sick days, or for more than a week's vacation, that there was no medical plan, or a pension. The rabbi was a decent man who respected my father's work and that was enough for him.

"What more can a man want out of life?" was a refrain that summed up Nachman's years in America. Now all that he needed to do was to help Mama get well. He thought of nothing else, wanted nothing more. Yet she had big plans for him.

I had come to Miami Beach in January for my father's birthday.

After our dinner, my mother said, "We have something to show you."

Why the plural? I wondered. "What do you mean *we*?"

"It's something your father and I made."

I couldn't imagine what it could be. I hadn't seen them working on any joint projects.

"Nachman, bring it out. It's on top of the bureau."

In a moment my father came out beaming and holding a wide strip of brown canvas. Mama walked toward him and held one end. They held up a collage of yellow, red, and green felt flowers on a brown background. The piece was stunning in its simplicity and reminiscent of an image that seemed familiar. I stood there awed.

"You two *made* this?"

"Yes," Mama said beaming. "We don't sit around and watch TV. We have more important things to do."

I laughed at her mock superiority.

"I had no idea," I mumbled, but she interrupted me.

"You know how talented your father is in art, but he needed a push, so I decided to join him in making a felt collage. You know I have so much felt left over from my doll-making."

"If it weren't for Mama, I'd not have had the *heyshekh*," my father said, using the Yiddish word for "desire."

"It kind of looks like something by Calder," I said getting closer and touching the narrowest strips of felt. They were cut with such precision that I couldn't imagine them being shaped by human hands. They laughed. "It is our tribute to Alexander Calder," Mama said looking very satisfied that I figured out the source of their inspiration.

"We call this piece 'Calderesque,'" my father said.

"Really? You came up with this name on your own?" I asked, surprised at the sophisticated English usage.

"What do you think? That we are dummies?" my father asked laughing. The crinkles around his eyes told me how happy the project had made him.

"No. I am just … I don't know. I'm so impressed. You have got to keep at it. You are so good."

"Don't worry we have plenty of ideas for collages of our own design, but we wanted to get a head start by copying a master artist," Mama said.

"What do you mean copying?" My father seemed annoyed now. "We didn't literally copy it. We did it in his spirit, as a kind of tribute."

"Yes, I can see it, an homage. Many artists do that," I said. "Do what?"

"Imitate one another's style, like the Cubists, Picasso, Gris, and Braque, for example. Remember their paintings of violins and guitar?" I said. "They all look practically the same."

"Yes, yes, exactly," they chimed in simultaneously.

Mama's interest in art did not surprise me. Though she did not paint or draw, she had an innate sense of design. One hint of her talent was the way she styled women's undergarments, dresses, or embroidered leather vests, without following any patterns. Later, when she retired, she began to create unusual dolls, like Shakespeare and his wife in period costumes, or four-foot Dressy Bessy and Dapper Dan, felt companions for my children. She made three-dimensional fabric images of Adam and Eve in the Garden of Eden, Hassidim with ear locks, and exotic fabric vases that held porcupine quills I had given her mixed with stalks of dried wheat. She did needlepoint pillows of whimsical designs, but was not happy following preprinted designs, no matter how complex, so after a while she made pillows of her own invention: exotic birds, geometric patterns, and abstract collages.

She loved museums and didn't like missing any new exhibitions. I took her to see the 1979 Edward Hopper show at the Whitney Museum. It was the last time she had been well enough to get out. I pushed her in a wheelchair until she saw every last painting in that exhibition and I remember how long she asked me to pause before paintings of Hopper's lonely women in hotels and diners. I hadn't known then, but it would be the last time she drank from the well of beauty.

When Daniel married his Canadian sweetheart, Nina Lewis, my father took much of the credit. After all, he'd been the one to send Daniel to the Yiddish-centric Camp Hemshekh, where the two met. And what a wonderful match it was. Nachman's new daughter-in-law had sterling provenance. She was the daughter of David Lewis who was the architect of the New Democratic Party and a member of Parliament in the Canadian House of Commons. A Rhodes scholar, Lewis, had been influenced by the ideas of the Jewish Labor Bund—a spiritual brother to Nachman!

Both our parents placed a huge premium on our success in school. Intense focus on our studies and excellent results were expected even when my brother and I were struggling with new languages in our adopted countries. It is impossible to directly attribute those high expectations to the ultimate results, but certainly in the case of my brother he more than met parental expectations. In 1970, he graduated Cooper Union with a summa cum laude in architecture and that was just the beginning of the honours and awards he would go on to amass.

By the late seventies, Daniel and Nina produced two more children: Lev, born while Daniel was practising architecture in Toronto; and Noam, when Daniel became the head of architecture at the Cranbrook Academy of Art in Bloomfield Hills, Michigan. One of my mother's last trips was a visit to Cranbrook to spend time with her two newest grandsons and to revel in Daniel's success. She walked the magnificent campus and sat for her last photo with Lev and Noam in her lap.`

Our second trip to Poland in 1992 was a detour from Berlin, Germany. Though Berlin was not at the top of my dream vacations, Jessica and I joined my father because Daniel was getting ready to build the controversial Jewish Museum. Located on Lindenstrasse in the Kreuzberg, the museum would defy history by commemorating the void left in Germany by the decimation of its Jews. Daniel had won an international competition for its design, first among 165 entries. The groundbreaking ceremony was a historic event my father would not miss, and that was reason enough for me to go.

Once I made the difficult decision to go to Berlin, Jessica did the nearly impossible: she convinced me that seeing Lodz— three generations together—would be an instructive and memorable experience for her. She was right, I had to admit, so metaphorically kicking and screaming I tagged Lodz onto our itinerary. To avoid focusing on the experience to come I packed haphazardly, throwing in a few permanent-press blouses, slacks and my raincoat, but forgetting my umbrella and comfortable walking shoes. Then we were off.

As soon as we arrived in Lodz, I could see that not much had changed. Jessica noticed the anti-Semitic graffiti first. "Jewish swine get the hell out! Go to Palestine!" "Hitler didn't finish the job!"

She whipped out her camera and proceeded to document it. But as she tried to take her fourth, or fifth photo, a young man with bloodshot eyes and a greasy mop of hair on his head emerged from the courtyard of the building whose facade was festooned with the graffiti and threatened her, waving his fist. "I'll smash your camera if you snap this picture," he said in Polish. I knew we shouldn't have come.

"What did he say, Mom?" she asked, and I translated under my breath, alert now as a rabbit.

"Look at this pig," Jessica hissed through her teeth. I was glad that he wasn't close enough to hear.

"Put away the camera, Jess," I said. "Now!"

"Tell him I'm writing an article for the newspaper and that I have enough photos already." She put the camera in her pocket and I tugged at her arm so we could move on. I could see the anger in her face, but I wanted us to get away from him. My heart was in my throat and my temples began to pound. When we turned the corner I said to her, "You can't teach this kind of person any lessons. It's too late."

In my heart of hearts I thought this was some sort of progress—at least he recognized that such slogans as "Jews get out of Poland," would be embarrassing. And the irony of the situation was not lost on us: of the three million plus pre-war Jewish population, by 1992 only 3,600 Jews were left in all of Poland.

Mama was on her fifth or sixth hospital stay at Montefiore Hospital as her remission periods became ever briefer. If one didn't know any better, her flushed cheeks might have appeared to be a sign of good health, or excitement rather than treatment induced.

She was very weakened by the disease that had ravaged her body, but she sat up in the hospital bed and patted the side of it. "Nachman, come sit here with me," she said resolutely. There was no hint in her voice of what she might say, or particular sadness. There was no signal that she would issue a directive for what would later save my father's life.

"Okay, I'm coming," he said, folding up the *New York Times* he was perusing when he thought she was napping. He'd not be immersed in reading if she were awake. All the hours he'd spent in the hospital room he filled with conversation. Nothing heavy or smacking of seriousness, just casual talk in their native Yiddish that made things feel normal. He was masterful in deceiving himself that she would come out of the illness and be well again. He was deaf to the doctor-talk in which I engaged daily. Her condition was deteriorating and all drug options for her leukemia had been exhausted. She was so insistent on getting better by the force of sheer willpower that he believed she could accomplish it. He smoothed the sheet and sat gingerly sideways on the edge of her bed. She was frail; he was careful not to make her uncomfortable in any way.

"Look at me, Nachman."

"Of course I am looking at you. Where else should I be looking?"

"When I die—"

"Stop, don't talk like that. Who is dying? What are you talking about?" he said swallowing hard.

"You are not listening," she said. "I am tired, let me say what I have to say, please."

He closed his eyes in a vain effort to slow the tears welling under his lids.

"I am not trying to scare you, but I have a good idea. I have been thinking about it for quite some time," Mama said, in an animated way as if she were perfectly well and proposing a trip. I had been sitting in the corner chair on the periphery of their conversation, uneasy that I was listening in. I considered if I should leave them alone, but concluded that walking out at this moment would be disruptive and disrespectful.

"*Nu, nu zog zhe.*" So tell me already, he said.

"You have always had talent and the soul of an artist, Nachman. Promise me that when I'm gone you will finally start painting."

"Gone, *schmann*, what are you saying, Dora?" The words tumbled out with panic. By the sound of his voice I thought his chin trembled.

"You are not listening. I'm tired. I can't repeat it again. Just say you promise." She looked at him intently with sunken eyes that bore into his own. There was a moment of expectant hush in the room marred only by the whirring of the machines to which she was connected. He could not avert his gaze from the plea written on her face.

"Do you promise? Do you?" She was not giving up.

"Okay, okay. I promise," he said with resignation and sat there with his head bowed and hands in his lap. Mama smiled wanly and reached for his hand.

I stood up and made an effort to break the tension. "I'm going down to the cafeteria. Can I bring you some tea? How about cheese Danish? You both love them." They looked at one another, then at me. Mama waved her hand.

"Go ahead, you haven't had any lunch and it's three o'clock already. I have no appetite."

My father sat staring past me, his stooped shoulders the only hint of his mood. I walked down the brightly lit corridor, bathed in the coolness of fluorescent light that seemed to be vibrating off the walls. By now the cafeteria's lunch crowds had diminished. There were more people wiping the plastic tables than those eating. The smell of tuna sandwiches and hot dogs clung to the air. I picked up a wet tray, went directly to the server, and ordered coffee and a Danish. As I played with the crumbs on my napkin I remembered that trip to Miami Beach to celebrate my father's birthday.

Someone tapped my shoulder.

"The cafeteria is closing, ma'am. We'll reopen in an hour," the woman in a blue hospital uniform said.

I looked at my watch. An hour had gone by. I had to go back upstairs to my mother's room, but I couldn't stop wondering if my father would keep his promise to her. *Death* ... I couldn't actually say that word to myself, not even in my mind. I just thought, *When she's gone*, as if she were going on an extended vacation. What if he doesn't have, as he said, the *heyshekh*? Would the start in collage making my mother had inspired sustain him?

"Jingle bells, jingle bells, jingle all the way ..." Christmas cheer penetrated the institutional ambiance of Montefiore Hospital with a vengeance. Smiling nurses festooned with flashing Christmas pins on their uniforms, doctors hurrying more than usually, sharing their skiing plans between patient rounds, a blinking synthetic tree in the visitor lounge, all these reminders of joy made it a particularly bad time to be dying. This wasn't our holiday, but I bought gifts for all the nurses on the floor and a basket of goodies to be shared by the interns in the hope they'd pay more attention to my mother.

Three days after Christmas 1980, my mother died amid the merriment, making our grief stand out like an unwelcome intrusion. The experimental treatments failed. My father was devastated and though I was thirty-seven, I felt as orphaned as he. When Mama was admitted to the hospital at the beginning of the month, we all had hoped for another remission. She had packed the suitcase for their annual migration to Miami Beach, which stood mockingly in their bedroom after the funeral, bursting with bathing suits and new beach towels she had packed. I did my best to console my father though my own despair mirrored his. About four weeks after the funeral he said, "I'm going to Florida." I knew that he would hate walking into their apartment alone and was taken aback by the suddenness of his decision.

"Are you sure, Dad?" I asked.

"Yes. I will feel better looking at her ocean. You know how she loved it," he said, and instantly he convinced me that it was the right decision.

"I will go with you," I said.

"What for? I can do it perfectly well by myself."

"I'll help you settle in and get some art stuff."

"What art stuff? What are you talking about?"

"Remember your promise to Mama?"

All he said was "Oh," and his eyes filled with tears.

He opened the suitcase she had packed and added two large framed photos of Mama.

"Okay. I'm ready, whenever you are," he said, wiping his eyes with the back of his hand.

In stark contrast to the dinginess of Bronx streets piled with mounds of soot-covered snow, Florida was dazzling. As we stepped out from the Delta terminal three weeks later, brilliant sunshine and profusion of pink impatiens and orange hibiscus flowers assaulted us. It was a shock to our sorrow-laden psyches and an antidote to sadness.

After I settled my father in the apartment and bought some basic groceries, I decided to venture out with him on the main mission. "Come, Tinku," I had said, "we have to do something important." He didn't ask what, just got up from his chair and walked over to the door putting on his sunglasses to cover his puffy, red eyes. I shopped like a crazy woman in the Easel Art Supply store while my father meandered through the aisles, reading the labels on various products with little enthusiasm. I had no idea what he needed to get started on this new career, but didn't want to ask him because I was sure he'd pooh-pooh the whole idea. I roamed the aisles looking for anything and everything that might spur him on to painting.

In the end I loaded up the cart with a palette, palette knife, canvases in different sizes, gesso, turpentine, and tubes of paint ranging from cerulean blue, which I knew would be his favourite colour, to cadmium yellow, which would reflect the Florida sun. Others I just tossed in at random, clueless about the themes he'd paint once his imagination was unleashed and his grief thawed. *Would he paint landscapes, portraits, animals, still lifes?* I had no idea then that it would be none of those. I suspected that he would not like watercolours because of their subtle, muted, washed-out quality. No, that definitely was not him. But there was no way to tell if he'd prefer oils or acrylics, so I decided to get both. *No sense giving him an excuse in case I got the wrong type of paint*, I thought.

Then I looked at the brushes and was confused by their sheer variety: student and professional brushes, squirrel hair and synthetic, square and pointy tipped, long and short haired. When he saw the shopping cart brimming he said, "Who needs all this stuff?"

"You do," I said emphatically to cut off any argument.

"But ... I have never painted on a canvas. I have no idea how to mix the paints."

"You'll learn. There's a first time for everything."

❖❖❖❖

In late fall of 1984, we returned to the United States with a sense of accomplishment and awaited word that the work on my grandparents' graves was completed. Spring came with gusts of warm air and shockingly green leaves. Renewal seemed to be everywhere. Many months had passed without any sign from Mr. Kaczmarek. I had not expected a call because he had no telephone, but I checked our mailbox for his letter and photos with increasing urgency as spring gave way to a scorching August.

By September 1985, I decided to contact Danuta and ask her to visit Kaczmarek to check on the cause for the delay. Almost a year had passed, but I didn't want to believe that he simply pocketed the down payment and decided not to do the work.

When we were still in Poland, Danuta had said she would be willing to tend the graves and lay flowers on anniversaries once the restoration was completed, but I hadn't wanted to bother her with something so personal. Now I felt I had no choice but to ask her for the favour. She didn't hesitate and promised to write me as soon as her mission was accomplished. Each day I checked my mailbox. After several weeks I finally received the envelope written in her large, childish script. I stood there in the lobby swallowing the contents of her letter. I read, then reread, but I still could not believe her words.

She had gone to the cemetery, but instead of Mr. Kaczmarek she spoke to his widow. Mrs. Kaczmarek told Danuta that her husband had been murdered one night. The widow believed that the vandals who had regularly stalked the cemetery at night looking for the choicest marble headstones to steal were offended by Mr. Kaczmarek's dedication to repairing Jewish tombstones. It was also possible, Danuta speculated, that the thieves might have known that he had been visited by foreigners and had the substantial stash of dollars he was paid. The police, she wrote, were not interested in finding the murderers. Perhaps they had been in on the heist, she said. I was stunned. The chilling message made me by turns sad then furious.

How would Mrs. Kaczmarek survive? Surely she wouldn't be allowed to continue living there. Would she and her girls be safe from the thieves? Over and over, my mind imagined the grizzly nocturnal murder scene. This was the stuff of horror films, not something connected with me, however indirectly. Danuta wrote that she paid the widow a sum of money and asked her to arrange for a horizontal glass plaque, instead of a marble headstone. This way, she reasoned, there would be nothing valuable for the vandals to steal. Immediately, I called Danuta to thank her. "How shall I send you the sum you laid out?" I asked.

"After what befell your people, this is the least I can do." Adamantly, she refused to be reimbursed. That Christmas my father and I assembled a beautiful package of non-perishable holiday treats: chocolates, almonds, pistachios, macadamia nuts, cookies, figs, apricots, and raisins. I also included a hand-painted silk scarf, a leather purse and a sweater trimmed with reindeer and sequins. Then we shipped it off to Danuta.

For several years running, on memorial days she would visit both graves, cut the new vines that had grown, sweep the fallen leaves, put candles and flowers and send me a photograph. "It's just as if you were here," she wrote. As I replied to her letters, my bitterness began to melt in tiny increments.

"More than a half century after their passing, my grandparents have a Polish friend," I wrote to her. But on some days I still wasn't so sure. The poisoned barbs, thrown at the young girl that was me forty years before, resisted eradication.

I left Dad in Florida that winter of 1981 and returned to New York with a heavy heart. He looked so overwhelmed, so shrunken, so alone. I had no idea how he'd manage and not much faith that he would find the oomph to embark on a new path. On my flight back I chastised myself. *He'd been through so much. He was resourceful and resilient. He always found a way to survive. Why wasn't I giving him the credit?*

We were in telephone contact daily and I began to sound like a broken record. "Did you start painting yet, Tinku?" I asked each time.

"Oy, don't be such a *nudnik*," he'd say. "I will start when I'm ready."

Several weeks had passed and he called me excitedly. "I did it," he said.

"What did you do?" I asked, unsure what he was talking about.

"*Nu*, you should know. What have you been asking me about every day?"

It couldn't be. Did he really paint something? I was busting with curiosity. "Tinku, what did you paint?"

"I didn't paint anything."

"So what are you talking about?" I was completely deflated.

"I made a collage."

My heart leaped up in a little somersault. "Really?"

"Why are you so surprised? I agreed to do artwork. It doesn't have to be a painting."

"Of course not!" I was so glad that he had finally put his reluctance aside I didn't even care that the stash of art supplies I had purchased laid unused.

"So ...?" I said.

"What do you mean 'so'?"

"Well, what is it a collage of?"

"It's kind of hard to describe. You'll have to see it for yourself. I used Mama's felt and glued it onto a piece of wood."

"Does this piece have a name?" I asked.

"Yes. I called it *Lonely Bird.*"

After we hung up I tried to form a mental image of the collage, but my mind was blank. It occurred to me that he had given birth to something creative and laden with emotion, as if he had given birth to a child. I desperately wanted to see it because it would give me insight into him. Maybe his paintings would reveal things that his words couldn't quite do. As winter waned and his spring return from Florida to New York loomed, my mind was filled with shapeless imaginings of my father's works. By now I knew that he had made several more collages and a few paintings and had shipped them to New York. I awaited their arrival as much as his and was as excited as if I were about to meet brand-new siblings.

When I finally saw them I was overwhelmed. The collages and paintings vibrated with colour. The compositions were abstract yet evocative. They hinted at music and dance and lush gardens filled with mythical creatures, magicians and maidens disguised behind odd shapes. They were neither landscapes, nor any other genre I could name, but I knew they were unique; they had style and flair and were so alive one could be forgiven for thinking they were done by a much younger person. By now my father was seventy-two years old, and these were his first artistic expressions. Aside from making beautiful handmade birthday cards and toy paper puppets with ingeniously moving body parts, he had never had the time or opportunity to engage in any artistic endeavours. It was stunning to think that all this had been locked inside him for decades and sprung forth fully formed so late in his life.

David and I stood over the display of my father's new collages and paintings laid out on the floor of our living room and standing against the furniture. We oohed and ahhed.

"Nachman, this is remarkable," David said.

"Tinku, you are a real artist. I'm so proud of you," I gushed. "Why didn't you do it sooner?" I asked and immediately realized how stupid my question was. He had been taking care of my mother during the eight years of her illness, and for thirteen years before that he had been a hard-working immigrant with a family to support, riding on the subway hours each day to his job and before that, well ... I was ashamed of being so insensitive.

"I'm glad you like my first steps," he said. "And please, take no offence, but I need a professional opinion."

"What do you mean, Tinku?"

"Well, I would like you to take some slides of these pieces, then send them to a museum curator somewhere and ask them what they think."

Museum curators? I was flabbergasted. Sure, I loved the work, but couldn't quite imagine what I'd say to a curator and besides, I had no contacts in the art world. I began thinking of how I might deal with this request. Frankly, I thought it would be the height of naïveté to expect a professional to comment on a work of a novice—even if that novice was my father and *I* thought his works were worthy of attention. But my father didn't give up. As much as I had nagged him about beginning to paint, now he kept asking me if I really planned to obtain a professional judgment of his work.

He'd ask every time we spoke, "So, Ania, did you send out the slides yet?"

"Don't worry about anyone's opinion, just keep on working," I would reassure him.

"I am not going to waste my time, or canvases, until I can hear from someone who knows art if this is worth anything," he said.

"What do you mean worth? Are you planning to sell them?" He looked at me as if I had lost my marbles.

"Who said anything about selling? These pieces are my children. They are not for sale. I just want to be sure I'm not playing with paints like a child. I don't need something to keep me occupied." He looked dead serious. I could read it by the intensity in his eyes. I exhaled. I was happy to hear that because I had fallen in love with the images and couldn't bear to see them put on the market like just another commodity. It would be like selling the soul he laid bare on those canvases.

"Okay, okay, I get it," I said. "I'll ask Jeremy to take the slides this week and start writing to museum curators." Jeremy was a talented photographer and I knew he'd relish the assignment.

"*Du bist aza min gute tokhter*, Ania," he said. He melted me by saying I was such a good daughter. After I mailed out the slides and the letters, however, I was overtaken by panic.

What if these curators laughed, threw them into the nearest wastebasket? How could I disappoint my father and destroy his budding artistic career? Every time I brought the mail in from the mailbox I quickly shuffled through the stack of letters looking for logos of the museums that I approached. When he saw me coming from the mailbox, my father would say, "*Nu*, anything?"

"Not yet, Tinku, be patient." In my heart I knew that at his age he couldn't afford to wait. Who was I to counsel patience? I had all the time in the world. He didn't. Maybe the inspiration that had welled inside him and rushed at his brain with the force of a cyclone would die down if not fuelled by the power of professional praise. What if the responses from the curators pierced his enthusiasm and passion?

Some weeks later I took a buff-coloured envelope out of the mailbox with trepidation, bearing the logo of the Metropolitan Museum and Art Center of Coral Gables. Initially, I was thrilled to finally have a reply, but in the moment it took me to open the door, I worried it might be negative in tone and that I would have to hide it from my father. *But why would they bother to write if they didn't like the works?* I argued with myself then ran into my study and opened the letter. I read it breathlessly in a single swallow. The assistant curator, Michael Spring, said, "[T]his work is very exciting ... a remarkable sense of design and color. The designs are very complex and advanced ... this is a work by a young exciting artist.... I hope to be seeing more of his work in the near future." I was glad I hadn't mentioned anything about my father's age.

I burst into the living room where my father was watching the news. He was a dedicated news junkie and I knew it would annoy him to be disturbed. "Look, look," I waved the letter in the air. "It's for you."

"What's so urgent?" he asked.

"It's from the Coral Gables Museum."

Instantly he reached for his glasses and said, "Let me see it." I could tell he was excited because he turned off the TV instead of muting it. I watched him read it. He stared at it for a moment and said, "See, they did write back," as if it vindicated his odd request.

"So, Tinku, what do you think?" I asked.

"What's to think? I have to get to work. Where did you put my painting supplies, Ania?"

A week later another letter arrived. This one was from New York. It exuded sophistication with its very typeface— Whitney Museum of American Art. The name of the museum filled me with awe. I was familiar with its vast collection and remembered well the last time I'd been there with Mama. Associate curator of the permanent collection, Patterson Sims, had taken the time to write back. It was heady, almost no matter what message the envelope contained. This museum, after all, had been meant to showcase little-known American artists when Gertrude Vanderbilt Whitney founded it in 1918. Suddenly I had a vision of an exhibition of my father's works there dedicated to Mama. Fortified by a feeling of confidence from the Coral Gables Museum letter, this time I was less frantic opening the envelope. Patterson Sims wrote, "I found your work amazingly proficient for a newcomer to the art scene ... the complex, more organic compositions struck me as your liveliest. I wish you well with your art."

My father read his words with as much enthusiasm as the letter from Miami, but at the end he said quite plainly, "So, you don't need to write any more letters, Ania. I have my answer." And that was all he needed to plunge into painting with the zeal of a youngster. It must have been like falling in love with Mama—an instant and powerful attraction.

I knew that my mother dreamed of a trip to Spain and intended to make it a reality in the spring of 1981, but her time ran out. This was an experience for which she had thirsted all those years when she worked, but could not afford a trip. Her pre-war friend Ruth had fought in the Spanish Civil War and told her so much about this country that pulsated with passions of every variety. I suspected my father wouldn't be enthusiastic about travelling anywhere in his abject sorrow and especially not if he had to go alone. He was used to travelling with Mama. The Spanish travel brochures my mother left behind on her dresser made me feel that it would have been her wish for my

Nachman Libeskind, *Insight*   Photo by Jeremy Berkovits

father to go there to assuage his grief by the sheer knowledge he was fulfilling her dream. I phoned him and offered to go with him in the fall. He surprised me by agreeing, but he said, "I guess from now on, Ania, you'll be my travel companion."

"I will do it with pleasure, Tinek," I said, happy that I could help lift him out of his mourning a little.

"But the *kinder*, what about them?"

"Ah, don't worry," I said. "They are teenagers already."

"That's when you have to be there for them," he said.

"David will be there to take care," I reassured him.

"*Eyer iz an oytser.*" He's a treasure, my father said and I thought he smiled, though I couldn't see him.

When we finally arrived in our hotel in Madrid, the first thing my father took out of his tiny suitcase was a large photo portrait of my mother and put it on the nightstand. "There, she is with us on this trip," he said, and I wondered how he managed to fit in his clothes. *Well, he's used to travelling light*, I mused, and turned away not wanting to embarrass him by looking at his eyes filled to the brim.

Our joint trip to Spain inaugurated a new phase of our relationship. We were rapidly becoming more than a parent and child: we were friends. I could speak to my father about anything—work, child rearing, books, politics—and he'd listen, really listen. And often he'd give me advice, but only if I asked. He never imposed his opinions. Having broken new ground with the trip to Spain, in 1983 we travelled together to China and Japan. But right after the trip he began having difficulties breathing and when I hauled him off to his cardiologist he protested, "Oy, Ania, you are such a worrywart. It must be time for me to slow down."

"No, Tinek," I said, "you are only seventy-four and Mama said you would live till one hundred." He smiled and stopped protesting. It turned out he needed a quintuple-heart-bypass surgery that very day! As I waited for the surgeon to emerge from the operating theatre, I chastised myself for having taken Dad for a very steep climb on the Great Wall of China. He was one of only three members of my tour group that made it all the way to the highest point. The rest had to be left behind on the lower section, huffing and puffing, bargaining for souvenirs with the vendors. What would I have done if he had a heart attack right there?

I was terrified by the details and risks of the surgery that Dr. Messina, the cardiac surgeon, spelled out all too clearly. My father laughed, and said, "If Dr. Messina is confident, so am I." When the nurses wheeled my father into the operating suite I was overcome with such fear that mindlessly I walked through the hospital and down the block to the Cathedral of Saint John the Divine. I had no idea why I went there, but if someone could have guaranteed a positive outcome to the surgery in exchange for conversion at that moment I am sure I'd have done it. I looked up at the stained-glass windows and my mind raced from images of the saw cutting through my father's chest to how he'd laugh if he knew I wandered into a church. I must never tell him!

I came to my senses and walked along Amsterdam Avenue thinking of the trip to China, now much calmer than before I entered. Neither of us had made a likely candidate for that trip. Though travel tested, at his advanced age my father might not have tolerated the rigours of travel in China's remote southern frontier. I wished I thought about it then. As a barely-qualified tour leader, I had to devote my attention to the trustees who had spent a bundle on the promised adventure. I knew there would be little time left to dote on my father. After much diplomatic haggling, my zoo had secured the rare permission for our group of thirteen travellers to visit the panda reserve in Sichuan Province. It was to be the highlight of that portion of the trip. My group members, seasoned travellers who had seen wildlife on all continents, chatted among themselves excited as kids at the prospect of coming nose to nose with the fluffy, endangered darlings of the conservation movement.

"Only six!" our Chinese minder informed me on the morning of our panda reserve day. "Only six permitted to enter the restricted area!" There was a hard edge to his voice and I hoped that no one in my group had heard him.

"But sir!" I pleaded and argued to no avail.

His eyes narrowed and he stood stiffer. "Only six can come in. Take it or leave it." He straightened the sleeves of his drab olive uniform.

My job was on the line. I turned to my secret weapon.

I left the bureaucrat fuming at my resistance and called my dad to my cavernous hotel room, down an endless hallway monitored at all times by a squat woman.

"Oh, Tinek," I said near tears, "these officials make me crazy. What would you do?"

"Ach, don't worry. It's not the worst thing in the world not to see pandas. There is so much more to China than just the animals."

"Yeah, like what?"

"Oy, Ania, don't be silly." He patted my hand and smiled. "I was speaking to some of the group members the other morning and it came out that they would love to visit the Stone Forest in Yunnan Province."

"Stone Forest? But it's not on our itinerary."

"Exactly! You should tell the Chinese official that they will need to rearrange it since they disappointed your group."

"But, but ... what about the pandas?"

"If you are asking me, no one should go. It's only fair. They won't mind as much if none of them goes. At worst, they'll be angry with the Chinese, not with you."

I was glad to have a solution, but worried that the Chinese may not take kindly to being forced to alter the itinerary. The next day our American group stood gaping at the odd rocky formations in the Stone Forest when several feet away a group of Chinese men and women engaged in animated conversation stood looking at us and pointing toward my father. I held my breath. Were they communist informers? Secret police? He stood addressing a circle of people from our tour group, who listened in rapt attention. A spectacle of fantastic natural sculptures stretched into the distance. We had no idea just how vast and magical this place would be when we travelled the seventy-five miles from bustling Kunming. The Chinese men who had been pointing toward my father approached me slowly and the elder of them asked in halting English. "Who is the leader of your group?"

"Why are you asking?"

"We have an urgent question," he said.

"Okay, you can ask me, I am the leader," I said.

"That man, the one in the green coat"—he pointed at my father—"we need him."

"What?" I was dumbfounded and began perspiring. "What for?"

"He looks like Lenin, we need a Western actor who looks like him for our movie. We are from the China Film Institute. We can make him a star."

I held my lips closed to keep the laughter in.

"He is not an actor. We are just tourists," I had said.

"No, no, is okay, is okay," they kept repeating.

My father thought it hilarious that he'd be asked to portray an arch enemy and would never have done it even if we were not tourists.

The memory of the trip was a soothing balm. And I should have known my father would breeze through a quintuple heart bypass as if it were the common cold. As soon as the doctor said, "Nachman, you are healing very well," my father put on his new "I Climbed the Great Wall" sweatshirt and went for a walk.

Chapter Nine

Of all the canvases my father produced in 1983, the one I was most smitten by was a painting he called *I Remember Zina.* By then he was already seventy-four years old but only two years into his artistic career. I suspect that Zina was among the very earliest memories he wanted to commit to canvas, almost as soon as he felt comfortable with a brush in his hand. In this painting he immortalized the teacher who taught him the Dutch *klompen* dance when he was selected to play a Dutch boy with clogs and a Dutch hat in a second-grade school performance.

Zina's blue figure glides across the canvas in a graceful movement holding an abstract instrument that may well be an artist's conception of a tambourine. Tambourines were often used in folk dancing and this was the kind of dance that was taught exclusively in the Medem School. Popular dances of the times such as the Charleston, the shag, or the shimmy were deemed to be bourgeois and inappropriate for young socialists.

In the painting, the crown atop Zina's head is a mark of my father's highest regard for her. Another graceful orange dancer follows Zina, but even a viewer who never met either of them will make no error telling who is the primary dancer.

Nachman Libeskind, *I Remember Zina*   Photo by Jeremy Berkovits

To Nachman, his dance and music teachers remained forever young and vibrant; not ghosts of the Lodz ghetto, but women who inspired him with an unending reservoir of ideas for his own music-making and painting. No wonder so many of his paintings were filled with whimsical musical instruments! As a child he dreamed of owning an instrument so he invented them all and played them in his mind.

In the spring of 1985, I unwrapped the painting *Sonata*. It seemed more enigmatic than his others. Who was that lone figure on stage cradling a note? And who were the faceless figures in the audience? The seating area below the stage was the first element I tried to interpret. On one level, it could have expressed my father's frustration that the war interrupted his involvement with the theatre. On another, it may have symbolized how he and other Jewish actors, songwriters, singers, and poets had lost their audience—gone in smoke of Auschwitz and other factories of human destruction. Perhaps now he was willing the audience to come back and listen, to hear the one note that survived. He gave the coveted front-row seats to women. Were these the ones he loved most? I was sure that my mother was among them. Perhaps the others included his mother and two sisters. But who was the fifth female figure? The devil-like form at the bottom of the canvas perplexed me even more. It bothered me I couldn't figure it out. I set these thoughts aside, but the painting haunted me and I knew I'd continue my quest to understand it.

In the early part of his career, Daniel was a brilliant academic architect and an inspiration to a generation of architecture students in Ivy League universities. He bristled against conventions and mindless glass-box architecture, and was not reticent about making his views known. His ideas were posted, manifesto-style, near water coolers in schools and offices by young rebel architects who were excited by his call for more creative design that had soul and history and something real to communicate at its core.

At Cranbrook, Daniel followed in the proud tradition of Eero Saarinen and Charles Eames, but broke new ground.

Dozens of students clamoured to study under him, and in 1986 he founded a post-graduate, not-for-profit institute for the study of architecture and urbanism, Architecture Intermundium, in Milan, Italy.

With his son and two grandchildren now a continent away, my father was forced to travel more than he might have otherwise. His daughter-in-law, Nina, welcomed his visits and included him in all of their family trips and activities, making him an integral part of their family, just as we had done in New York. Daniel showed him models of all his latest projects, including his scheme for the Berlin Jewish Museum competition. My father was immensely proud of it, but Daniel assured him there was little chance his design would be chosen out of hundreds of submissions. In fact, Daniel had been invited to assume a prestigious position at the Getty Museum in California and the family was preparing to move.

Although I no longer had to accompany my father on every trip, often I did because I enjoyed his company. He was full of amusing observations, made lists and notes about what we had seen and people we met. He insisted on exploring local art and music, like fado in Portugal and the silent Macedonian dances in Yugoslavia. He hummed every new piece of music he heard and made his own cryptic notations so he could play it later on his keyboard. We also travelled to Germany, Italy, France, Norway, Denmark, Sweden, Israel, and through the American Southwest long after our early trips to Spain, China, and Japan. Each trip gave him a myriad visual impressions that he would later immortalize in his paintings: an abstract composition incorporating the traditional roosters and neon lights of Lisbon became *Lisboa Noite,* and in *Kibbutz Hora* he captured the dynamic Israeli dance movement.

As art and music began to fill the void in his heart, my father grew emotionally and intellectually. His age was no obstacle, nor was his quintuple-heart-bypass surgery. He was a voracious reader and to this day I am stunned as I peruse the lists of forty to fifty books he read each year. The majority were in English, with a smattering of books in Yiddish and a few in Polish. Here was a man with a seventh-grade education, who studied English in night school while he worked a forty-hour work week and cared for his ailing wife, but he acquired sufficient facility that he could enjoy the written word in a language he found so difficult when he first arrived in America.

After Dora's death, Nachman became a diehard snowbird. He gravitated to what he always called my mother's ocean because this is where, I suspect, he felt her spirit most. He painted almost exclusively in Florida from December through April. He said the winter angle of the Floridian sun magnified the colour of the water. The intensity of the sky and the ocean mesmerized him. Both, just slight variants of his eye colour, served as his muses. He couldn't paint without them. Because he could not carry back on the plane the ten to twelve canvases he produced each winter, he would pack them ingeniously and mail them to my office at the Bronx Zoo in New York. For several weeks before his April departure, he hauled home large cartons discarded by the supermarkets, cut them down to the exact size he needed and fashioned a custom-sized crate to hold the canvases. After securely taping the box so that it resembled a professional container, not something scrounged, he would label it with my address in a most exquisite handwriting, boxing in the recipient's and sender's address with a black magic marker.

When they arrived, the neat and distinctive boxes immediately signalled to everyone in my office that I received another shipment of treasures. The paintings were a welcome diversion from watching monkeys and sea lions. Staff gathered to see the contents, but I rarely opened the boxes in public because I wanted to savour each painting privately and at my leisure. I thought of each as a child of his imagination and hoped it would provide me with the key to understanding his heart.

One of the early paintings that my staff and I hauled out of the crate was titled *The Rehearsal*. Two dancers moved their bodies to an unheard rhythm, their ample skirts flared, heeled shoes clicked, and a tambourine raised high accompanied their performance. There was so much movement in those skirts and so much colour that we felt as if we were participating in some exciting fiesta, all conveyed with a mixture of chemicals and a bristle brush. It was intoxicating that one could possess such an inner repository of energy and joy in one's seventh decade.

One day when my father was already in his late seventies he received a call from his old friend, Blima.

"Nachman, I did not know you had become a writer in your old age," she said.

"I have no idea what you are talking about," he said mystified.

"I just bought a book titled *Yiddish Folktales*, and I see it includes one of your fables."

"Impossible, you must be mistaken," he replied.

"I believe this is a collection of oral traditional tales collected in the 1920s and '30s," she clarified.

And then the memory rushed at him with the velocity of a rocket taking him sixty years into the past. He was transported to Lodz, to the pine table his father had made. Nachman and his father sat there late into the night with the oil lamp flickering and the smoke smudging its glass chimney. He greedily caught each word that issued from his father's lips and wrote them in tiny, elegant Yiddish script. Every now and then he would hold up his hand and ask Chaim Chaskel to stop. "Papa, slow down, I can't write that fast," he'd say.

"*Oy, genug, genug.*" Enough, enough. It is so late already. I am tired, I will tell you the rest of the story tomorrow, the father would say.

"No, please don't stop now. You are at the best part," Nachman pleaded. "I want to mail my whole stack of your tales to Vilna tomorrow."

By now Nachman was so deeply engrossed in that long-ago memory that he almost forgot that his friend was still on the line.

"Nachman, are you still there?" She sounded alarmed.

"Where else would I be?" he replied and adjusted the receiver, moving it closer to his ear. "It can't be. It just can't be," he said to her. "I had sent these stories when I was just a kid. And I didn't send them to America. I sent them to Vilna, Lithuania, to the YIVO headquarters. And then ... well, you know what happened. More than 195,000 Jews murdered! How could my papers have survived when hardly any Jews did?"

"I don't know, Nachman. Maybe you should go to the YIVO offices in New York and inquire."

The next day Nachman took the subway to YIVO headquarters and headed directly to the head librarian's office. First, he asked if he could have a look at the original handwritten manuscripts. Astonished and nervous when the librarian carried in a box of folders, my father carefully leafed through the yellowed sheets of paper. "Be very careful handling them," she had said. "They are very fragile."

"Yes, I know. Thank you for letting me take a look." He removed each page gingerly, glanced to see if the handwriting looked familiar, then set it down gently on the growing stack of yellow paper. And then they were there! He recognized his childish handwriting immediately and with a pang. He was now an old man. How is it possible that such an ephemeral substance as paper had survived? He couldn't stop marvelling at YIVO's prescient vision. It could not have known back in 1926 that these accounts would be silenced only fifteen years later. That made the collection effort all the more remarkable. With a trembling hand he held the page on which he had recorded his father's fable. His eyes misted. He read and reread it several times. The story struck him as very old-fashioned and silly, but there it was, a testament to a vanished world. In his head, he could hear his father's deep voice narrating into the night. But it was one of dozens he had mailed. Where were the rest?

The librarian told him of the Vilna YIVO's heroic efforts to save the manuscripts and how the Nazis had treated these materials. It seemed that a large portion was destroyed and the rest designated for transfer to Frankfurt where they would become a part of the Nazis' exhibition in their planned Institute for Research on the Jewish Question. If it hadn't been for the Allied officers discovering them, fifty thousand bound volumes and thirty thousand archival folders would not have found their way to New York. "A few years ago a young folklorist found these handwritten narratives in our files and compiled them into this book," the librarian said reaching above her desk for a hardcover volume in a blue jacket.

"Remarkable," she said.

"You have given me a piece of my youth back," Nachman said, still barely able to speak. "*A groysn dank*." Thank you so much, he said.

"No, thank *you*," she replied. "It's a privilege to meet you."

My father's eightieth birthday was approaching and he was as excited as a kid. There was more than one reason for this. Besides a spectacular celebration in Disney World as he had dreamed, he was expecting his fifth grandchild. Now that Daniel's boys were approaching their teen years, a new baby was a wonderful, unexpected surprise.

Daniel travelled from Europe to join the birthday celebration. My father said he never had so much fun in his life as when the orchestra at the Contemporary Hotel played "Happy Birthday" for him and the entire restaurant broke into applause. Seven weeks later he got the best birthday present ever—a granddaughter, Rachel, who was honoured with Dora as her middle name. My father was ecstatic and soon set out on a trip to Milan to meet her. How proud he would have been when she graduated from Harvard University and had her first art exhibition in a SoHo gallery in Manhattan, just twenty-one years later!

All five of Nachman's grandchildren were a grandparents' dream. Jessica became an attorney and served in the US Air Force as a JAG. Jeremy led a group of Bard College seniors and graduate students from University of Witten-Herdecke in Germany in an audience with Pope John Paul as part of their year-long Peace Studies around the World Program. Lev, Daniel's oldest, worked for the European Union monitoring Holocaust education in EU nations and later became CEO of Libeskind Design and Libeskind Architecture. Noam, the younger son, received his doctorate in astrophysics in his mid-twenties.

In the fall of 1992 my father and I would take another trip to Europe, but this one was nearly as controversial as the trip to Poland had been. Like many Jews, I felt that Germany was not a place I'd want to visit, but circumstances forced me to reconsider.

In 1989 having won the international competition to design the Jewish Museum in Berlin, Daniel embarked on an arduous struggle to have it built. Admired by many and reviled by some, his controversial design would take years to complete, but my father was bursting with pride and had no doubt that it would ultimately be built. Daniel and family were now living in Berlin, and the groundbreaking ceremony for the museum was about to take place on the fifty-fourth anniversary of Kristallnacht. My father persuaded me to accompany me to Berlin the same way he stood up to the vocal protests of his friends.

"Nachman, I am surprised you would set foot in Germany after what happened to your family," a chorus of them said, as if he had forgotten.

Each time he heard a variation of this theme he would respond, "Yes, I want to show something by my very presence."

"Like what?" they'd ask, irritated by his insistence.

"It will say simply, *Ikh bin do*, I am here," he'd reply.

So we were there in the flesh, very much alive, riding on the Kurfursterdam bus. My father who normally spoke in a gentle soft voice, suddenly addressed me in a loud Yiddish. I looked at him surprised, but he continued. It was then that I noticed an older woman whose corpulent body barely fit into the seat next to ours who seemed to be eavesdropping with a look of disdain on her jowly face. She adjusted her fancy hat, leaned toward my father and asked him in a conspiratorial tone of a neighbourhood gossip, "*Was für einen Deutsche Dialekt sprechen Sie?*" What sort of a German dialect are you speaking?

My father turned to face her directly and said with emphasis, "I am speaking Yiddish, madam." She must have understood him because she looked stricken as if he had hurled an obscenity, but he couldn't say more because we had reached our stop and I tugged at his sleeve to remind him to disembark. When we got off the bus he was high as a kite. "I was itching to tell her, to tell all of them—*mir zenen do*—we are here and we do not speak a bastardized German. We are speaking *mame loshn*, our mother tongue."

As became our custom, David and I would visit Nachman each winter in Florida and take him on a shopping spree for art supplies. He was very particular about the colours he selected and always looked for black markers to outline his figures, "So they stand out," he'd say. "So they would not melt into the background."

Too many people in his life had already melted, I thought.

Often when we arrived at the canvas section David and my father would haggle as if they were in a Middle Eastern bazaar.

"Nachman, let's get six of these and six of the larger ones," David would say.

"You must be kidding. That's a whole dozen," my father would say. "What do you think? I'm a factory?"

"You'll be here for four whole months. I don't want you to run out. What if you have a great idea and no canvas?"

We encouraged my father to keep painting because it became evident that it gave him a new direction in life and that it restored his optimism that had been so muted after Mama's death. While David and my father negotiated, I roamed the aisles looking for new shades of paint and anything else that would foster his creativity: X-Acto knives, coloured pencils, sharpeners, sketch pads, easels, adhesives, hardwood manikins, French curves, T-squares, tracing papers, and erasers. If I could, I'd have gladly bought the entire store, if only he'd continue creating. At the checkout counter he'd laugh and say, "It'll take me a lifetime to put these to use. Who has the time?"

As he gained confidence, my father became more interested in exhibiting his work. But he was very clear about his goal: "My paintings are not for sale; they are meant to make people happy and to illustrate that it is never too late to start doing something you love." This meant that art galleries were not a particularly viable option, so I communicated with varied exhibition venues where sale of the works was not required.

Libraries presented the best opportunity and as soon as I showed slides of his works to the chief librarians, public libraries throughout Westchester County wanted to mount a show. From 1982 onward, his works were shown widely. Larchmont, New Rochelle, Eastchester, Bronxville, White Plains, Chappaqua, and Scarsdale libraries had excellent exhibition galleries. The paintings, carefully framed by David, attracted a steady viewership. Each time David framed a painting for him, my father would say, "Just like a woman in a lovely dress."

In 1983, the *Chappaqua Journal* published a review of his show with the headline: "A Brilliant Exhibit Follows Chappaqua Library Tradition." The review went on to say, "[H]is work is abstract, reminiscent sometimes of Picasso, sometimes of Leger, in the pattern he uses and the way he chooses to represent a musical instrument, or a thought."

Nachman Libeskind, *Lady with the Green Hair*   Photo by Jeremy Berkovits

The reviewer commented that the exuberant works contained a wistful seriousness, sly humour, or both. "His work is an object lesson to all of us," he wrote. Articles praising his work appeared in local and regional newspapers, such as the *Gannett Westchester Herald Statesman* and others. The Jewish press also chimed in with a major story in the *Forward*.

As he became bolder about displaying his paintings, my father began submitting works to juried shows. The Maria Hagadus Studio Gallery in Bedford Hills exhibited his work in 1984. The Pelham Art Center exhibition followed in the same year. When he won first prize at the World Trade Center art show, he was in all his glory at the reception cocktail party, greeting guests, and chatting about how they started in their art careers. An exhibition in the Arsenal at Central Park in Manhattan followed and then his greatest source of pride: a show at the Bronx Museum of the Arts. The museum focused on American artists and now he was one of them! He looked forward to each show's opening with as much anticipation as if it were his first. It didn't matter if the venue was humble, like a nursing home, the Amalgamated Houses Vladeck Hall Community Gallery, the Riverdale YMHA, or his doctor's office. He reviewed all promotional copy, sketched advertising flyers, made lists of invitees to the opening receptions, and made suggestions for the refreshments. He would dress in a crisp white shirt, a jacket, and a tie he wore only for these occasions. He enjoyed shaking people's hands, chatting about the paintings, answering questions and being the centre of attention. He loved seeing people sign his guest books and writing their comments. He seemed to derive strength and inspiration from viewers' comments on his works.

"If only Mama could see this," he'd sigh.

By far what he enjoyed most was when people would ask him where he trained to paint. He was immensely amused by this question. "You don't need training if you have an idea here." He would point to his head. "Then it will flow right here." He would hold up his hand. He made it sound so simple.

"The most important thing to remember is that it is never too late to start. Never," he would say. When the public TV station in Miami invited him for an on-air interview, he accepted instantly because he wanted to convey this philosophy to as many people as he could. "Look," he told me, "if I can persuade even one person to make a new start, I will have been successful. It'll all be worth it."

When I heard those words I remembered his teacher's letter from Paris in which she imagined his paintings at the Louvre. How proud she would be of him now, the blue-eyed blond dreamer who drew so beautifully in her fourth-grade class. Wouldn't she be surprised that it took Niemele more than sixty years to become an artist? Yet, it would surely not surprise her that his paintings bubbled with life and music— that was just like the little boy she had known all those decades ago.

We hung *Sonata* in our dining room. I was still completely transfixed by the image and stared at it each morning sipping my coffee. It was unlike any in my father's other works and for some reason it moved me deeply. The figure on the stage commanded the attention of her audience and mine too. Though it was clear it was sexless, at first I interpreted it as female because of its sinuous body shaped like a violin. With exquisite tenderness in her gesture she cradled a single note as if it were a precious infant. Now I noticed that the female figures closest to the stage were protectively encircled. But who were the male figures, each a clone of the others? What did this painting mean to my father? Like many puzzles about him, I felt a need to unravel its mystery. As much as he enjoyed his newly found artistic talent and as exhibiting his works, he never discussed their meaning. Left alone in my quandary, I turned them over in my mind's eye at every angle. I squinted. I looked for pentimento.

"What did you have in mind when you painted this?" I would sometimes ask him, looking at a new painting. I always got the same answer.

"I can't really say. It was in my head and just had to come out."

"Well, what were you thinking when you sketched it?"

"I never make sketches."

"Never? So how do you know what to do each time you pick up the brush?" I asked in sheer amazement.

"I can't really say. It just flows directly from my brain to my hand."

My father was warm, open and easy to talk to, but for many years I did not think of him as a complex person, because he often said, "I am a plain man." And it was true. There was no artifice of any kind about him. But he sure fooled me. It took my mature mind to understand just how complicated he was; that he turned his deepest wishes, fears, loves and obsessions into the complex language of art. Anyone looking at his paintings would discover his rich inner life. He immortalized his love of music in countless paintings of whimsical instruments, both real and imagined. His lifelong desire to play an instrument and his childhood inability to acquire one were transformed in paint into a virtual musical instrument factory. Guitars, balalaikas, pianos, harmonicas, trumpets, flutes, and all manner of string, and percussion instruments populated his canvases as soon as he realized that he could now create an unlimited number of magical, musical objects.

But it was the painting of the figure cradling the note that summed up his feelings about music. And the more I thought, the more sense I made of his creation. Music, the songs sung by his family, had been the earliest imprint on his developing brain and his first pleasure. It was singing, as he always said, that saved his spirit in prison before the war, in the brutal Soviet gulags and when he and Mama were starving in Kyrgyzstan.

NACHMAN LiBESKiND·1983

Nachman Libeskind, *Evening at the Pops*   Photo by Jeremy Berkovits

As odd as it might sound to say about a man in his eighth decade, once my father immersed himself in his new life as an
artist he opened up like a flower. He threw himself into each
new painting with the zest and excitement of a young man.

He reveled in playing the keyboard several hours each day and read up a storm. And if his own life took a turn for the better, his children's successes brought him even more satisfaction.

By 1997 Daniel's achievements in his field had been widely recognized. That May my father opened the envelope from the American Academy of Arts and Letters with a mixture of awe, pride, and astonishment. He and I were invited to attend the ceremony in New York where Daniel would receive the Arts and Letters Award alongside such towering figures as poet John Ashbery and author Margaret Drabble. My father walked in sporting a carved African cane I had bought for him on my work trip to Kenya. His demeanour was so splendid and dignified that even now at five foot three, he looked taller than most of the distinguished guests. It was this particular award, more than all the others bestowed on Daniel before that impressed my father most—it was, after all, The *American* Academy. After this event my father was convinced that Daniel was the most important architect in the world. To anyone who'd struck up a conversation with him, if children came up as a topic, he'd say, "You must know my son, he's the famous architect." This was years before Daniel won the competition for rebuilding the World Trade Center with his inspired master plan that landed his name in headlines around the world.

My father had also followed my career at the Wildlife Conservation Society from the start. He was a good listener and became so familiar with the issues I dealt with that he was able to give me helpful tips based on his long years as an administrator at Centrala Textylna. His love of animals made my job especially interesting to him and he became a frequent visitor to the zoo. After a while, he knew almost all of my staff by name. They liked him too and whenever there was a special event at the zoo staff members would ask, "Is Nachman coming? I hope you are bringing him." Sometimes he gave me advice about handling difficult staff situations and sometimes he had ideas about updating exhibits. "Why don't you have kangaroos in the Children's Zoo? I think kids would love them," he once asked me. *Why not, indeed?* I wondered. I spoke to my animal supervisor. "Our enclosures aren't big enough for kangaroos," he said, "but they might work for wallabies." A short time later we opened the wallaby exhibit which quickly became a favourite for children and adults alike.

Though few women made it in what was at the time a man's profession, after a series of promotions I managed to break the glass ceiling: I became a senior vice-president for education, the first in the Wildlife Conservation Society's one-hundred-year history. Whenever I encountered an obstacle, I kept the image of my parents' struggle, my mother's ability to fight fire with fire when she tried to run a business in communist Poland, or fought for better working conditions at her fur-making sweatshop in New York. I also remembered her adage: I had become the stone grown over with moss.

Jessica's wedding was to be held in the spring of 1999 and I was concerned about my father's reaction to it. He would soon be ninety and I wanted nothing to upset him, to disturb the equanimity of his waning years. Yet these nuptials presented a plethora of potential trouble spots: the groom wasn't Jewish. He was a military man from a Pentecostal Christian family, and eleven years older than Jessica. And if that wasn't enough, he had been married before and had a grown son. Then there was the clash of sensibilities: Jessica's conception of a dream wedding was dramatically at odds with my father's. He was satisfied with his five-ruble marriage performed under Stalin's steely gaze; Jessica imagined something more akin to a royal fete. And—I will admit to all the problems—a rabbi would be the officiant. I remembered too well my father's negative reaction to my synagogue wedding and knew this would be the biggest grenade of all.

But what I didn't know was that even so late in his life there was still a great deal I'd learn about Tinek.

Though concerns about the wedding persisted, I had another major and more immediate affair to plan. My father's ninetieth birthday was approaching and he had indicated he wanted to celebrate this one in Israel. His choice surprised me; he seemed to have no emotional attachment to it. My mother's brothers and sisters were long dead, but their children were delighted to host a celebration at Gvat for their uncle Nachman, in the kibbutz dining hall. I was excited about this rare gathering of our entire family in a place that had been so pivotal to my growing up. I set about searching out all of my father's old friends—those that were still alive. But there was another twist that would make this event special. The BBC was filming a documentary about Daniel and wanted to interview my father and film the birthday celebration.

We landed in Lod airport on the outskirts of Tel Aviv on a balmy January day in 1999. An entourage of cousins awaited us and spirited us to the kibbutz in a convoy of vehicles. Then they rolled out the red carpet. They had prepared rooms for all ten of us: David and me; Jeremy; Jessica and her fiancé, Steve; and Daniel, Nina and their three children who came from Berlin, Germany. We hadn't all gathered in one place since my mother's funeral, nearly twenty years before. Ruthi, my closest cousin, the one who had made my adjustment to Israel forty-two years earlier more bearable, invited us to see what was going on in the huge industrial-size kitchen of the kibbutz. We went over right after we deposited our luggage in our rooms. Several cousins stood, enveloped in vapour, around a giant stainless steel vat. A delightful smell of broth wafted into the huge kitchen.

"What's cooking here?" My father was touched by the abundant warm welcome.

"Gefilte fish, for your party tomorrow," one of the cousins replied.

"It looks like enough for an army," my father said. He still had no idea how many guests I had invited.

The BBC crew scurried around like ants setting up lights and cameras on the hillside near the house in which we were lodged. They were preparing to interview my father. He seemed quite unsure why the fuss was about him. "They should be interviewing Daniel, not me," he said.

"They already have, " I said. "Now they need to speak with you."

"But why? My age is not an achievement," he said.

"No, Dad, they want to talk to you about your life and your art."

"Okay," he said and settled into the interview chair while one of the sound technicians attached a mic to his lapel. My father wore a jacket, despite the warm weather, so I knew he thought this was special.

He was awed when we entered the dining hall. Not only was the place decorated with streamers, balloons, and flowers, but everyone he loved was gathered there and applauding him as he walked in. I managed to locate two friends who had been through Opalicha with him; a friend from his first-grade; Mrs. Yoffe and her daughters who had been with us in Kyrgyzstan; and one of my elementary-school friends who came with her mother, a woman my parents had been friendly with in Poland. Rosa's two daughters came with her grandchildren. All in all, about one hundred friends and relatives came to celebrate. I planned a part of the event to be a review of the significant events of his life through music, poetry, and reading of excerpts of old letters. I knew he would enjoy an emotional program, but never anticipated what would happen.

When I read a portion of the letter Rosa had sent him informing him she was alive, searching for him and recounting the fate of everyone who perished, I heard sobs in the back of the dining hall. A moment later, my cousin, Rosa's daughter ran out of the room. When I was done reading. I looked for her and found her sobbing back in the kitchen. "What happened?" I asked, quite shaken at her unusual reaction.

"My mother never told me she had been married before and had a baby," she said, wiping her eyes. I gasped. I didn't know I'd be revealing such a deeply buried family secret. Then I remembered. Rosa did say, "We must forget."

"I am so sorry," I said and hugged my cousin.

"No, don't be sorry," she said. "I needed to know. It explains a lot about my mother. I wish she had told me before she died."

The grand finale of the evening came when Nachman's youngest grandchild, ten-year-old Rachel Dora, wheeled out a cart with a giant cake shaped like an artist's palette and topped with ninety flickering candles. After he blew out the candles, the grandchildren gathered around him and asked questions.

"*Zayda*, how does it feel to be ninety?" Rachel, the youngest, asked.

"Just the same as forty," he said. "I feel just as young."

Then one of the others asked, "What present would you like for your one hundredth birthday?"

"Oy, not so fast, I have to wait another ten years, and anyway I have everything I ever wanted," he said with a twinkle in his eyes.

"But, *Zayda*, just think. What if you could get anything in the world?"

"Well, actually, yes. I would like to get a birthday card from the president of the United States."

The notion that a Jewish Museum would be built in the heart of Berlin aroused great passions. The proposed project survived more than one attempt to cancel it, but Daniel and Nina never gave up. They moved their young children to Berlin, to be closer to the action, leaving much of the family aghast, but not my father. He was glad that Daniel gave up the cushy Getty Museum job offer and set his mind to completing the much debated project, even if the children had to grow up among German peers whose grandfathers may have been Nazis. It took eleven years to build the angular museum in the shape of a broken Jewish star. Though construction had been largely completed by 1998, changes of directors had caused delays in the exhibition installations. However, the building itself was deemed so remarkable that it was worthy of being exhibited as a kind of sculpture; a decision was made to open the still-empty building in January 1999. My father went to Berlin to attend the opening ceremonies directly from his birthday celebration in Tel Aviv, accompanied by Daniel's sons.

He had watched the entire saga of the museum's birth from the moment Daniel entered the competition. He followed with intense interest every media story and every behind-the-scenes manoeuvre to scuttle the project. He walked the construction site in a hard hat with Daniel and collected every newspaper and magazine article written on the subject. The opening couldn't have come soon enough for him. And nothing could have prepared him for the opening celebration of this museum. Seeing this building dedicated would be the realization of a father's and an immigrant's dream—international success for his son.

The international press was there in full force. The guest list included dignitaries from various strata of German society and notable political figures including German chancellor Gerhard Schröeder. Civic leaders, representatives of the Jewish community and patrons of the arts were all in attendance. So was one Nachman Libeskind, a small, elderly Jew whose son's creation was to be celebrated. The guests approached the massive zinc-clad building jutting out assertively toward the sidewalk, shaped like a broken Star of David and stood dumbfounded gazing at a structure unlike any they had ever seen. Some even saw it as a broken swastika. Decked out in tuxedos, murmuring words of astonishment, they filed into the largest museum space still echoing with the sounds of construction machinery. They stared at the enormous zigzag windows placed at vertiginous angles. Sounds reverberated against the empty space as the orchestra played a welcome concerto. The music fell silent and one could only hear the rustling of the taffeta evening gowns. Then the speeches began.

Each speaker seemed more eager than the next to emphasize his sincere appreciation that the contributions of German Jews would now be recognized, that they would no longer be remembered as victims, but as a vital part of the fabric of German society. They expressed regret at the lives lost and creative potential that would never be realized. In flowery speeches they lauded the award-winning design for its imagination and ability to evoke the void in German life wreaked by the extermination of its Jewish thinkers, authors, composers, and everyday productive citizens. Gerhard Schröeder approached the podium to deliver *the* speech of the evening. He was a beefy man whose father had served as a lance corporal in the Wehrmacht. Members of the press jockeyed for positions. An expectant hush fell over the room as the chancellor changed his path. Slowly he stepped toward my father, seated in the front row, leaning on his African cane. Then Schroeder bent on one knee to speak with the diminutive man whose son was responsible for the evening's event. He took Dad's small, leaf-dry hand and welcomed him, thanked him for coming, and then he *apologized*. The audience broke into wild applause. My father just smiled.

When it was completed, the building became an instant magnet for tourists from around the globe. My father's pride could not be measured by any known scale. After what he had survived, to see his son's building erected in the heart of Germany, to see his name in every German newspaper was not only satisfying, it was a victory for Jews, a vindication of his beliefs that an open attitude could lead to reconciliation with even the worst enemies. When he returned to New York, I asked my father how he had felt at that moment, what had been going through his mind. He said, "All I could think about was what Yankel, Natan, and Pola would have said if they were alive." Then he added, "Now the Germans will know for sure that we have endured. They will know it every time they look at this building. I am glad I lived to see that."

After he returned from Berlin, David and I presented my father with his birthday present: a website of his artworks.

Those were the early days of the Internet and its use as a medium for displaying art had hardly been touched. We wanted to give my father something spiritually enriching. He didn't need any more things. My father could not get over it. *"Meyn nisht a gelekhter!"* You are kidding! he exclaimed when we told him anyone with a computer could now look at his work and enjoy it. "That must be thousands of people," he said shocked.

"And not only that," I had said. "They can send *you* comments."

"Impossible, impossible," he said. "Really? Show me again how this thing works." He'd practise logging on. "So fast! Look at it, here they come. Wow, my pictures look so professional here. I like them myself." Then he laughed and the crinkles around his eyes multiplied. When the online exhibition was fully operational, my father updated his calling card with his website address. He always carried it in his wallet to give people he wanted to persuade that age should not be a barrier in pursuing a goal.

The Memorial Day weekend of 1999 came faster than any of us anticipated. The beastly heat was unexpected so early in the spring, and I was terribly worried how my ninety-year-old father would hold up in an outdoor wedding, thinking how the men in the wedding party would perspire heavily in their dark Air Force uniforms. I made myself a strong cup of coffee before anyone was up and smiled remembering how when time came to discuss Steve, the groom, before my father had met him, I tossed out the troublesome bits of information like hot potatoes, wanting desperately to move on to other topics.

"Dad, Steve is an Air Force major," I began.

"Oh, that says a lot," he said, pushed the glasses down his nose and set aside the paper.

"How do you mean that?" I steeled myself for an argument.

"Well, Ania, he and Jessica are serving the greatest country on earth. It's a *mitzvah*," he said and a smile lit up his face. I smiled inwardly: *mitzvah* is a Talmudic concept. But it gave me an opening to mention the participation of a rabbi in the ceremony. And I did, quickly, so perhaps he wouldn't focus on it.

"Okay, you know how I feel about *that*, but I'm sure he won't bite. I got along with my boss, Rabbi Levy, remember?" my father remarked without any tension in his voice or posture.

Ooh, this is going better than I expected, I thought, so I moved on to the personal stuff. I sighed. "There is more, Dad."

"More than one rabbi?"

"No, not that. Steve is eleven years older than Jessica," I blurted out.

"What's wrong with that? I am ... let me see, I am fifty-seven years older. Why should that matter if they are both adults and in love?" By now he was laughing out loud.

"Well, that's not all either. He is divorced and has a son," I spat out.

Tinek knitted his eyebrows and stopped laughing. "I see, I see," he said slowly and I feared for what would come next. But he sat up and said, "He is an experienced man and by now must know how to avoid mistakes with women.... Not so bad," he pronounced after a pause.

I felt lighter, but there was one more revelation I needed to disclose. I wanted to get it over with, "Steve comes from Ohio from a Pentecostal Christian family."

"Does he go to church?" my father asked, visibly disturbed now.

"No, he doesn't, even though he was once groomed for the priesthood," I said, knowing it would please my father that Steve veered so far from religion.

"This man has a brain, a *kluge kop*, a smart head," he said nodding approvingly. "And he doesn't mind having a rabbi at the ceremony?"

"Apparently not," I said, "even though both his parents will be in attendance."

"*Nu*, I can see he is open-minded. *Dos iz zeyer vikhtig*. This is the most important thing, open mindedness," Tinek said. He added, "My granddaughter will marry a real American, from Ohio. Ania, Ohio is the heartland!" He smiled from ear to ear. So Steve had passed the critical judgment of the family's elder statesman. I was relieved but still worried about my father's reaction to the wedding itself. Little did I know there were revelations to come that would show me more of my father's emotional resilience.

When Jessica found her exquisite dupioni-silk wedding dress, she fell in love with it instantly. She twirled around to show it to me. I was excited at the perfect fit, but my immediate thought was *This thing must cost a fortune*. We had already maxed out our financial contribution to the wedding. "Jess," I said slowly, fearing I'd burst her bubble, "why don't you ask the price, or see if there are other dresses for you to try on."

"I am not trying other dresses. This dress is mine."

"But—"

I couldn't even finish when she said, "Mom, if are you concerned about the cost, don't worry. *Zayda* already gave me the money. He said he wants me to have whatever gown I choose. It's his wedding present."

What? It wasn't my father's generosity I was questioning, but his ability to pay for it; this gift might have equalled his lifetime clothing budget! He lived on social security and had very little money to spare for non-essentials. At first, it didn't seem like him, he who was the paragon of frugality and simplicity, who'd always chose to spend his few spare dollars on worthy social causes. Then I realized she was his first grandchild, the one in whom he first invested all his hopes for the future.

I still had much to learn about my father.

And the surprises kept mounting. Jessica and her *zayda* were complicit in hatching plans I couldn't fathom. Two perfectionists, scheming to get everything just so. One of the biggest surprises were the sabers. "Mom, it's not as easy as you think to get the requisite number of swords."

"Swords? What are you talking about? This can't be something connected with the wedding?" I asked as we discussed details on the phone.

"Yes, Mom, haven't I told you? I want to have an arch of swords and *Zayda* loves the idea of a military wedding." A desire to please her grandfather shone through her words.

"Where in the world would I have seen such a spectacle?"

"I don't know, Mom, but we are going to have it all, the swords *and* the uniforms. I want it and *Zayda* will be so happy." I shook my head and couldn't imagine my father approving such an over-the-top plan: fairy-tale gown, swords, spiffy Air Force uniforms festooned with medals, and a silk, flower-decorated *chuppah*! I had no experience with lavish wedding arrangements and thought they'd conflict with her grandfather's ideas for simplicity and modesty. Needlessly I had spent months worrying over my father's reaction; now he was behaving in ways that left me totally puzzled. Jessica had insisted on making dancing a big part of the wedding celebration. My father had expressed to her his opinion about dancing many times in the past. "I don't like it. Dancing is for empty heads." It was a very strange attitude from a man so musically talented, but the austere socialist upbringing of his youth had left him permanently opposed to frivolous pursuits, dancing among them.

"But, *Zayda*, will you dance with me at my wedding?" Jessica had asked him repeatedly, even years before there was a prospective groom on the horizon.

"*Ach*, Jessica, don't be a *noodge*. I don't dance," he would say. She would persist and eventually he would pacify her, "We will see, we will see." He would then wink toward me with a look that I interpreted as "In your dreams, kid." What would happen to Jessica's plan to dance with her ninety-year-old grandfather at the wedding? Would he turn her down? I didn't ever want her to be hurt, and especially not on her big day. My father also adhered to his diabetic diet with no exceptions. No one could compel him to violate his dietary code—no desserts, and no cake, in particular. "But, *Zayda*, will you eat just a small piece for me?" Jessica beseeched him whenever they discussed the wedding.

"What do you care what I eat?"

"It wouldn't be right if the people most important to me didn't get to taste the wedding cake. It's an important ritual. It brings luck."

"*Ach*, ritual, shmitshual," he would say with a laugh and a wave of his hand.

So many seemingly small things for me to worry about!

As the rabbi delivered his lines, my father sat at the edge of a chair, spellbound by the unfamiliar proceedings. A large grin stretched from one side of his face to the other. Momentarily, at least, his reservations about rabbis, ceremonies, and big public productions seemed to have evaporated completely. The minute the rabbi pronounced the couple husband and wife and Steve crushed the glass with his spit-shined shoe, my father stood up and made his move. I knew what he wanted. He was positioning himself to watch the arch of swords. The bride and the groom were officers in the American military, something that unequivocally confirmed his own status as an American. His granddaughter was repaying his debt for admission to the country. And her having achieved a rank he never could as a Jew in the Polish military was sweet and singular redress. The music resumed triumphantly and the two lines of swordsmen looked like a miniature army ready to do battle. On cue, their swords shot up in the air, the sun glinting off the metal and the newlyweds walked under the arch with blissful expressions. I looked at my father again. His eyes were moist. A rivulet of sweat ran down his temple and he took out his handkerchief.

"Are you okay, Tinku?" I asked. "Are you crying?"

"No, it's just the heat." He dabbed at his eyes.

After the ceremony and cocktails the guests moved into the ballroom to await the arrival of the newly married couple for their first dance as husband and wife. Jessica floated into the room more radiant than I'd ever seen her. The newlyweds danced. When the music stopped, Jessica bowed to the assembled and gestured toward the DJ. All at once the nostalgic tunes from *Fiddler on the Roof* filled the room. Jessica walked over to her grandfather and said, "*Zayda*, may I have this dance?" All eyes were now on them.

I froze.

But without a moment's hesitation he stood up looking not a day over seventy, took her hand, and all five foot three of him sashayed toward the centre of the dance floor. Everyone watched with amazement. The room burst into a round of applause. This man, who hadn't danced since his Dutch *klompen* dance in third grade, was now gliding gracefully as if dancing were his life's profession. *It must be his musical ear*, I thought, because I knew that he had never done this before. Later the dancing became more intense: enthusiastic tunes of the hora burst out of the loudspeakers, the couple lifted into the air, twirled in the ceremonial chair dance paying homage to our Jewish tradition. Around them an ecstatic circle of guests headed by my father stood clapping. Of all the voices singing the infectious tune of "Havah, Nagila Havah," his was the loudest.

The day had been so emotional that I was hardly prepared for another surprise, but there it was at the end of the evening. The sight of my father lifting a forkful of chocolate cake to his mouth made me giddy.

For years after my mother passed away, we had been urging my father to move in with us, but each time the topic came up he said, "No, thank you. I am not ready to give up my headquarters," as he called his apartment in the Bronx. And we didn't press because we knew how much he valued his independence. But after his eighty-ninth birthday, he finally decided to do it.

"Nachman, why did you agree to do this now?" David asked.

"Because it is time," my father replied.

Although he seemed to have come to terms with his decision, every so often a look crossed his face as if he was gathering his emotional resources for what he knew would be the final move of his life. It seemed like a paradox. Our kids were now living on their own, but we needed a larger house. Trying to make my father's transition as painless as possible, I felt a need for a house large enough to accommodate some of his furniture that would remind him of the home he and my mother had made together. Given my father's age, I felt pressed for time. We needed to find a house quickly, one that had a downstairs bedroom for my father because his mobility was worsening, and would have enough space for two men with very different needs. David was running a small consulting business and needed a quiet office and a place to meet with clients. My father had recently taken up playing the keyboard, practising many hours each day. Regardless of their great relationship, I was worried that they might encroach on one another's activities.

Fortunately, we didn't need to accommodate pets. Our Airedale terrier, Tess, was gone and my father ... well, he had not had a pet for eighty years. As a young boy he had a beloved dog—Filozof, or, as we would say it—Philosopher. He was truly a Jewish dog. Rather than being preoccupied with gnawing on a bone, or chasing cats, Filozof had more important things on his mind, or at least my father thought so. He and his dog were inseparable. Filozof died under the wheels of a tram and my father's pain at this loss lingered in his eyes eighty years later. It must have been this love affair that predisposed him to pay so much attention to animals. He, more than almost any member of our household, enjoyed playing with Tess. Each spring, on his return from Florida he would beam when Tess barked her welcome while he was still outside the door. She would jump on him, reaching his shoulders with her paws, lick his face and hands, and he would say with enormous pride, "See she remembered me, she really did. *Aza min kluge hunt.* What a smart dog, all these months and she still hasn't forgotten me." Tess wagged her stump of a tail agreeing enthusiastically. In his preoccupation with animals and their behaviours, my father stood out among his peers. I noticed a peculiar trend among many of my parents' Jewish friends and acquaintances. Very few of them had had pets of any kind. I speculated it had something to do with the fact that most of these people had grown up in poor homes in crowded Polish cities. There had been barely food enough to feed their large families, let alone a dog or a cat. For those from religious homes, pets were out of the question, as if they were obeying a prohibition against harbouring creatures not made in God's image.

Not only did my father feel a deep attachment to animals, his way with them was consistent with his politics. I had a vivid demonstration of this on one of my annual visits to Florida to celebrate his January birthday. We had hard-boiled eggs for lunch and I noticed he was doing something odd with them. He was carefully separating the egg yolks from the egg whites and placing the yolks in a plastic baggie. "Tinku, what are you doing?"

"I don't eat the yolks. They have too much cholesterol."

"So why are you saving them?"

"You will see later. I need them."

After lunch we went to the beach. My father unfolded his beach chair and placed his book and towel on it then walked along the shore. I read my book. When I looked up I saw him surrounded by dozens of sea gulls, squawking and jockeying for position. My father stood among them like a captain throwing up handfuls of egg yolks for them to catch and calling out, "No, it's not for you, you *khazer*, you already got some. This one is for the little guy."

"Tinku, are you talking to the gulls?"

"Yes. Can't you see this one, the one with the darker wings? He's such a bully. He doesn't let the smaller ones get their share. I want them all to get some."

So it was that our search for a house began with a great sense of urgency. We looked at scores of homes before we fell in love with a Victorian in New Rochelle that had been built by a sea captain. The house once had a view of Long Island Sound. Though the beech trees now obscured that view, we could see Beechmont Lake from the home's three terraces. David now worked at the Port Department of the Port Authority of New York and New Jersey, so water was of great interest to him personally and professionally. When we first entered the home on a rainy November day, all of its three fireplaces had been lit. The roaring fires emitted a sweet smell of wood, mixing with the aroma of freshly baking cookies that, as we shortly discovered, emanated from a renovated cook's kitchen. From the central hallway— a beautiful square room with stained-glass windows—a magnificent mahogany staircase with beautifully detailed balusters wound its way to the next level. I had to have this house. There was much still to see, but I was already smitten. Then I stepped into a huge stone sunroom with arched windows running along its length. It faced the lake and was perched above the tallest stand of rhododendrons in the county. On its southern wall was a magnificent working stone fountain. The water gurgled out of the gargoyle's mouth and I could hear it whispering to me, "This will be your castle." I looked at David and could see that he too was hooked. Maybe not quite the way I was, but I could tell that he was willing to be persuaded.

We made the offer hastily to discourage the other couples that started arriving and inspecting our house. I already felt as if we owned it even though we had been in it for no more than fifteen minutes. I wanted all those intruders out. And not just them, the owners too. We got home, threw off our wet raincoats and took a deep breath. A terrible realization hit me. The house had no bedroom on the main floor. How could we have overlooked our prime requirement? It wasn't that there were not enough bedrooms. There were bedrooms galore. The master suite alone could have easily filled the pages of *House Beautiful*. But there was no way around it, the house had an enormous flaw—it lacked a first-floor bedroom. I was so upset when this occurred to me that I wanted to scream. David suggested we call my father, that he'd know what to do. He was already in Florida for the season and would not be back until the spring. Nervously I dialled his number.

"Hallo," he answered, cheerfully, as always.

"How are things, Tinek?" I asked.

He gave me his standard Yiddish answer, *"Alles gut un gornisht."* All's well and nothing's new. "You should be here, Ania. Aahh, Florida. The ocean is so blue today." This gave me just the opening I needed.

"Tinku, how would you like to live in a house overlooking the water?"

"I am overlooking the water right now."

"I mean here, in New York."

"Since when are you millionaire? Where can you afford a house with a water view?"

"Don't worry about that, we found one in New Rochelle." I stalled trying to find the right words about the lack of a main-floor bedroom.

"So ... what's wrong?" he asked.

"Well ... there is one problem."

"What kind of problem?"

"It doesn't have a bedroom on the first floor and it is a very tall house with four levels and lots of stairs."

"That's great!"

"Great?"

"Yes. Don't you see? It will force me to exercise. Go ahead and buy it if you two like it. *Mazel tov.*"

I still felt guilty at having overlooked my key requirement, but I was thrilled he had given me his blessing. The castle on the hill would be ours. I could hardly believe it. Both David and I worked in not-for-profit institutions, but we were savers and David had made some wise financial decisions early in our marriage. In June 1999, five months after my father celebrated his ninetieth birthday, he moved into the castle on the hill.

The packing up of his household in the Bronx turned out to be more complex than we expected. At first when I asked him what he wanted to bring along, he said, "Nothing. I really don't need much of anything." But it turned out his attachment to the artifacts of his life was much stronger than he had realized. Each piece of furniture we wanted to mark for the dump, or for charity, each platter, or vase, or book, he would say with disbelief, "You aren't going to throw *this* out? Are you?"

"Well ... I thought you didn't need it." I tried to be rational.

"But look at it, it's perfectly good," he would say no matter how long any item had been in his possession, no matter how worn or chipped or useless. In the course of packing I opened up his desk drawer to box its contents and came across what had once been a pencil. By now it was a diminutive stub, no more than half an inch long, with both ends sharpened. I saved it. It would be a good lesson for my grandchildren, I thought, an object of wonderment worthy of the old lunch bag.

In the end, I had no heart to discard anything he really wanted. I could not dispose of the pieces of his life he cherished. He even argued persuasively that we keep his loose-handled, ancient toaster oven encrusted with years of grilled cheese remnants, chicken drippings, and assorted breadcrumbs. I congratulated myself on getting such a big house as we would have no trouble accommodating everything he wanted to keep. When we finally all moved in, my father walked through the rooms mumbling in disbelief about its vastness and beauty. "*Dos iz a hoyz far a gvir.*" This is a house for a rich man, he'd mumble, walking through his suite of rooms. He had never lived in any home with more than one bedroom, let alone five.

Shortly thereafter I extended a brunch invitation to eight of my father's friends from his old Bronx apartment house. I knew he'd want to show the place to them. Like my father, they had all been socialists before World War II, members of the Jewish Labor Bund. Two of the women were his Medem School classmates. I wondered what they'd think of my father living in this place. He'd been so consistent refusing anything extravagant that my mother often called him "Bontshe Shveig" ("Bontshe the Silent") after a character in a Y.L. Peretz story. Bontshe's only wish when he got to heaven after a life of exemplary piety and toil was a buttered roll.

One friend who would come to brunch, Carl, had been my father's camper back in Poland. Now Carl was an eighty-year-old man himself and was the first to arrive. He entered our huge foyer where a two-storey stained-glass window let in morning light in a diffuse display of colours. My father stood at the bottom of the grand staircase leaning against the polished wood banister. On his face was a look of pure pleasure. At his foot, on a delicate Persian rug, stood a small antique statue of a butler pointing upstairs with the word "welcome." Carl looked stunned by the interior and he had barely crossed the threshold. Looking up at the chandelier and the imposing window he said with a wink, "*Nachman, du bist a sotsyalist. Shemst zikh nisht voynen in aza min palats?*" Nachman, a socialist like you is not ashamed to live in such a palace?

"*Neyn,*" said my father, a smile growing on his lips. "*S'iz zeyer laykht zikh tsugevoynen tsu aza min lebn.*" It's very easy to get used to living like this. He laughed in a way that made my heart sing.

For days, my father couldn't believe that he actually lived there and when he got used to the idea he designed calling cards with this and his Florida address—"Like a real American," he said with pride. He never failed to hand out the card to new people he met. They were better than a passport in proving where his heart belonged.

Though I worried about how my father would adapt to living away from his familiar Bronx neighbourhood and his well-established routines, he behaved as if he'd always lived with us in the house. He especially enjoyed his music room with a huge terrace overlooking the lake. The room was flooded with sunlight and his paintings hung on the walls. The white Persian rug he and Mama had bought years before covered the floor and the wall unit he had commissioned from the Russian carpenter when we moved into the elevated Bronx apartment fit exactly. It was a warm and private refuge with excellent acoustics. He loved to invite guests to come up and to select pieces he'd play for them on his keyboard. Kathleen, a young woman who worked for me and cared for our Children's Zoo animals was one of his fans. She not only loved to listen to his music, but to his stories as well. With a twinkle in his eye he would ask her, "What kind of songs would you like to hear today? Italian? Russian? The Beatles? Frank Sinatra?" He knew them all by heart. He referred to his notes rarely, but they were not what any musician would recognize as musical notation. As he never studied music, he invented his own musical notation made of dots, dashes, and slashes. He would write down the first few bars in his notebook as a piece of music came to his mind, or as he heard it on the radio—the rest he memorized. His musical memory was prodigious. He remembered literally hundreds of songs and lyrics, most of them in Yiddish, but for Kathleen he'd sing in any language.

By far, the best parts of the house for my father were the terraces. As his mobility declined he would sit outside where nothing escaped his attention. He didn't just watch the birds and small mammals, he became a behavioural scientist.

One day he asked me, "Do you have any unshelled peanuts?"

"No, but I have peanut butter. Do you want some?"

He laughed. "No, I need the whole nuts with shells on. Can you get me some?"

"Sure, but what do you need them for?"

"You'll see."

I bought what he wanted and promptly forgot about them. One day when I returned from work, I found him sitting on the terrace looking intently at his watch, then shifting his gaze from side to side toward the terrace railing.

"What are you doing, Tinku?"

"Shh ... be quiet. You'll disturb my experiment," he whispered.

And then I noticed it. A chubby squirrel with a luxurious tail sat at one end of the railing holding a peanut in its dainty paws, whiskers trembling. At the other end of the railing lay a small stash of nuts.

"I am timing how long it takes to eat one peanut and then how long before it goes for the next one. I already timed its friend."

"Oh," I said, glad that he was finding relationships, even if they were among squirrels. In addition to observing the squirrels, my father loved to watch the various species of birds that regularly visited the garden around the terrace. He was partial to the blue jays because he loved the lavender-blue hue of their plumage, a colour that was his signature. He loved to use it in his paintings as well as in selecting his shirts and sweaters. One day he called my attention to the bird perched on a tree limb overhanging the upper terrace.

"*Ania, kuk oyf di oysergeveyndlekhe bloy kolier.*" Look at that magnificent blue, he said in Yiddish. "If I could only find paint this exact colour."

"Actually, there is no blue pigment in the feather," I said. "It is only the peculiar way the light is refracted by its structure."

"*Meyn nisht a gelekhter.*" You must be joking. Henceforth he was amazed not only by the bird's ability to mimic art, but by his newly acquired knowledge of how the magical hue was made visible to the human eye.

The jays may have sported his favourite colour, but they could not hold a candle to the pair of swans that ruled

Beechmont Lake. He could not stop remarking about their grace, the way they glided so silent and powerful toward one another. When I told him that swans mated for life, his eyes widened and he said, *"Azoy vi dayn mame un ikh."* Like your mother and I. He kept track of the swans religiously. If one of them wandered off to the far end of the lake where he could not see it, he would ask, "Did you see the mate as you drove past the lake?"

"Yes, yes, I did."

"Gut, zeyer gut." Good, very good, he would say.

The following week, though, when I hadn't seen the mate, I had to tell him the truth. "No, Tinku, I didn't see it today. I have no idea what happened to it."

One day while walking around our property, I noticed several crows and a sparrow lying in the grass. They were below the terrace level where my father could not see them from his chair on the terrace. I was taken aback when I saw the bodies of the fallen birds, but had no idea what may have caused them to die. An unusual stealth attack by hawks? Pesticide from something sprayed by the gardener? Nothing reasonable came to mind. I decided not to mention it to my father because I knew how much he would worry about his beloved birds.

The next day he asked me about the swan with more urgency and concern. "I am sorry," I said, "I really don't know."

"You work at the zoo. Why can't you ask the bird curator why one member of a pair would just disappear."

"Okay," I said, but thought, there is no way I'll bother our busy curator with such a question.

A few days later he noticed that the other swan was missing.

"You must speak to the bird curator, Ania," his voice rising in alarm. "This is an emergency. You must find out."

"Okay, Tinek, I will try, but I don't think it's serious."

His anxiety made me nervous so later that week when I ran into the bird curator, I asked. I was appalled by her answer:

Nachman Libeskind, *Holocaust*   Photo by Jeremy Berkovits

West Nile virus. A brilliant Bronx Zoo pathologist had made the discovery. Our Beechmont Lake swans were proof positive that the virus was rampant in both wild and captive species in the entire area. When I finally informed my father, he was heartbroken. "I will gladly buy a new pair to put on this lake," he said. "Can you ask the curator where we can get a pair?" He was like a child who had lost a pet. Inconsolable. His usual sunny expression had changed. The furrows on his brow deepened.

"Tinku, the epidemic will likely kill a new pair. This is not a good time for birds."

He gave me a look that could only mean one thing: *I have known whole groups of living things being wiped out. This is not so new to me as you think.*

I pulled up a chair and sat next to him on the terrace. I took his papery hand in mine and sat with him in silence wondering if he was thinking about his family—innocent victims, like the swans.

✧

Presidential and senatorial debates fascinated my father almost as much as watching animals. He enjoyed political discourse more than sport and followed arguments of even those parties he opposed. "You have to hear all ideas," he used to say, "otherwise you have no basis for making decisions." On the few occasions he had been hospitalized during an election, he had made sure to get absentee ballots. So it is no surprise that he had followed Hillary Clinton's bid for the Senate seat in 2000 and sent all he could in support of her campaign—two $10 cheques, written with flair. I enjoyed seeing how excited he was about her candidacy. "What a smart woman she is," he would comment whenever he saw an interview with her on television, "Smarter than her husband." He reminded me that he'd been taught to value women ever since his days as a schoolboy and that women's rights had been very much a part of the Jewish Bund party platform as far back as the turn of the century. Despite his age, he was a modern man ahead of his time, more comfortable with women in authority roles than many men of his children's generation, and he was particularly impressed with Hillary Clinton.

A few days before the November election we were having breakfast in our New Rochelle home. "*Zayda*," Jeremy asked him, "did you know that Hillary Clinton is visiting our neighbourhood this morning?"

"Really? Right around here?" My father was not surprised that she was in the campaign mode, but that she was almost in our back yard.

"Yes, I heard that she'll be right near the Barnard School, just a few blocks from here," Jeremy replied. "Would you like to meet her in person, *Zayda*?"

My father smiled spreading margarine on his toast, "Sure, but she must be surrounded by a hundred Secret Service men. How can I get through with this?" My father pointed to his wheelchair. By then he had serious mobility problems and even his favourite African cane was inadequate to the task of getting around.

"Look, *Zayda*, I'm going to get over there right now and see what the situation is," Jeremy said as he pulled on a sweatshirt. It was already quite cold and a light drizzle began. "I'll be right back," he yelled as he closed the front door.

We continued our breakfast and talked about the upcoming election. "She is very, very smart—a *kluge kop*. I think she can win against Lazio," my father remarked. It was clear he was speaking of Clinton because he had expressed this opinion frequently. Then he added, "That *kholerya*, Lazio, is accusing her of having made anti-Semitic remarks twenty-six years ago. I don't believe a word he says."

I had poured my second cup of coffee when the phone rang. It was Jeremy. "Mom, quick put *Zayda* on. I have Hillary Clinton with me. She wants to speak with *Zayda*."

"Who? Are you putting me on, Jeremy?"

"No, Mom, quick get him on. The media are here. Their cameras are pointed at her standing here with the phone in hand."

I passed the phone to my father, "Here, Tinku. Hillary wants to speak with you." He pointed toward his chest with question marks in his widened eyes and put the receiver to his ear.

"Good morning, Nachman," I could hear her voice. She sounded cheerful, amused almost. My father was beaming. Light flickered in his eyes and his cheeks stretched in a huge grin.

"Good morning, Mrs. Clinton," he replied.

"What are you up to today?" she asked.

"Well, I am just having my breakfast," he said casually, as if a morning chat with the First Lady was what he did each day. Then I could see from the intense concentration on his face that he figured out what he needed to say. "I am a Democrat and have never missed an election since I came to this country. You can be sure of my vote."

"That's wonderful, thank you, Nachman," she said.

When he hung up he was quiet for a moment, still overwhelmed by the call. "Can you believe that? Hillary Clinton calling *me*? How did she know our number?"

"I bet Jeremy had something to do with it," I conjectured. Only a few minutes later Jeremy burst through the door yelling. "*Zayda*, where's your coat? I'm taking you to meet Hillary in person. Hurry, she won't be at the school much longer."

"But ... but I just spoke with her," my father said.

"Yes, yes I know, but now that she met you over the phone she wants to meet you in person."

"How will you get the wheelchair past the Secret Service barricades?" I asked, but Jeremy was already handing my father his jacket and steering the wheelchair out the door.

They returned a half hour later both on a high. "She is so nice," my father said, "A real mensch. And I met Congresswoman Nita Lowey too. She is very gracious. She had planned to run for the Senate seat herself, but stepped aside for Hillary. These women ... ach, they are fantastic."

By December 2000, my father was in very poor health and I didn't want him to spend his snowbird months alone. He had serious mobility issues and I worried he'd find it too difficult to shop and prepare his meals. One thing I didn't need to worry about was his mind. In January 2001, he'd be ninety-two and was as sharp as ever, anxious to get to work on his next painting. I was unable to take extended leave from work and said to him, "Tinek, maybe you'll skip Florida this year?"

"What are you saying?" He was incredulous that I'd ask such a ridiculous question.

"Please hear me out," I said. "It's too risky for you to be alone. I'll do nothing but worry about you."

"I have plenty of good neighbours in the condo," he said, but I could tell from the way he responded that he saw my point.

"They can help you occasionally, but not every day," I said. He looked at the fire in the fireplace and rubbed the stubble on his cheek.

Then he brightened suddenly and said, "Ania, I have a great idea."

"Let me hear it," I said.

"Why don't I call Danuta in Poland and ask her to come?"

"Danuta?" I was agape. "What do you mean, Danuta?"

"Don't you think she would like to spend two or three months on the beach with me, all expenses paid? She has never been out of Poland." He was grinning at his novel idea.

"But, Tinek ... well ... I hardly know what to say. She won't leave her husband and come running here," I said. Slowly, I began to realize that she might and the idea that she'd spend so much time with him made me jealous. I was wishing I could do it. *Still*, I calmed myself, *let's be real, she'll never come.* My father brimmed with enthusiasm as he reached for the phone. A short conversation later my father had his answer: Danuta was on her way! Mixed emotions churned in my stomach. On the one hand, it would allow him to paint and spend time away from the cold. She would shop and cook for him, keep him company and take him to the doctors. On the other hand, she would be with him and I would not.

Danuta did her best to make my father comfortable as he became sicker. She cooked him his old favourite Polish soups and told him stories about Poland. He taught her Yiddish words and played his favourite pieces of music on the keyboard, but by March it was clear he had to return to New York for more intensive medical care. He was annoyed that he left a half-finished painting on his easel in Florida, but he did not protest the return to New Rochelle.

By April I became even more fully aware of just how sick he was. He was not able to come to the ceremony at city hall in New York where Peter Vallone, speaker of the city council, honoured my professional achievements as part of the Jewish Heritage and Culture Event. Had he been able, my father would have not missed this ceremony for the world. Nor would he have missed the black-tie award ceremony in Washington, DC, that May, in which the National Science Foundation presented me with its highest honour for my division's distinguished service to science education nationwide. If he were able to attend, I think I might have even managed to get my father into the tux, but not easily. He had never worn one.

By June Nachman was hospitalized and in pain, but fully conscious. He kept inquiring about Jessica. She was pregnant and expected to give birth to his first great-grandson in August. When she arrived at his bedside from Europe he tapped gently on her belly, "Come out, come out," he encouraged the baby to make an early appearance. He knew he couldn't hold on much longer. Michael was born eight weeks to the day after my father died.

Looking at the young crowds spilling all the way down the staircase of the funeral home, one might have mistaken the event for a rock concert or a club, not a memorial gathering for a simple old man. That was the first positive thought that entered my mind on that black day. People from all walks of life had shown up though I made no effort to notify them. They filled more than one hundred seats, crouched on the floor in every empty spot, stood at the back and sides of the auditorium, spilled into the hallway and sat on the stairs. Young people: my children's friends, my coworkers. Old people: his one remaining Medem School friend, age ninety-one; and his camper, Carl, age eighty-two. Emil, who had taught him to operate the photo-offset press, with his wife and daughter. The rabbi, his wife, and their six children. Zoo employees from many departments. Jimmy, an assistant at the print shop, and Carlos, a handyman. Professionals in suits: lawyers who travelled with us to China, his doctor and his nurse who closed the office for the morning, architects from my brother's office. And workaday people in chinos and sweatshirts: Sammy the elevator operator in the building where the print shop was housed. I smiled inwardly at the unusual aggregation of assembled mourners. My father was like a potent gravitational force.

Through my fog of grief I had made a decision to display his paintings on easels positioned around the auditorium. With the crowds and paintings the service looked more like an opening of an art show. I knew he wouldn't have wanted to miss such a good opportunity for an exhibition. "Ania, look at that beautiful light coming through the stained-glass windows. It'll illuminate the paintings," he'd have said. We ended the service with the Warsaw Ghetto Fighters' hymn "Zog nit keyn mol" and I explained it meant "Never Say That This Is Your Last Road." The music, originally written for the 1937 film *Sons of the Working People*, became part of Holocaust Day observances. Everyone stood to the march-like hymn. Those who knew the words sang. Those that did not mouthed the transliterated Yiddish lyrics. I closed my eyes as the song rose and filled the space. All I could see was my father's approving smile. He did not instruct me on how to conduct his funeral because death was a concept he refused to acknowledge. He erased it by never, ever speaking of it. But I knew he'd have approved.

We returned to our house after the memorial service in Manhattan and subsequent burial in Paramus, New Jersey. On the way back home, my mind wandered absurdly: *New Jersey? He has to spend eternity in New Jersey! And that means that I will be a frequent visitor there as well.* I was seeking anything to keep out the image of him being lowered into the ground. Back home, immediate family and close friends—ours and my father's—joined us to mourn and remember with the aid of food. Of course, Jews don't gather without food. Platters brimming with bagels and lox, whitefish, sliced meats, fruit salads, and rugelach—a regular feast, as if all were well. I carried on like a proper hostess, a wind-up doll.

"Please help yourself to the canapés and fruit. The coffee will be on soon," I said as if this were one of the luncheons

I gave each spring for my father's friends. They had always looked old to me, but on that day they seemed younger somehow and I found myself resenting that they were still alive. Carl began to tell some of the others how as a young boy he looked up to my father in the Children's Republic in Poland. "He was our hero, our leader," he said, blinking away tears. In the living room people reminisced, looked at my father's paintings that covered nearly all of the wall space. A few guests stepped out onto our terrace overlooking the lake. A friend called me from the open door and pointed at the sky, "Annette, look up!" I stepped out, squinting at the June brightness and looked toward the sky. A huge rainbow stretched directly over our house on that clear day.

"Let's find Steve," I said urgently. "He is a meteorologist. He must have an explanation for this." Someone went into the living room to find him, our learned son-in-law. He came out puzzled.

"What's going on?" he asked.

"Look up. You have got to explain this bizarre celestial phenomenon," I said.

"Hmm ... I'm not sure. From everything I know this shouldn't be happening, but—" And I couldn't hear what else he said because suddenly I knew the answer.

A moment before the rainbow appeared I thought, "Now I am a real orphan, abandoned by both parents," but now a feeling that this was not true flooded me. I mumbled something and walked off to the farthest corner of the long terrace and stared at the rainbow. The conversations receded as I remembered a day when I had visited my father in Florida a year before. Though then it was January, the sky seemed the exact blue as this June day and the weather as warm.

The two of us sat on the balcony of his Florida condo sipping afternoon tea and chatted. He was a vision in blue: blue shorts, blue shirt, and his favourite blue baseball cap. He was deeply tanned and looked like the picture of health. He had hardly any wrinkles, a skin I hoped I'd inherit. "I have an old secret to tell you," he said suddenly.

"What? There's something I don't know?" I said. "Tell me, tell me."

"I want to tell you a piece of history about your grandmother, Rachel Leah," he said. "I have already told you what a wonderful woman my mother was, but what I'm about to tell you is the true measure of her character. You know that she was a deeply religious woman, don't you?"

"Yes," I replied. "You have mentioned that."

"Well, now I want to show you how truly open-minded she was, how she respected other points of view."

I must have not have looked interested enough.

He said, "Really, this is something I haven't yet told you." He looked very serious.

"I didn't know you kept secrets, Tinek," I said and leaned closer so I wouldn't miss a word.

"When she was on her deathbed, very, very ill, my mother called me to her bedside and in a barely audible voice said, 'Nachman, I know that you don't believe in religious rituals. When I die I don't want you to say the mourner's Kaddish.' Her words hit me like a ton of bricks." I said, 'Why, *Mame*?' And she said, 'I don't want you to be forced to mouth words you don't believe.' Yes, yes, that's what she said. For a deeply religious woman this was truly a heroic act! Do you understand that, Ania? For a religious Jewish woman to die with the awareness that her son will not say the Kaddish? An extraordinary act of courage! Unheard of in our day, in our community."

"So what did you do instead?" I asked. "I mean, at her gravesite, how did you avoid this obligation without offending the other mourners?"

"When the rabbi approached to conduct the service, Natan, who wasn't very religious either—and who understood my predicament—waved me away. I hid behind a tall tombstone nearby. The only thing I heard were the thuds of soil dropping on my mother's coffin. I was glad to be hidden because I didn't want everyone to see me bawling like a baby."

"How old were you then, Dad?"

"Twenty-seven."

Epilogue

Within a few days of the appearance of my father's obituary in the *New York Times* dozens of emails and letters from around the world filled our mailboxes. Nachman's Medem School classmates who were still alert enough to pen letters wrote remembrances of their childhoods and lifelong bonds. Men who had been my father's campers in Poland sixty years before wrote how the experience changed their lives. They all commented on how my father's artistic soul had inspired them and how his passing would diminish them. Fellow inmates from the Soviet gulags wrote about how he had kept up their spirits when it looked as if they would not have the stamina to hang on. Tributes poured in by the bucketful and each one tore open my fresh wound. There was one so special and unexpected that I gasped when I saw the envelope. Hillary Clinton wrote a letter commenting on Nachman's remarkable life. I knew he'd have liked that even better than the presidential birthday card.

Shortly after the funeral I received a most unusual call. Kathleen, the young woman who cared for the collection of Children's Zoo animals asked me somewhat haltingly, "I have just received a baby wallaby [a small species of kangaroo]. Its mother has rejected it. He is so tiny and beautiful, I would like to name him Nachman, after your father."

"A wal-la-by?" I said slowly. "Is that what you said, Kathleen?"

"Yes."

I was still grieving and not inclined to smile at anything, but a wide grin grew on my face. My father would have gotten such a kick out of this unusual tribute. This would be the only wallaby in the world with a Yiddish name. I chuckled and said, "Yes, of course, go ahead, and take good care of him," all the while wondering if my father's friends would see this as a disrespectful tribute. "Naming a wild animal after a man? What were you thinking?"

Kathleen was delighted and reminded me how my father played her favourite songs whenever she visited. What was most remarkable about her tribute was that she didn't know that indirectly my father had been responsible for the Children's Zoo acquiring the wallabies for exhibition in the first place. When the furry Nachman was old enough to make a public debut, he got his own employee photo nametag and Kathleen chauffeured him around in a silk-lined pouch while traversing the zoo on her electric cart. In no time at all it became a Bronx Zoo tradition that every celebrity from President Bill Clinton to numerous stars of screen and television and sports figures who visited the zoo had to have their photo taken with the wallaby.

Kathleen would take them behind the scenes and say, "Now that you have come to see this wonderful creature, I must first tell you how he acquired his name." The audience would look a bit baffled and eager to touch the wallaby's incredibly soft fur, but Kathleen continued, "Once I met a man who inspired me with his art and his music. He taught himself how to play and paint when he was well into his old age. His name was Nachman and he made me believe that anything is possible if you put your mind to it ... even raising such a vulnerable animal as this Nachman." Her words made me think again of my father's painting, *Sonata*. I had been deciphering it for years. And it struck me that he, himself, might be the beautiful central figure on stage, cradling the note, showing the world the nurturing music requires and the conditions that make it flourish. He seems to be saying, "I am here. I am playing out the rhythm of life. Watch me."

Again, I thought about the devilish figure at the very bottom of the theatre, way below the audience and its gruesome teeth grew more frightening. I thought that over the years I had squeezed out as much meaning from this painting as was possible, but now it was clear I had missed one essential message. Very slowly a concept took shape. It was my father who occupied the centre stage in the painting, sustained only by a single note—the only note he needed for survival—optimism. But he was reminding the viewers that below the vibrant life on the world's stage there is always danger and evil lurking, gnashing its terrible teeth, searching for victims to fill its maw. The only way to avoid falling prey to it is to keep singing and cradling that single note of hope.

I was dumbstruck by this realization. I am on a mission to find this note. I must listen for it in the unlikeliest places and revel in its otherworldly sound.

LIFE WRITING SERIES

In the **Life Writing Series**, Wilfrid Laurier University Press publishes life writing and new life-writing criticism and theory in order to promote autobiographical accounts, diaries, letters, and testimonials written and/or told by women and men whose political, literary, or philosophical purposes are central to their lives. The Series features accounts written in English, or translated into English from French or the languages of the First Nations, or any of the languages of immigration to Canada.

From its inception, **Life Writing** has aimed to foreground the stories of those who may never have imagined themselves as writers or as people with lives worthy of being (re)told. Its readership has expanded to include scholars, youth, and avid general readers both in Canada and abroad. The Series hopes to continue its work as a leading publisher of life writing of all kinds, as an imprint that aims for both broad representation and scholarly excellence, and as a tool for both historical and autobiographical research.

As its mandate stipulates, the Series privileges those individuals and communities whose stories may not, under normal circumstances, find a welcoming home with a publisher. **Life Writing** also publishes original theoretical investigations about life writing, as long as they are not limited to one author or text.

Series Editor
Marlene Kadar
Humanities Division, York University

Manuscripts to be sent to
Lisa Quinn, Acquisitions Editor
Wilfrid Laurier University Press
75 University Avenue West
Waterloo, Ontario N2L 3C5, Canada

BOOKS IN THE LIFE-WRITING SERIES
Published by Wilfrid Laurier University Press

Haven't Any News: Ruby's Letters from the Fifties edited by Edna Staebler with an Afterword by Marlene Kadar • 1995 / x + 165 pp. / ISBN 0-88920-248-6

"I Want to Join Your Club": Letters from Rural Children, 1900–1920 edited by Norah L. Lewis with a Preface by Neil Sutherland • 1996 / xii + 250 pp. (30 b&w photos) / ISBN 0-88920-260-5

And Peace Never Came by Elisabeth M. Raab with Historical Notes by Marlene Kadar • 1996 / x + 196 pp. (12 b&w photos, map) / ISBN 0-88920-281-8

Dear Editor and Friends: Letters from Rural Women of the North-West, 1900–1920 edited by Norah L. Lewis • 1998 / xvi + 166 pp. (20 b&w photos) / ISBN 0-88920-287-7

The Surprise of My Life: An Autobiography by Claire Drainie Taylor with a Foreword by Marlene Kadar • 1998 / xii + 268 pp. (8 colour photos and 92 b&w photos) / ISBN 0-88920-302-4

Memoirs from Away: A New Found Land Girlhood by Helen M. Buss / Margaret Clarke • 1998 / xvi + 153 pp. / ISBN 0-88920-350-4

The Life and Letters of Annie Leake Tuttle: Working for the Best by Marilyn Färdig Whiteley • 1999 / xviii + 150 pp. / ISBN 0-88920-330-x

Marian Engel's Notebooks: "Ah, mon cahier, écoute" edited by Christl Verduyn • 1999 /viii + 576 pp. / ISBN 0-88920-333-4 cloth / ISBN 0-88920-349-0 paper

Be Good Sweet Maid: The Trials of Dorothy Joudrie by Audrey Andrews • 1999 / vi + 276 pp. / ISBN 0-88920-334-2

Working in Women's Archives: Researching Women's Private Literature and Archival Documents edited by Helen M. Buss and Marlene Kadar • 2001 / vi + 120 pp. / ISBN 0-88920-341-5

Repossessing the World: Reading Memoirs by Contemporary Women by Helen M. Buss • 2002 / xxvi + 206 pp. / ISBN 0-88920-408-x cloth / ISBN 0-88920-410-1 paper

Chasing the Comet: A Scottish-Canadian Life by Patricia Koretchuk • 2002 / xx + 244 pp. / ISBN 0-88920-407-1

The Queen of Peace Room by Magie Dominic • 2002 / xii + 115 pp. / ISBN 0-88920-417-9

China Diary: The Life of Mary Austin Endicott by Shirley Jane Endicott • 2002 / xvi + 251 pp. / ISBN 0-88920-412-8

The Curtain: Witness and Memory in Wartime Holland by Henry G. Schogt • 2003 / xii + 132 pp. / ISBN 0-88920-396-2

Teaching Places by Audrey J. Whitson • 2003 / xiii + 178 pp. / ISBN 0-88920-425-x

Through the Hitler Line by Laurence F. Wilmot, M.C. • 2003 / xvi + 152 pp. / ISBN 0-88920-448-9

Where I Come From by Vijay Agnew • 2003 / xiv + 298 pp. / ISBN 0-88920-414-4

The Water Lily Pond by Han Z. Li • 2004 / x + 254 pp. / ISBN 0-88920-431-4

The Life Writings of Mary Baker McQuesten: Victorian Matriarch edited by Mary J. Anderson • 2004 / xxii + 338 pp. / ISBN 0-88920-437-3

Seven Eggs Today: The Diaries of Mary Armstrong, 1859 and 1869 edited by Jackson W. Armstrong • 2004 / xvi + 228 pp. / ISBN 0-88920-440-3

Love and War in London: A Woman's Diary 1939–1942 by Olivia Cockett; edited by Robert W. Malcolmson • 2005 / xvi + 208 pp. / ISBN 0-88920-458-6

Incorrigible by Velma Demerson • 2004 / vi + 178 pp. / ISBN 0-88920-444-6

Auto/biography in Canada: Critical Directions edited by Julie Rak • 2005 / viii + 264 pp. / ISBN 0-88920-478-0

Tracing the Autobiographical edited by Marlene Kadar, Linda Warley, Jeanne Perreault, and Susanna Egan • 2005 / viii + 280 pp. / ISBN 0-88920-476-4

Must Write: Edna Staebler's Diaries edited by Christl Verduyn • 2005 / viii + 304 pp. / ISBN 0-88920-481-0

Pursuing Giraffe: A 1950s Adventure by Anne Innis Dagg • 2006 / xvi + 284 pp. (photos, 2 maps) / 978-0-88920-463-8

Food That Really Schmecks by Edna Staebler • 2007 / xxiv + 334 pp. / ISBN 978-0-88920-521-5

163256: A Memoir of Resistance by Michael Englishman • 2007 / xvi + 112 pp. (14 b&w photos) / ISBN 978-1-55458-009-5

The Wartime Letters of Leslie and Cecil Frost, 1915–1919 edited by R.B. Fleming • 2007 / xxxvi + 384 pp. (49 b&w photos, 5 maps) / ISBN 978-1-55458-000-2

Johanna Krause Twice Persecuted: Surviving in Nazi Germany and Communist East Germany by Carolyn Gammon and Christiane Hemker • 2007 / x + 170 pp. (58 b&w photos, 2 maps) / ISBN 978-1-55458-006-4

Watermelon Syrup: A Novel by Annie Jacobsen with Jane Finlay-Young and Di Brandt • 2007 / x + 268 pp. / ISBN 978-1-55458-005-7

Broad Is the Way: Stories from Mayerthorpe by Margaret Norquay • 2008 / x + 106 pp. (6 b&w photos) / ISBN 978-1-55458-020-0

Becoming My Mother's Daughter: A Story of Survival and Renewal by Erika Gottlieb • 2008 / x + 178 pp. (36 b&w illus., 17 colour) / ISBN 978-1-55458-030-9

Leaving Fundamentalism: Personal Stories edited by G. Elijah Dann • 2008 / xii + 234 pp. / ISBN 978-1-55458-026-2

Bearing Witness: Living with Ovarian Cancer edited by Kathryn Carter and Lauri Elit • 2009 / viii + 94 pp. / ISBN 978-1-55458-055-2

Dead Woman Pickney: A Memoir of Childhood in Jamaica by Yvonne Shorter Brown • 2010 / viii + 202 pp. / ISBN 978-1-55458-189-4

I Have a Story to Tell You by Seemah C. Berson • 2010 / xx + 288 pp. (24 b&w photos) / ISBN 978-1-55458-219-8

We All Giggled: A Bourgeois Family Memoir by Thomas O. Hueglin • 2010 / xiv + 232 pp. (20 b&w photos) / ISBN 978-1-55458-262-4

Just a Larger Family: Letters of Marie Williamson from the Canadian Home Front, 1940–1944 edited by Mary F. Williamson and Tom Sharp • 2011 / xxiv + 378 pp. (16 b&w photos) / ISBN 978-1-55458-323-2

Burdens of Proof: Faith, Doubt, and Identity in Autobiography by Susanna Egan • 2011 / x + 200 pp. / ISBN 978-1-55458-333-1

Accident of Fate: A Personal Account 1938–1945 by Imre Rochlitz with Joseph Rochlitz • 2011 / xiv + 226 pp. (50 b&w photos, 5 maps) / ISBN 978-1-55458-267-9

The Green Sofa by Natascha Würzbach, translated by Raleigh Whitinger • 2012 / xiv + 240 pp. (5 b&w photos) / ISBN 978-1-55458-334-8

Unheard Of: Memoirs of a Canadian Composer by John Beckwith • 2012 / x + 393 pp. (74 illus., 8 musical examples) / ISBN 978-1-55458-358-4

Borrowed Tongues: Life Writing, Migration, and Translation by Eva C. Karpinski • 2012 / viii + 274 pp. / ISBN 978-1-55458-357-7

Basements and Attics, Closets and Cyberspace: Explorations in Canadian Women's Archives edited by Linda M. Morra and Jessica Schagerl • 2012 / x + 338 pp. / ISBN 978-1-55458-632-5

The Memory of Water by Allen Smutylo • 2013 / x + 262 pp. (65 colour illus.) / ISBN 978-1-55458-842-8

The Unwritten Diary of Israel Unger, Revised Edition by Carolyn Gammon and Israel Unger • 2013 / ix + 230 pp. (b&w illus.) / ISBN 978-1-77112-011-1

Boom! Manufacturing Memoir for the Popular Market by Julie Rak • 2013 / viii + 249 pp. (b&w illus.) / ISBN 978-1-55458-939-5

Motherlode: A Mosaic of Dutch Wartime Experience by Carolyne Van Der Meer • 2014 / xiv + 132 pp. (b&w illus.) / ISBN 978-1-77112-005-0

Not the Whole Story: Challenging the Single Mother Narrative edited by Lea Caragata and Judit Alcalde • 2014 / x + 222 pp. / ISBN 978-1-55458-624-0

Street Angel by Magie Dominc • 2014 / viii + 154 pp. / ISBN 978-1-77112-026-5

In the Unlikeliest of Places: How Nachman Libeskind Survived the Nazis, Gulags, and Soviet Communism by Annette Libeskind Berkovits + 2016 / xiv + 380 pp. (colour illus.) / ISBN 978-1-77112-248-1